Rethinking Asset Management

From Financial Stability to Investor Protection and Economic Growth

Report of a CEPS-ECMI Task Force

Chair **Jean-Baptiste de Franssu**
Chairman of Incipit
Former President of the European Fund
and Asset Management Association (EFAMA)

Rapporteurs **Mirzha de Manuel Aramendía**
ECMI-CEPS Researcher

Karel Lannoo
CEPS-ECMI Chief Executive Officer
and Senior Research Fellow

Centre for European Policy Studies
European Capital Markets Institute
Brussels

Disclaimer

This report is based on the discussions in the CEPS-ECMI Task Force on Rethinking Asset Management, which met on four separate occasions in 2011. The policy recommendations offered at the beginning of this report reflect a general consensus reached by Task Force members, although not every member agrees with every aspect of each recommendation. A list of members, observers and invited guests of the Task Force can be found in Annex 3. The members were given the opportunity to comment on the draft final report, but its contents may only be attributed to the rapporteurs.

CEPS and ECMI gratefully acknowledge the financial support received for this Task Force from the CFA Institute, a global not-for-profit association of investment professionals.

The author, Mirzha de Manuel Aramendía, wishes to thank his co-rapporteur Karel Lannoo for his valuable supervision and guidance, as well as for all his input; Diego Valiante for his constant advice and his emphasis on substance; Jean-Baptiste de Franssu for his commitment to this project; the Task Force members for their active participation and insightful comments; Claire Fargeot of the CFA Institute for her support; the European Commission and the European Securities and Markets Authority for their useful involvement as observers; Jean-Pierre Casey for inspiring this project; Anne Harrington for her careful editing and advice; and the rest of the CEPS staff for all their help and encouragement. All errors/omissions are the sole responsibility of the author.

ISBN 978-94-6138-180-4

European Capital Markets Institute
Centre for European Policy Studies
Place du Congrès 1, B-1000 Brussels
Tel: (32.2) 229.39.11 | Fax: (32.2) 219.41.51
www.ceps.eu | www.eurocapitalmarkets.org

CONTENTS

List of Tables

List of Figures

List of Boxes

PREFACE

It is my pleasure to introduce this ambitious and comprehensive ECMI-CEPS Task Force Report on "Rethinking Asset Management", which concentrates on financial stability, investor protection, product integrity and economic growth.

The asset management industry has thrived in capturing the opportunities offered by the single market and the regulatory framework put in place in 1985 under the leadership of the European Commission. UCITS has been so successful that it has grown outside the European Union. It has become one of the most reliable and innovative pooled vehicles worldwide, serving tens of millions of investors in building their long-term financial security. The strength of flows before and after the financial crisis testifies to the trust that investors place in UCITS, accounting for half of the industry's assets under management – notwithstanding that all managers may not have delivered relative positive returns net of fees.

The strength of the asset management industry in Europe means a great deal to its economy. Beyond the number of jobs created, the €15 trillion under management is a significant force when it comes to supporting growth and financing investments, hence an important resource for citizens in Europe and beyond.

The asset management industry was heavily impacted by the financial crisis as reflected in the overall reduction of assets under management and the associated fall in revenue. The industry has seized this opportunity to review its role, as well as some of its practices and instruments – including some alternative funds, certain money market funds strategies, the use of derivatives, product complexity, securities lending and the compatibility between daily valuation and long-term investing. A number of initiatives have been already taken to regulate these practices, which are reviewed in detail in this report.

But the industry also faces a significant level of regulatory activity addressing the wider financial markets: MiFID II, Solvency II and shadow banking, to name only a few, as well as foreign initiatives with extra-territorial reach, such as the Foreign Account Tax Compliance Act (FATCA) or the Volker rule enacted in the US. We should not underestimate the amount of work and expense entailed by such reforms over a short time frame and their sometimes ambiguous impact on investors.

The challenge today lies also in navigating between more regulation and better supervision. To that extent, the entire industry welcomes the creation of ESMA with its pan-European mandate but at the same time questions its relative lack of resources and the evolution of its positioning vis-à-vis the European Commission and national regulators.

Beyond systemic risk and prudential regulation, investor protection at the point of sale (and this is one of the highlights of this report) is probably the one area where more needs to be done. Progress on depository aspects, investor compensation, disclosure and transparency has been notable in the last few years. However, we should avoid the errors of the past when some rules did not see the expected degree of transposition and implementation. To date, investor protection has not been approached holistically at pan-European level, or with a level playing field in mind, to the detriment of investors. Many national regulators have or are in the process of introducing rules on marketing, product approval and sales that create new barriers to the single market and limit the free circulation of capital.

But we know that the key to successful development of long-term financial savings lies in the quality of investment solutions, distribution and selling practices. So it is high time to bring forward pan-European legislation addressing all (packaged) retail investment products and harmonising all aspects of distribution, including advice, disclosure, fees, inducements - and all other sources of potential conflicts of interest, training of sales and advice teams, and product-to-market principles. This report considers abundant evidence and examines different reform options in many of these respects. A level playing field is indispensable to avoid regulatory arbitrage in favour of less transparent or more expensive products, or across different distribution channels. Failing to take these steps would severely affect competition, choice and the value for money that investors receive.

All these points are discussed and documented in this thorough and timely report prepared and issued by ECMI and CEPS, with a view to offering critical thinking as well as creative direction to the industry and policy-makers. I would like to thank them in the name of the entire working group whose inputs have been critical.

Jean-Baptiste de Franssu
Chairman of Incipit
Former President, European Fund and Asset Management Association

EXECUTIVE SUMMARY AND POLICY RECOMMENDATIONS

Fresh prospects are opening for asset managers as Europe seeks to reduce its historical reliance on banking and to promote capital markets. At the same time, however, the industry faces a dual challenge: regaining investors' trust and coping with the post-crisis regulatory reform. Retail investors require more protection in the sale process to facilitate their access to the best-in-class products in order to save for their future. Distribution is the major stumbling block to competition and the area where substantial reform is needed to serve retail investors' interests. The single market should be exploited to remove inefficiencies and promote competition among providers for product integrity to increase and feeds to decrease. Piecemeal solutions and distinctly national approaches will no longer suffice. We must insist on a holistic (and horizontal) approach across products, players and countries that prevents regulatory arbitrage, preserves financial stability and protects the investor. We must also work to unleash the potential of the asset management industry to benefit the real economy. The stakes are high to make investment funds and other investment products deliver to European investors.

In view of these imperatives, this Task Force report puts forward policy recommendations in seven main areas aimed at strengthening investor protection in the sale process, product integrity in UCITS, the management of non-market risks, long-term and responsible investing and venture capital.

1. RETAIL INVESTOR PROTECTION

- **Pre-contractual disclosure should be comparable for all retail investment products.**

  The KIID (key investor information document) standard should apply across investment funds, insurance-based investment products, retail structured products and banking saving products – in line with the PRIPs (packaged retail investment products) initiative. Ultimately, uniform standards of pre-contractual disclosure should apply to all retail investments, whether packaged or not, and including pension products, to the benefit of investors.

- **Selling practices should be regulated in the same manner across products and channels.**

  The proposed extension of the rules governing MiFID (markets in financial instruments directive) to structured deposits is a step in the right direction to stop regulatory distortions. Uniform rules on conduct of business and conflicts of interest should apply across products and distribution channels. MiFID and the IMD (insurance mediation directive) should converge in this respect also in their implementation.

- **Investor protection at the point of sale should be clearly distinguished from product integrity and financial stability concerns.**

  It is important to draw a distinction between concerns over financial stability and product integrity, on the one hand, and the protection of retail investors at the point of sale, on the other. Complexity in *product structuring* should be addressed by product regulation to the extent necessary to ensure the integrity of retail investment products. By way of contrast, complexity in the *risk-reward profile* should be addressed by distribution rules.

- **Retail investors should be encouraged to request investment advice for products with a complex *risk-reward profile*.**

  Execution-only services should be reserved for investment products whose *risk-reward profile* may be understood by the average retail investor. Investors should be strongly urged to request investment advice when purchasing an investment product with a complex *risk-reward profile*. Both market and non-market risks (operational, counterparty and liquidity risks) are relevant in understanding the risk profile of a given product.

- **Retail investors need more information about investment advice.**

  Distributors should be completely transparent in describing to investors the character of the services they offer. The Task Force supports the proposal of the European Commission to require distributors to disclose whether advice is provided on an independent basis and whether advice is based on a broad or more restricted analysis of the market. Investors should also be informed about the cost of advice, whether in the form of inducements or up-front charges. Disclosure in these three respects should be meaningful for investors and where appropriate, standardised.

- **Professional standards for advisers should be raised and harmonised.**

  Europe needs a uniform approach to raise the professional standards of investment advisers and distributors. Ultimately, better advice would improve capital allocation by directing savers to the most adequate and cost-effective product solutions. Ongoing training is also needed to keep advisers up-to-date on market developments.

- **A level playing field is needed to stop regulatory arbitrage.**

  Additional steps are needed to close the gaps that allow the marketing of non-regulated products to retail investors. Two issues are of particular concern: the sale to retail investors of structured products and exchange-traded notes that are not subject to product rules nor the approval of supervisors, and the different standards that apply to regulated products.

2. PRODUCT INTEGRITY

- **UCITS needs to be governed by a single rule book; partial harmonisation can no longer be justified.**

  The UCITS rules are loosely harmonised and implementation diverges across member states with respect to essential aspects, such as eligible assets, concentration limits and investment practices. Insufficient harmonisation also affects key elements of disclosure, such as total expense ratios. To strengthen product integrity and provide clarity to investors, UCITS needs a single rule book.

- **The current rules on derivatives and financial indices should be fine-tuned.**

  The current rules on the use of derivatives and structured financial instruments in UCITS should be revised to strengthen product integrity. It would not be a matter of producing a major overhaul but of closing gaps to reduce the opportunities for arbitrage and deepen harmonisation to improve consistency. Chapter 3 (section 4 and Box 4) provides some ideas in this respect.

- **Legislation should consolidate best practices on collateral management.**

  The Task Force supports ESMA in its work to clarify collateral requirements for UCITS. The same rules should apply, however, to all retail investment products in the form of binding legislation instead of guidelines. Since collateralised transactions are a common practice in financial markets, a horizontal approach is needed, in coordination with international regulators.

- **Legislation should require more transparency on securities lending.**

  EU legislation is needed to bring more transparency into securities lending by UCITS and other retail investment products. Any broader issues related to securities lending in financial markets need to be considered horizontally and in coordination with international regulators.

3. NON-MARKET RISKS AND DEPOSITARIES

- **Non-market risks should be better communicated to retail investors.**

  In a context where market risks are often transformed and repackaged, resulting in novel operational, counterparty or liquidity risks, it is essential to clearly communicate these non-market risks to investors. UCITS are already required to communicate these risks in the KIID, but closer supervision would ensure meaningful compliance. The effectiveness of the current standard of disclosure should be reviewed under PRIPs and extended to all retail investment products.

- **The implementation of depositary rules should make sure that custody risks are managed instead of insured against.**

  The depositary rules in the AIFMD (alternative investment fund managers Directive) should be implemented in a manner ensuring that custody risks are managed and not insured against. Strict liability should only fall on depositaries for the safe-keeping of instruments over which they have effective control, as recommended by the European Securities and Markets Authority (ESMA). Depositary rules for UCITS should be aligned with the AIFMD, but with retail investors in mind.

- **National rules should fully converge before a depositary passport is introduced in Europe.**

  The Task Force would like to see a depositary passport in future. However, full convergence of national rules should be achieved beforehand, based on the AIFM and UCITS V Directives, to avoid distortions of the kind identified by the Committee of European Securities Regulators (CESR) in 2010. Member states should conscientiously implement these directives and the Commission should enforce compliance.

4. LONG-TERM INVESTING

- **Investment horizons should be better communicated to retail investors.**

  Pre-contractual disclosure and investment advice should more carefully consider investment horizons. While UCITS may mention any 'minimum recommended holding period' in the KIID, investors would nevertheless benefit from consistent and more positive disclosure in this respect. Advisers should be expressly required to consider the investment horizon of their clients.

- **A new long-term vehicle for retail investors should be introduced in Europe.**

  Retail investors would benefit from having access to relatively illiquid asset classes to channel part of their long-term savings, including part of their retirement savings. A harmonised regulatory framework for long-term retail funds (LTRFs) should therefore be considered. Chapter 5 (Box 6) offers some initial ideas in this respect.

- **Prudential rules should not hinder the ability of institutional investors to make long-term investments.**

  The importance of long-term investing cannot be sufficiently stressed both to foster sustainable growth and to generate the returns needed to meet pension liabilities. In this respect, prudential rules should be reconciled with long-term investing.

5. RESPONSIBLE INVESTING

- **Institutional investors should consider engagement in their investment mandates.**

  Environmental, social and governance (ESG) indicators are useful tools to mitigate risks and potentially increase returns. Policy-makers should actively support the development of integrated reporting standards for non-financial corporations. Institutional investors should pay more attention to engagement and ESG criteria in their investment mandates and voting policies.

- **Harmonised rules are needed for funds that present themselves as responsible.**

  Responsible investment funds have the potential to combine attractive returns for investors with the achievement of ESG objectives. Europe needs a harmonised framework for retail funds presenting themselves as responsible, including responsible UCITS. This framework should be robust and ensure that the funds are indeed invested in a manner consistent with the ESG goals they purport to seek.

- **The industry should commit to the success of the EU initiative on social entrepreneurship funds.**

  Forthcoming legislation on social entrepreneurship funds is a useful instrument to promote impact investing. The Task Force invites the asset management industry to commit to the success of this initiative aimed at small and medium enterprises whose primary goal is to achieve positive and measurable social impacts.

6. VENTURE CAPITAL

- **The proposed rules on venture capital should be flexible enough to unleash its full potential.**

The proposed regulation on European Venture Capital Funds (EVCFs) is of key importance for the economy, given the role of venture capital in financing entrepreneurship and innovation. Sufficient flexibility should be extended to qualifying funds and qualifying investments so that the passport becomes truly attractive for managers. Beyond building the single market, additional incentives will be needed to boost the 'venture capital ecosystem' in Europe.

7. THE SINGLE MARKET

- **The standard of harmonisation should be upgraded to complete the single market.**

  Completing the single market is essential to foster growth and competitiveness in Europe. As highlighted recently by several heads of state and government, "The single market must be brought to its next stage of development, by reinforcing governance and raising the standards of implementation".[1] The single market for asset management products and services is of particular importance, given its role in financing the economy and providing retirement income. Divergent national rules on investor protection risk reversing the single market for retail investment products.

- **Beyond issuing new rules, Europe needs better implementation and supervision of existing rules.**

  The Task Force found that some of the rules recently reviewed, while not flawed, were ineffective due to the lack of appropriate implementation and supervision. More resources should be made available to make legislation work in practice. The role of ESMA should become more central, and the body should be endowed with adequate resources to carry out its tasks.

- **The single market would benefit from promoting competition but also its competitiveness.**

  Resolving the distribution conundrum is essential to foster competition, rationalisation and lower fees in retail markets. The European Parliament and member states should step-up their efforts to find a satisfactory solution in this respect. Next to fostering competition, policy-makers should also strive to promote the competitiveness of the EU in global markets for investment funds and asset management services.

---

[1] Joint Letter to President Herman Van Rompuy and President José Manuel Barroso of 20 February 2012, by David Cameron, Mark Rutte, Mario Monti, Andrus Ansip, Valdis Dombrovskis, Jyrki Katainen, Enda Kenny, Petr Nečas, Iveta Radičová, Mariano Rajoy, Fredrik Reinfeldt and Donald Tusk.

INTRODUCTION

A Task Force was set up in late 2010 by the Centre for European Policy Studies (CEPS) and the European Capital Markets Institute (ECMI), an independent research institute managed by CEPS, to investigate four seminal issues, in view of their importance for the European economy, the single market and investors:

1) The future of the asset management industry after the financial crisis and the adoption of AIFMD (Alternative Investment Fund Managers Directive),
2) Product innovation in UCITS (Undertakings for Collective Investment in Transferable Securities) and the way forward to complete the single market and strengthen product integrity,
3) The distribution of investment funds and other products to strengthen the choice and protection of (retail) investors and
4) The contribution of the asset management industry to the economy and how to unleash its untapped potential.

For this purpose, CEPS and ECMI brought together a wide range of stakeholders, including asset managers, custodian banks, academics, experts and policy-makers, under the chairmanship of Jean-Baptiste de Franssu, Chairman of Incipit and former President of EFAMA (European Fund and Asset Management Association).

This report has two objectives: to serve as a reference work on asset management regulation and to carefully examine the desirability and feasibility of the multitude of ongoing regulatory reforms. It was acknowledged during the Task Force meetings that the nature and role of asset management products and services is not always clear to investors and other stakeholders. This report is aimed therefore at raising awareness of the asset management industry, its contribution to the economy, and the detail of its regulation in Europe. It was also felt during the Task Force meetings that recent and forthcoming regulatory reforms will have profound effects on asset managers, investors and the economy at large. This report considers therefore most of the legislative proposals that were on the table at the time of drafting, including the implementation of the AIFMD, the review of the markets in financial instruments Directive (MiFID), and the packaged retail investment products initiative (PRIPs). It also examines the potential for further regulatory reform in some areas such as long-term and responsible investing. The drafting attempts to combine clear language and straightforward introductions with detailed and technical analysis and illustrations.

This report is structured following a horizontal approach by substantive issues (financial stability, product integrity, investor protection and economic contribution), presented in five chapters.

Chapter 1 Setting the scene: Asset management and its regulation in Europe

Provides an introduction to the industry and its regulation. It argues that the AIFMD radically alters the picture and embodies in terms of substance the basic regulatory framework of asset management in Europe. It also anticipates the five regulatory trends that will contribute to shaping the future of the asset management industry in Europe.

Chapter 2 Financial stability: Scoping the issues and navigating the regulatory reform

Reflects on the issues of financial stability that concern the asset management industry and the progress achieved so far by regulation in addressing each of them. It also considers the examples of money market funds and exchange-traded funds.

Chapter 3 Strengthening product integrity: Which way for UCITS?

Considers product innovation in UCITS and the rules governing the use of derivatives and financial indices by presenting their strengths and shortcomings. It also elaborates on non-market risks and the role of fund depositaries.

Chapter 4 Distribution: Single market, investor protection and investor choice.

Examines the current state of distribution in Europe and a wide range of policy instruments to consolidate the single market, improve investor protection and foster investor choice. It refers to disclosure and comparability, product complexity and investment advice, among other aspects.

Chapter 5 Nourishing the real economy: Today and tomorrow

Assesses the contribution of the asset management industry to the financing of the economy, and in particular the need to foster some practices such as long-term investing, responsible investing and venture capital.

1. SETTING THE SCENE: ASSET MANAGEMENT IN EUROPE AND ITS REGULATION

This first chapter provides an overview of the asset management industry and its regulation in Europe, starting with the distinct characteristics of asset managers and investment funds, compared to other intermediaries and financial products. It then considers the size and organisation of the industry in comparison with that of the US, with special reference to the real level of dispersion that lies behind the high number of funds and management houses. The chapter then turns to investors - both retail and professional - and some key trends in their participation across industry segments. Before examining the regulatory aspects, the ground will be prepared by referring to the process of convergence between traditional and alternative asset management. Asset management regulation will be explained first with regard to its role and objectives, introducing the distinction between 'product' and 'manager' rules. After this conceptualisation, the section will offer a broad overview of the current regulatory framework after the adoption of the alternative investment fund managers Directive (AIFMD) in 2011. Finally, reference will be made to two additional issues: the execution of the single market and the success of European funds and managers abroad.

1.1 The distinct characteristics of asset management intermediation

The asset management industry plays a distinctive role in capital markets by pooling the savings of investors and investing them strategically in financial instruments and other assets with the aim of generating returns (see also Chapter 5). It is an agency business where managers offer chiefly two types of vehicles: i) mandates where the assets of a single investor are managed separately and ii) funds where the assets of several investors are managed jointly. Mandates service institutional investors and 'high net worth' individuals with a big pool of wealth to invest, whereas funds more frequently service small investors. In both instances, the investor benefits from a professional approach to asset allocation whereby experienced managers select and monitor the assets that become part of the investor's portfolio. Investment funds bring in additional value by allowing investors to pool their savings, achieving risk reductions via diversification.

It was felt during the Task Force discussions that the nature of the asset management business and its role in the economy are not always well understood by investors and politicians, as compared to that of banking or insurance. The asset management industry fulfils an essential economic function by directing savings towards productive activities. It i) facilitates the participation of small investors in financial markets; ii) takes part in both primary and secondary equity markets; iii) provides short and long-term credit to corporations, financial institutions and governments and iv) participates in price discovery. Crucially, asset managers perform these functions on behalf and in the interest of investors who retain direct ownership over the assets managed - which are usually segregated or placed under the overview of independent entities called depositaries. These features are unique to the asset management industry and differentiate it from other intermediaries, such as banks and insurers (see Table 1). Asset managers are also different from other intermediaries in the way market risk is borne by investors; in contrast to bank deposits, market risk in investment funds is openly carried by investors and is not insured by sovereign governments.

In spite of their distinct nature, asset managers interact with banks and insurers in different ways, to a similar extent as other players in financial markets and the real economy. In effect, asset managers can be commissioned by banks and insurers to manage their portfolios. Even when they are not externally commissioned, managers are nevertheless present within banks and insurers as part of their in-house teams or subsidiaries. Moreover, asset managers employing leverage frequently source it from banks under so-called 'prime-brokerage agreements'. Finally, banks and insurers act as distributors of funds manufactured by independent asset managers to their captive clienteles. In distributing third party funds, next to their own products, banks benefit from a direct access to the clients for which they primarily provide deposit and payment services.

A further link among players is found in their corporate ownership structures, in spite of which asset management subsidiaries are frequently managed as stand-alone businesses. At the end of 2009, an important part of asset management companies were owned by banking and insurance groups. France presents the largest number of independent management houses (over

60%) followed by the United Kingdom, where over 50% of the houses are independent, similarly to the US (EFAMA, 2011a, p. 14). Bank affiliates remain the largest players in the asset management industry in Europe although some banking groups have substantially reduced their support for their captive business as a result of i) conditions linked to the receipt of state aid and ii) a commercial shift to deposits to comply with stringent capital requirements. Insurers also hold significant stakes in asset management companies, particularly in some jurisdictions, such as the United Kingdom, Germany and France.

Table 1. A comparison of asset management and other forms of intermediation

	ASSET MANAGEMENT	BANKING	INSURANCE
Main function	To manage savings by strategically investing them in financial instruments or other assets to generate returns, providing financing to the economy	To accept deposits and provide credit to the economy	To gather funding and pool risks to provide compensation for the damages insured
Ownership of assets	Assets are owned by the individual investor and placed under the overview of an independent entity	Deposits are owned by depositors but pooled together and lent to third parties	Premiums are transferred to the insurer who acquires their ownership to compensate future damages
Maturity and liquidity transformation	When present can be limited by redemption restrictions	Main business model	Insurers need to match their liabilities
Distribution of risks	The risk of losses due to market risk is borne transparently by investors	Deposits are insured up to a maximum amount	The insured risks are pooled and borne by the insurance company and reinsured

1.2 Industry size and industrial organisation

Europe has come to hold a prominent position globally in the asset management industry. It accounts for about 30% of global assets under management (AuM), making it the second largest player in the world after the United States (see Figure 1). The size of the asset management industry appears directly related to the degree of economic development, the size of the relevant market and the level of market integration. If only US mutual funds, UCITS and similarly open-ended investment funds are taken into account, the market shares remain roughly the same. The 2% market share that Europe gains in mutual funds may be well explained by the 2% that Asia loses, given the relative success of UCITS among investors in Asia. UCITS is the harmonised framework for the structuring and 'passporting' of mutual funds across Europe.

Figure 1. Total global assets under management, end 2010 ($ trillion)

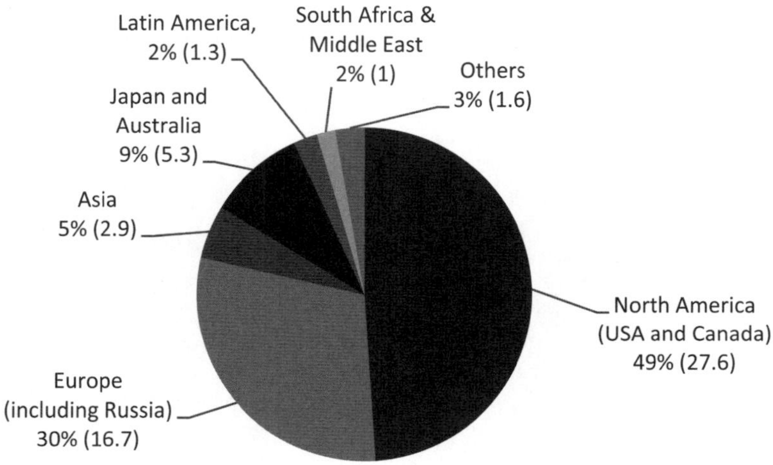

Source: Adapted from BCG (2011).

Figure 2. Assets under management in mutual funds, end 2010 ($ trillion)

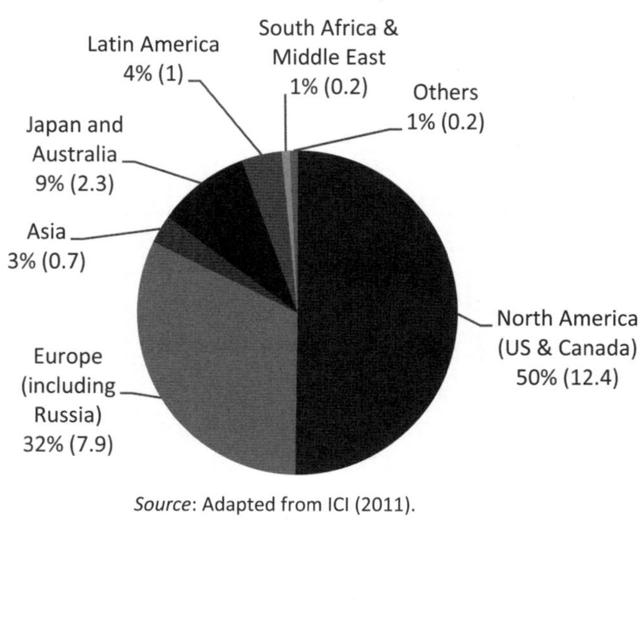

Source: Adapted from ICI (2011).

Industrial organisation is characterised by moderate (but rising) barriers to entry and high dispersion of intermediaries. Yet dispersion is much more prominent in Europe than in the United States. It is estimated that over 3,100 asset management companies operate in Europe, including small specialised firms (boutiques), in contrast to less than 1,000 firms providing investment management services in the US market to fund investors (EFAMA, 2011a, p. 12; ICI, 2011, p. 14). Only a small number of European firms manage assets in excess of €100 billion - eight in the UK, three in Germany and six in France, where data are available (EFAMA, 2011a, p. 13). The difference with the US is due mainly to the fragmentation of national markets. If funds rather than firms are considered, the average UCITS fund holds €150 million net assets while the average US mutual fund holds $1.5 billion (EFAMA, 2012, p. 9; ICI, 2011, pp. 187-188).

In effect, there are 54,000 open-ended funds in Europe, 67% of which are structured as UCITS, in contrast to 7,000 to 8,000 mutual funds in the US (EFAMA, 2012; ICI, 2011). However, assets under management in Europe are unequally distributed and concentrated in a small number of players. Using data of Strategic Insight on long-term UCITS,[2] it appears that the top 10% largest funds in Europe hold approximately 65% of the assets in their category - UCITS funds excluding money market funds. By the end of Q3 2010, this top 10 was formed by 1,884 funds, each of which held €1.13 billion assets on average while the biggest fund in the sample held €26 billion. Conversely, 80% of European funds held just 20% of the assets. Figure 3 represents the level of concentration.

Figure 3. Fragmentation in the EU asset management industry, 3rd qtr. 2010

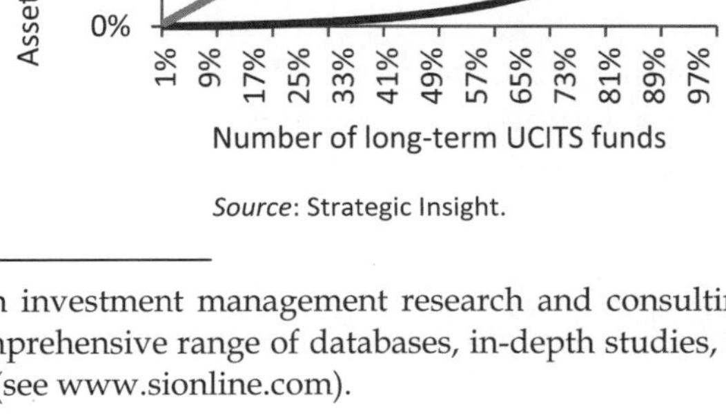

Source: Strategic Insight.

[2] Strategic Insight, an investment management research and consulting company in New York, produces a comprehensive range of databases, in-depth studies, internet libraries and on-demand research (see www.sionline.com).

To overcome this state of relative fragmentation, changes were made to the UCITS framework so that management companies could operate cross-border and merge their funds (UCITS IV, 2011). Mergers allow managers to rationalise their fund structures and exploit economies of scale. Ultimately in a competitive environment, the efficiencies generated would be passed through to investors in the form of lower fees and higher returns. The UCITS IV legislation facilitates both mergers and master-feeder structures. Given its recent entry into force, it is too early to pass judgement. However, important barriers to industry consolidation remain, including taxation. In effect, fund mergers become a tax event for investors in some member states, which could dissuade fund mergers, in spite of the cost efficiencies (EFAMA & KPMG, 2010). For as long as tax harmonisation requires a unanimous decision by member states, the only feasible way out is coordination promoted by the European Commission, based on the jurisprudence of the Court of Justice of the European Union (European Commission, 2006, p. 7).

1.3 Investors' weight and trends

It is estimated that institutional investors account for about 68% of assets under management in Europe while retail investors make up the remaining 32%. These figures do not reflect the indirect participation of retail investors in investment funds via 'wrappers' such as unit-linked products offered by insurance companies. Unit-linked policies are life-insurance contracts for which the cover and premiums are expressed in terms of investment units, such as shares in investment funds. They are very popular in Denmark, Sweden and the Netherlands but also in large markets such as the UK, France and Italy.[3] Inflows to unit-linked products totalled €112 billion in 2010 - a sizeable number if benchmarked to the net sales of UCITS funds over the same period (€290 billion) (CEA, 2012; EFAMA, 2012b).

The large majority of retail investors hold their assets in investment funds rather than mandates, with the possible exception of high net worth individuals, given minimum assets under management thresholds. In effect, investment mandates are used extensively by institutional investors looking to externalise the management of their portfolios and find expertise in certain practices such as asset-liability matching. Discretionary mandates account on average for 50% of assets under management in Europe, although there are large differences among member states (EFAMA, 2011a, p. 13).

---

[3] Popularity is measured in terms of annual premiums paid as a share GDP, based on 2010 data from CEA (2012).

Figure 4. European assets under management per type of investor (€ trillion)

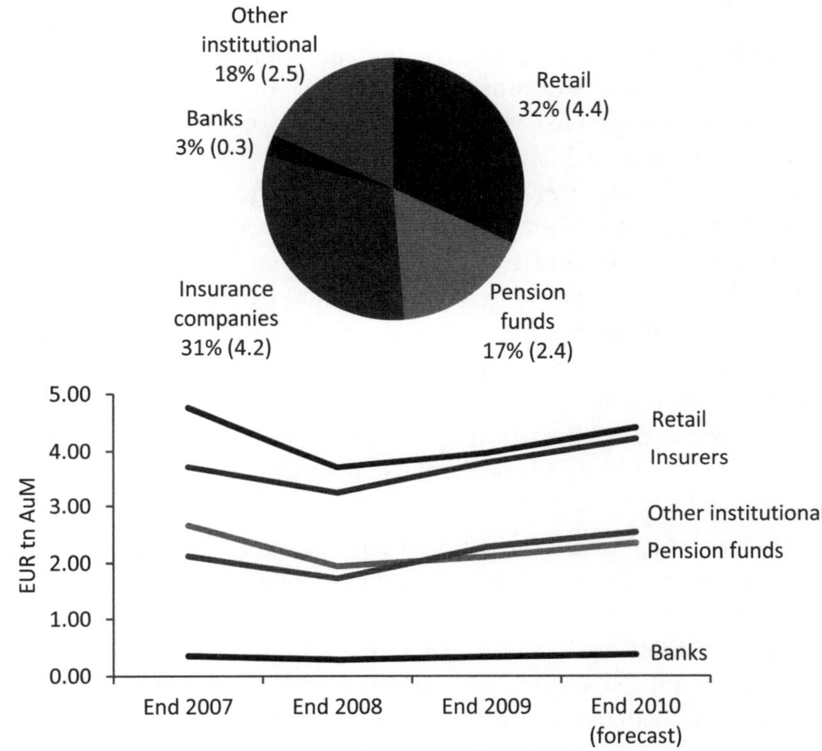

Source: EFAMA (2009 and 2011a).

Institutional investors also invest in funds, including UCITS, given product quality and eased due diligence. In some countries the share of institutional participation in investment funds is well over 60%, in contrast with the US market where only 15% of net assets in mutual funds are held in institutional accounts (EFAMA, 2011a, p. 29; ICI, 2011, p. 184). Besides financial intermediaries, governments and non-financial corporations also invest in funds and discretionary mandates for a variety of purposes. It is notable in this regard the use of money market funds to manage corporate cash in some member states such as France (€340 billion net assets by end 2011 - AFG, 2012). This cash management function, however, is much less developed in Europe than in the US - net assets in money market funds in Europe accounted for approximately €1.2 trillion in 2011, in contrast with $2.6 trillion in the US (EFAMA, 2011b, p. 5; ICI, 2011, p. 164).

1.4 Convergence between traditional and alternative strategies

Traditional and alternative investments have been converging for some years, following the path of financial innovation, and changes in markets, correlations among asset classes, investor demand and regulation. The line between traditional and alternative asset management is sometimes difficult to draw. At the margin, traditional managers are those who invest in plain vanilla stocks and bonds and only pursue long-term strategies characterised by strong diversification and no leverage. This profile has been the object of regulation in the US (mutual funds) and Europe (UCITS) since 1940 and 1985, respectively, aimed at allowing the marketing of traditional funds to retail investors under conditions of high liquidity and transparency. By way of contrast, the concept of alternative strategies is all-embracing, comprising every style other than simple diversified long-only plain vanilla. The most general categorisation of alternative managers is made with reference to the asset class in which they primarily invest: i) hedge funds, invested in financial instruments; ii) private equity, in non-listed companies; iii) real estate funds and iv) commodity funds.

The common ground among all alternative funds is that they attempt to provide investors with returns that are uncorrelated to other asset classes. For instance, hedge funds may invest in similar instruments as traditional managers but they are different in that they strive to provide returns even when markets fall (so-called 'absolute returns'). For this purpose, they use a wide range of instruments and practices, including derivatives, structured products, leverage or short-selling in order to profit from unstable or falling asset prices. Of course, as in any other fund, returns are not guaranteed and there is no principal protection.[4] The hedge-fund universe, however, is far from homogenous, with some managers for instance running significantly leveraged funds while others do not. Another typical hedge-fund strategy is the arbitrage of price differentials and other market inefficiencies, based on the managers' in-house research capabilities.

The convergence of traditional and alternative strategies is reflected both in hedge fund managers registering their own mutual or UCITS funds, and traditional managers investing in some asset classes or employing some practices that were previously seen as the exclusive realm of alternative funds, such as investing in (OTC) derivatives or running leverage. Overall, convergence has been the result of four main forces:

---

[4] The reference to 'absolute returns' has been heavily criticised from this perspective, given that it may confuse retail investors and misrepresent the risks embedded in alternative products.

i) *innovation*, given the generalisation of the use of derivatives, structured instruments and other practices in financial markets;

ii) *supply*, given the interest of managers in expanding their investor base and product range;

iii) *demand*, given the growing funding gap in institutional investors' balance sheets and their search for long-term returns and expertise in portfolio management in declining markets and

iv) *regulation*, given the convergence of the rules that apply to both types of managers.

The interest of institutional investors in alternative investments has resulted over time in a significant expansion of their allocation to these strategies. The trend has been well documented both before and after the financial crisis (BIS, 2006; McKinsey, 2006; Deutsche Bank, 2011; P&I, 2011). Institutional investors have demanded higher transparency and better governance from managers, particularly after the crisis, prompting for instance hedge funds to abandon their 'black-box' approach to investing in order to expand or retain their business. At the same time, asset managers have implemented some of the features of alternative strategies in UCITS. The move is believed to be the consequence of latent demand by retail investors, the uncertainties that surrounded the adoption of the AIFMD and the effect of prudential and other rules in shaping the preferences of institutional investors. The UCITS Directive has been permeable to alternative strategies by gradually opening up to innovations that had become commonplace elsewhere in financial markets, such as derivatives, structured instruments and others. Ultimately, financial innovation has changed the conception of traditional asset management, where the use of derivatives has been generalised both to mitigate risks and to generate returns (EFAMA, 2011c, p. 7; City Fund Services, 2010). Despite institutional investors leading the way, the 'new' traditional funds are also present in the retail space - albeit subject to (increasingly tight) regulatory requirements with regard to counterparty and operational risks.

In the coming years, additional changes in regulation that were adopted to take stock of the lessons learned notably in the financial crisis (such as the AIFMD) are expected to deepen convergence. On the one hand, the registration requirements, conduct of business rules and transparency obligations that used to operate only for traditional managers have been extended to the alternative space, thereby reducing the gap in terms of administrative burden - which acted as a major disincentive for alternative managers to launch their own mutual and UCITS funds. On the other hand, prudential rules, which influence the allocation of institutional investors by establishing capital and solvency charges, have been revisited to give more weight to the ultimate underlying rather than the legal form of the fund. It follows therefore that managers will increasingly offer customised solutions to institutional investors, where they will apply the best tools at their disposal, whether traditional or alternative, and thereby furthering convergence. In the retail space, convergence will probably continue unless a deterioration of product integrity or any risk of misselling brings regulators to restrict the access of retail investors to certain products.

1.5 The role of regulation in asset management

Asset management regulation pursues a number of objectives, including financial stability, investor protection and the development of capital markets. Regulation has traditionally targeted retail investors, providing a framework for asset managers to structure and sell funds in the retail market. Mutual funds in the US and UCITS in Europe are the two most important examples, next to other less liquid structures in some member states. The goal of these frameworks is both to protect retail investor savings and promote their participation in capital markets. Retail investor protection does not attempt to deny market risks since these are inherent to any investment and in the case of investment funds are transparently and directly borne by investors. Protection refers instead to ensuring that retail investors can access funds that fulfil three basic criteria: i) are well diversified, ii) are well managed and iii) are transparent and well governed, thereby permitting investors to understand the risks embedded and choose in line with their investment objectives, risk profile and financial ability to bear possible losses. For this purpose, regulation addresses different areas, notably:

- product structuring (e.g. eligible assets, issuer concentration and leverage limits),
- risk management (e.g. risk management function, liquidity and redemptions),
- conduct of business (e.g. operating requirements, conflicts of interest) and
- disclosure to investors (e.g. transparency obligations, pre-contractual disclosure).

Legislation that addresses all or most of these items, and in particular product structuring, is known as 'product regulation'.

Protecting retail investors was the primary concern of asset management regulation until the financial crisis of 2007-08, when it became apparent that regulation should more intensively target two other goals: financial stability and the 'protection' of professional investors. The work carried out by regulators to understand the causes of the crisis and devise the regulatory response concluded that asset managers were not at its source but still merited more attention from a financial stability perspective (Turner, 2009; de Larosière, 2009 and FSB, 2011a). In pursuit of more resilient and stable financial markets, existing asset management regulation revealed itself to be partially inadequate. Not only did it not cater specifically for financial stability but it was also patchy across jurisdictions and industry subsectors. In effect, some subsectors of the asset management industry were largely unregulated or subject to significantly different approaches across jurisdictions – in spite of the industry experiencing strong convergence and being eminently cross-national in its operation. To overcome these deficiencies, in 2011, the EU adopted the alternative investment fund managers Directive (AIFMD) with a distinct and overarching financial stability objective.[5] In contrast to the UCITS legislation, the AIFMD is not 'product' but 'manager' regulation. In effect, the AIFMD does not consider product structuring and instead applies horizontally to all asset managers (except those operating under the UCITS rules). It introduces minimum operating requirements and extensive reporting to enable supervisors to effectively monitor financial stability. The US Dodd-Frank Act follows a similar approach in this respect, by mandating registration and reporting for systemic risk oversight.

The crisis also revealed the importance of affording an adequate level of 'protection' to professional and institutional investors. In effect, the road to the crisis proved that micro-risks, such as poor due diligence, have spill-over effects that may ultimately undermine financial stability (Turner, 2009 and de Larosière et al., 2009). Yet, the use of the word 'protection' carries a fundamentally different meaning in the professional space in comparison to retail investor protection. Where it comes to professional and institutional investors, the protective role of regulation is limited chiefly to: i) mandating a level of disclosure from managers that enables their clients to conduct meaningful due diligence processes and ii) making conduct of business principles explicit in regulation so that investors are better equipped to ensure that managers abide by their fiduciary duties. These two elements complement strictly prudential rules in the AIFMD and, by their connection with financial stability, are also integral parts of 'manager regulation'.

Manager and product regulation are cumulative, meaning for instance that most of the rules in the AIFMD are built-in the UCITS Directive. The question arises therefore whether product rules should be imposed on the different subsectors of the asset management industry. From a retail investor perspective, product rules may have a role to play in enabling investor access to particular products or strategies. By way of contrast, for professional and

[5] Directive 2011/61/EC (AIFMD).

institutional investors, product rules would prove counterproductive. Notably, product rules would: i) reduce the incentive of professional investors to perform their own due diligence, ii) unduly restrict the range of available investments in the market place and iii) induce relative simple and transparent intermediation in the asset management industry to move into other areas of financial markets that are comparatively more complex and opaque. In effect, product rules are no substitute for the prudential objective embedded in management rules, which are called upon to have a broader scope and therefore follow different principles than product rules.

Table 2. Management versus product rules

	Management (prudential) rules	Product rules
Goals	- Financial stability - Investor protection - Fostering capital markets	- Investor protection (retail) - Other public policy goals
Level	- Macro-prudential - Micro-prudential	- Micro-prudential
Object	- Profession - Provision of service	- Product structuring
Content	- Operating requirements - Conduct of business - Transparency and disclosure	- Portfolio composition and asset allocation - Risk management

Finally, it is worth noting that asset management regulation may have other public policy objectives beyond financial stability, investor protection and fostering capital markets. Some of these other goals are promoting *long-term savings* by providing for instance product rules for illiquid investments, or promoting *socially responsible investment* (SRI) by introducing a framework for the consideration of environmental, social and governance criteria in asset management (ESG). Two examples in these areas are open-ended real estate funds and SRI funds in Germany and France, respectively. Besides, regulation may also promote the participation of asset managers in not-for-profit activities, as in other parts of the financial services industry. In this latter respect, the European Commission proposed in 2011 a regulation on *social entrepreneurship funds* (SEFs). Last but not least, Europe has the opportunity to develop the AIFMD into a *competitive management framework* that would see EU managers offering their services around the world, generating jobs and wealth at home.

1.5.1 *Regulatory coherence and future steps*

The AIFMD radically alters the picture of asset management regulation in Europe. In contrast to UCITS, the AIFMD is a mandatory regime that applies to all managers, regardless of their market classification or business model. In effect, hedge funds, private equity, real estate funds, commodity funds and in sum all other non-UCITS funds will be affected by the AIFMD – the Directive applies however to the manager rather than the fund since it does not regulate product structuring. While most member states had legal forms to accommodate alternative investments before the adoption of the AIFMD, the added value of the Directive lies in its distinct macro-prudential approach and in aligning national rules to create a single market for the distribution of AIFs (Alternative Investment Funds) to professional investors in Europe.[6]

Despite having been referred to as *the hedge-fund Directive*, the AIFMD embodies the basic regulatory framework of asset management activities in Europe. While formally independent from the UCITS Directive and ulterior in time, the AIFMD borrows a significant part of its content from the principles in the UCITS framework – for instance the parts concerning minimum operating conditions, conduct of business rules or segregation principles. In terms of substance, UCITS adds to the AIFMD framework product structuring rules and standardised disclosure for retail investors. In spite of the reference to 'alternative investment fund managers' in its title, the substance of the AIFMD applies both to alternative and traditional asset managers, and to UCITS funds by virtue of the UCITS Directive and given its many similarities to the AIFMD. In the words of Amenc & Sender (2011, p. 8), "by including the depositary regulation in the AIFMD, and by explicitly relying on some of the UCITS objectives and references, regulators and politicians confirm that the AIFMD is a general framework that could encapsulate UCITS".

The role of the AIFMD as a general framework instead of a hedge fund regulation should be asserted both to clarify the substantive structure of asset management regulation in Europe and to open a new window of opportunity for managers and investors. The introduction of the AIFMD will encourage managers to reposition their business models in the next few years. The UCITS experience proves that there is sizeable demand for transparent and well-governed financial intermediation. By extending these principles horizontally across the asset management industry, the AIFMD may generate similar success and industry growth, although challenges to implementation remain. At the same time, it may provide the ideal launch platform for specialised

---

[6] For a survey of national rules for hedge funds, private equity and real estate funds, see EDHEC-Risk (2010a).

regulation in domains such as long-term or socially responsible investments, where latent investor demand has arguably not yet been satisfied. In this regard, the proposal of the European Commission to tailor the AIFMD to promote venture capital illustrates that the Directive is already playing this role for the promotion of other public policy objectives - such as, in this case, facilitating innovation and the development of new businesses.

Figure 5 provides a fairly comprehensive *picture of asset management regulation in Europe* today, followed by a brief description of its main elements.

Figure 5. The new picture of fund management and related regulation in Europe

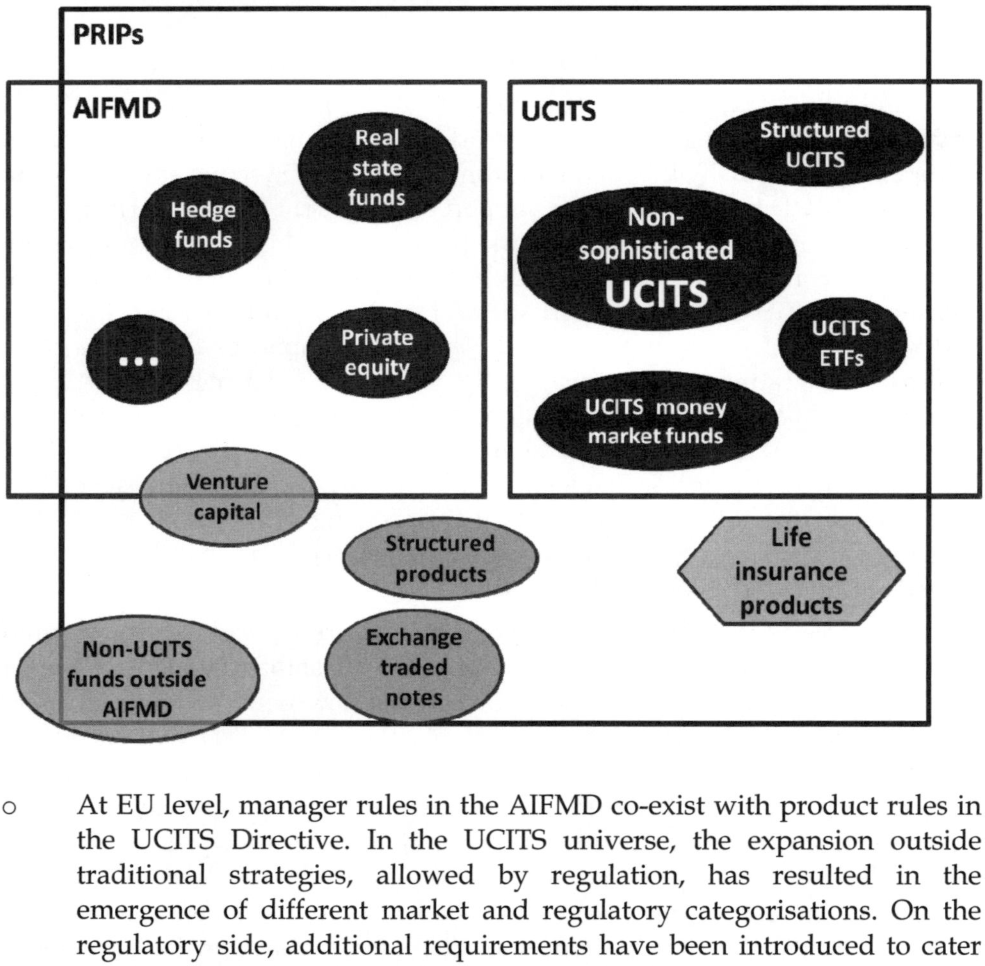

- o At EU level, manager rules in the AIFMD co-exist with product rules in the UCITS Directive. In the UCITS universe, the expansion outside traditional strategies, allowed by regulation, has resulted in the emergence of different market and regulatory categorisations. On the regulatory side, additional requirements have been introduced to cater for the specificities of some fund types, including:
  - i) *sophisticated UCITS*, at the level of managing and measuring the risk embedded in derivatives,

ii) *structured UCITS*, at the level of pre-contractual disclosure and (in the review of MiFID proposed by the European Commission in 2011) sale practices,

iii) *exchange-traded UCITS*, at the level of pre-contractual disclosure and the redemption of units, among other aspects and

iv) *money-market UCITS*, at the level of eligible assets and maturity of the underlying.

On the market side, concepts such as alternative UCITS and others have been coined to identify funds pursuing alternative investment strategies in compliance with the UCITS Directive.

- In its turn, AIFMD, by not considering product structuring, will encompass broadly speaking all non-UCITS managers and in particular hedge-funds, private equity and real state funds.
- Against the background of the proliferation of product types in asset management and other areas of financial intermediation, in 2012 the European Commission will propose to extend the model of standardised pre-contractual disclosure in UCITS (the key investor information document or KIID) to other retail investment products with an element of packaging, including notably unit-linked insurance policies and structured banking products, in the interest of retail investor protection. This proposal falls within the packaged retail investment products (PRIPs) initiative.
- Beyond EU rules, member states may still apply local legislation in some instances, including to: i) non-UCITS managers who are exempted from the AIFMD due to their size, ii) non-UCITS funds that are sold to retail investors and their managers and iii) funds whose managers have to comply with the AIFMD as long as no discrimination is introduced against managers domiciled in other member states. In cases in which managers are domiciled outside the EU, the AIFMD follows a phased approach that should end up by requiring foreign managers to comply with most of the provisions in the Directive if they market funds in the EU. Until that moment arrives, national rules (sometimes called national placement regimes) will continue to apply to non-EU managers.

1.6 Success of the single market project

In the context of European integration, the realisation of the single market appears as an additional objective in asset management regulation. The rationale is that market integration stimulates competition and allows providers to reach optimal operating scales, with the consequential gains in efficiency, reductions in costs and increases in returns. As for most other products and services, the execution of the single market for asset management is based both on harmonisation and mutual recognition. In effect, common EU rules on the structuring of products (funds) and/or the operating conditions of intermediaries (managers) are the initial step that makes mutual recognition work in practice. Mutual recognition then enables funds to be marketed in member states other than the one where they are domiciled. The mechanism is known as a 'passport', which in the case of UCITS extends to retail investors but is restricted in the AIFMD to professional clients, in line with the different scopes of the two directives. The AIFMD passport is scheduled to enter into force in July 2013.

So far market integration in UCITS has been a success, building up slowly since 1985. Initially, management companies would clone funds using local subsidiaries given the reticence of local supervisors to grant mutual recognition of funds domiciled in other member states. Over time the passport was perfected allowing for the emergence of two main cross-border fund domiciliation centres, Luxembourg and Ireland, from where the bulk of cross-border UCITS funds are marketed in the EU through local branches. Locally domiciled funds in other member states are also exported cross-border thanks to the passport. In 2011, a further step was taken by creating a management company passport (MCP), which allows the centralisation of asset management activities. Before the introduction of the MCP, management groups had to establish a fully functional management company in each member state where they domiciled a fund. The introduction of the MCP is aimed at reducing the large number of intermediaries (mergers and master-feeder structures also became possible in 2011 for this same purpose).

While no complete figures exist on the penetration of foreign funds in national UCITS markets in terms of assets under management, good proxies are available. Data from Lipper FMI, which monitors the source of assets for Luxembourg retail funds and other cross-border retail funds, suggest that the share of penetration of foreign players in national markets may not reach 20% on average (Lipper, 2010, p. 44). Where UCITS sold to institutional investors are taken into account, the share of cross-border assets is thought to have exceeded 40% in 2011, in contrast to just 21% in 2001 (Lipper, 2012, p. 6). In terms of registrations, the number of funds distributed in at least three countries reached 7,907 in 2010 with the average fund in this group being distributed in eight countries, including its own member state of domicile (PwC, 2011). The former figure represents a share of approximately 20% of UCITS funds. Given the introduction in 2011 of a simpler procedure to passport UCITS funds across member states, the penetration of foreign funds in national markets is expected to increase at a faster pace over the next few years.

Figure 6. Assets sourced by foreign UCITS in national retail markets (estimation)

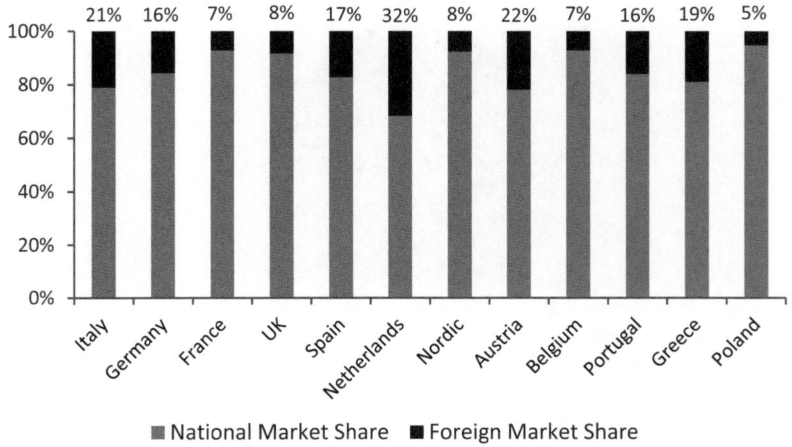

Source: Lipper (2010, p. 44).

As to AIFs, no figures are available yet pending the introduction of the passport, but the stakes are high so that a single market for alternative funds and management services emerges in the EU despite the difficulties found in the adoption of the Directive and its implementation. In 2011, UCITS accounted for approximately 70% of the net assets in investment funds in Europe (EFAMA, 2012a, p. 9), but future growth, hopefully propelled by the AIFMD passport, could increase the share of non-UCITS funds in overall net assets over the next few years.

1.7 Opportunity abroad for EU managers

Regulation has proven that it can help industry development and open opportunities for European asset managers in other areas of the globe. According to data from Lipper, as much as 25% of AuM in UCITS funds are sourced outside the European Union, with the majority of those assets coming from Asia and an increasing share from South America (Lipper, 2010, p. 39). In a period of slow growth in Europe, emerging economies represent a significant opportunity for European asset managers to market both their funds and their management services. For instance the client base of UCITS funds has become fairly international over the years – estimations by EFAMA indicate that over 40% of UCITS net sales took place outside Europe in 2011 (EFAMA, 2011c, p. 7). The challenge today is to develop the AIFMD into a competitive framework that would see EU managers successfully offering not only their funds but also their management services around the world.

Figure 7. Geographical origin of cross-border sales in UCITS

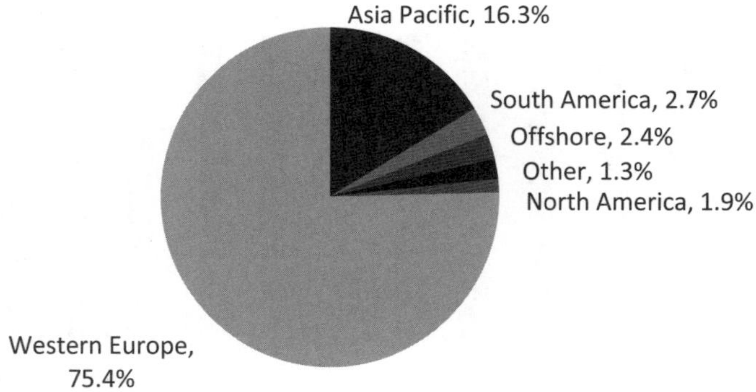

Source: Lipper FMI Sales Watch Project. Moisson (2010).

Box 1. Five regulatory trends that will contribute to shaping the future of the asset management industry in Europe

The regulatory focus will shift to investors...

Having addressed most of the prudential concerns in relation to fund management through the AIFMD, the regulatory focus in Europe will shift to investor choice and investor protection. The review of the markets in financial instruments Directive (MiFID) and the initiative on packaged retail investment products (PRIPs) represent a significant opportunity to revamp the panorama of retail distribution in Europe and promote greater competition among intermediaries.

... but targeted rule-making to strengthen financial stability will continue.

Concerns about maturity and liquidity transformation, and imperfect risk transfers, outside the regular banking system (shadow-banking) are likely to result in restrictions to practices such as securities lending or the re-hypothecation of collateral. The Financial Stability Board (FSB) will coordinate international action in this regard. Some industry sub-sectors, such as money market funds with stable net asset values, are likely to see fundamental changes in the way their business is regulated.

Funds under AIFMD will attract the interest of institutional investors...

As AIFMD (alternative investment fund managers Directive) comes into force and gains momentum, the allocation of institutional investors to non-harmonised investment funds is set to increase further. Moreover, as prudential rules turn their attention to the ultimate underlying rather than the legal form of investment funds, the access of institutional investors to non-harmonised funds will be eased. The challenge will be to implement the AIFMD successfully, achieving its objectives without undermining the competitive position of the EU asset management industry.

... while new fund types will be pushed forward by regulators.

Fragmentation of the UCITS brand is likely to come either at the point of sale (through immediate changes in the regulation selling practices) or at the level of product structuring (through future changes in product rules). At the same time, the AIFMD will prove that it encapsulates the general regulatory framework for asset management and will serve as a sort of launch platform for regulatory spin-offs aimed at promoting public policy goals such as long-term investing, responsible investing, venture capital and social entrepreneurship.

And competition will be increasingly tough.

The likely expansion of exchange-traded funds will commoditise some investment strategies, forcing other managers into lower fees or radical specialisation. Size will become ever-more important for mass-market funds to remain competitive, while continuing polarisation of passive and active management will further erode middle product ranges. Ambitious distribution reform could intensify competition for retail clients and introduce additional pressure on fees, forcing industry consolidation and rationalisation. At the same time, the AIFMD will intensify competition from non-EU managers.

2. FINANCIAL STABILITY: SCOPING THE ISSUES AND NAVIGATING REGULATORY REFORM

The asset management industry was fundamentally affected by the financial crisis, but is not seen to be one of its main causes. Still, asset management is interwoven with most if not all financial sector activities, and the industry will be strongly impacted by many of the measures taken in the meantime in the pursuit of more resilient and stable financial markets. In addition, parts of the asset management industry are strongly associated with the banking system, a connection that attracts increasing attention by policy-makers.

Financial stability may be broadly defined as the absence of disruptions in the ordinary functioning of financial markets that would significantly undermine the wider economy (Allen & Wood, 2006; Čihák, 2006 and Schinasi, 2004). The events that took place in financial markets from 2007 onwards positioned financial stability at the centre of the regulatory agenda at global and regional level. The G-20 nations meeting in Washington, D.C. in November 2008 pledged to improve the regulation and oversight of all financial markets, products and participants as appropriate. In Europe two comprehensive reports – one commissioned by the Financial Services Authority (FSA) to Adair Turner (2009) in the UK and the other, by the European Commission to Jacques de Larosière (2009) – explored the causes of the crisis and the regulatory response that should follow. Both reports concluded that the asset management industry did not play a major role in the financial crisis.

Acknowledging the limited role of asset managers in the financial crisis did not prevent regulators from further investigating the links between asset management and financial stability. In effect, the crisis prompted a step-change in the approach of authorities to the regulation and surveillance of all financial intermediaries, including asset managers. The new approach of regulators highlights the importance of: i) targeting the economic substance of financial intermediation rather than its legal form, ii) challenging business models and strategies instead of focusing supervision on systems and processes, iii) monitoring markets continuously from a financial stability perspective and iv) taking action at an early stage before perverse developments become endemic and pose immediate threats to financial stability (Turner, 2009 and de Larosière, 2009). This new approach explains most of the regulatory and supervisory developments that are reshaping the asset management industry in Europe and globally, such as the enactment of the alternative investment fund managers Directive (AIFMD), the role of depositaries or the FSB monitoring of non-bank financial intermediaries (or 'shadow banking').

This section will consider the links between asset management and financial stability by first discussing the role of the industry in the crisis; then referring to selected issues of financial stability in asset management; and finally considering the major regulatory reforms undertaken to strengthen the resilience of the industry. The section will elaborate in particular on how the rules in the AIFMD address the links between financial stability and fund management. It will also consider in detail maturity transformation, as illustrated by the case of money market funds with stable net asset values, and the role of the new financial stability watchdogs, as illustrated by the case of synthetic exchange traded-funds.

2.1 The role of the industry in the crisis of 2008

Regulators worldwide have acknowledged that the asset management industry did not play a principal role in the crisis, with the exception of some money market funds. Notably the size of the industry and its volume of leverage did not make it systemically important (Turner, 2009 and de Larosière et al., 2009). Data from the IMF (2008) and the World Bank (2009) reveal that the levels of leverage in the asset management industry were moderate and significantly lower than in the banking industry. In 2008, the most leveraged asset managers, e.g. hedge funds pursuing capital of relative value and fixed-income arbitrage strategies, were on average three times less leveraged than the 10 largest banks in continental Europe (see Figure 7). Pooling all hedge-fund strategies together, their average leverage was 20 times lower than the average leverage of banks in Europe in 2008. In terms of size, over 3,000 asset management companies hold an average of €4 billion assets under management, which is roughly 50% of the average assets in domestic banks in the EU27. In rounded figures, assets under management in investment funds represent €6 trillion, in contrast to €34 trillion in domestic banks in the EU-27 (EFAMA, 2011a and ECB, 2011). While banks provide a useful benchmark with regard to size, the activities of asset managers and banks are intrinsically different in nature. Crucially, the risk of loss in investment funds is borne transparently by investors, i.e. the direct owners of the underlying assets, and is not insured by sovereigns.

In spite of their limited size, leveraged funds logically played a role in depressing asset prices (Turner, 2009 and de Larosière et al., 2009). Precisely because of their use of leverage, some hedge funds were part of the deflationary spiral. Those funds relied on banks and other counterparties to fund their exposures (under so-called 'prime brokerage' agreements). Where market conditions deteriorated, drops in asset prices prompted prime brokers to cut down on the financing and ask for more collateral or higher margins. In a deflationary spiral, financing restrictions forced hedge funds into fire sales and depressed prices further, restarting a vicious cycle in which prime brokers' conditions would worsen further. Some hedge funds failed (about 1,500 in the US), but it is worth noting that the impact of these failures on the counterparties was not very significant probably given the difference in size (BIS, 2010, p. 56). In conclusion, while asset managers did not play a major role in the emergence of the crisis, some funds behaved pro-cyclically in a transmission capacity due to their leverage (de Larosière et al., 2009, p. 24).

Figure 8. A comparison of hedge fund and bank leverage, 2nd qtr. 2008

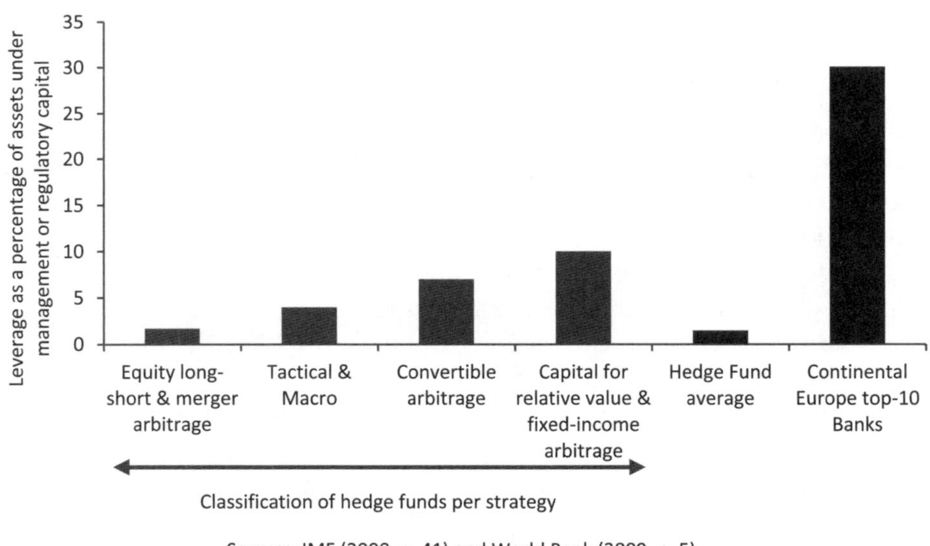

Sources: IMF (2008, p. 41) and World Bank (2009, p. 5).

In comparison to the rest of the asset management industry, money market funds (MMFs) were the most affected by the financial crisis. In September 2008, a fast-growing US MMF "broke the buck"[7] by acknowledging a difference of 30-basis points between the face value of its units ($1.00) and their mark-to-market value. Contagion became widespread, involving large redemptions across the industry and further deterioration of conditions in money markets. The run prompted the US Treasury to introduce a temporary guarantee in favour of investors. The Federal Reserve was also forced to step in by extending credit lines in favour of banks to restore liquidity in money markets. In Europe, despite the lack of a harmonised definition of MMFs, some funds experienced similar problems as their US counterparts. Losses in Europe were borne primarily by asset management companies and their parent undertakings - either directly or indirectly. The ECB was also forced to intervene by providing assistance to restore liquidity in interbank and money markets. European interbank markets suffered dearly due to the reliance of European banks on USD-denominated MMFs, prompting the ECB and the Federal Reserve to increase their swap lines (McCauley et al., 2009).

The problems experienced in 2008 were the consequence of i) poor investment decisions, ii) the deposit-like promises made by some MMFs, iii) the direct losses caused by the failure of Lehman Brothers and iv) the loss of confidence in the quality of the commercial paper issued by banks. In effect, some funds commercialised as 'money market' were invested in illiquid assets, including subprime CDOs (collateralised debt obligations), which significantly undermined their resilience to market shocks and their ability to meet redemptions. Some funds were performing significant maturity transformation while making deposit-like promises that misrepresented the risks to investors. Widespread reliance on 'liquidity through marketability' proved flawed where market conditions deteriorated (Turner, 2009, p. 21).[8] Growing redemptions and worsening conditions in money markets exhausted the ability of fund sponsors to keep stable NAVs.

The run in 2008 revealed the relative systemic importance of MMFs, given their size and economic relevance, as well as their deposit-like promises (in some instances). MMFs are a very significant source of short-term funding for governments, corporations and financial institutions, including interbank markets - assets under management totalled more than $3.8 trillion in the US and $1.3 trillion in Europe in 2008 (McCauley et al., 2009).

---

[7] If a fund's net asset value (NAV) falls below $1.00, it is said that the fund "broke the buck".

[8] 'Liquidity through marketability' is the ability to recover the value of assets before their maturity by selling them in the marketplace.

2.2 Issues of financial stability in fund management

Beyond the limited role of asset managers in the financial crisis, regulators have reconsidered their approach to the industry in their efforts to strengthen the overall resilience of the financial system. The Financial Stability Board (FSB), established in 2009, is coordinating under a G20 mandate an effort to strengthen financial stability through regulatory and supervisory reforms. Among several other work streams initiated, the FSB is considering non-bank financial intermediation from a financial stability perspective, including fund management (FSB, 2011a). The work of the board in this regard follows three main steps: i) building global monitoring capabilities to capture the scale and trends in non-bank financial intermediation, ii) indentifying broad themes that concern financial stability and iii) assessing in detail specific concerns and proposing concrete actions (FSB, 2011b, p. 7). The approach of the FSB consists therefore of first *casting the net wide* and then *narrowing down* the scope of its analysis (FSB, 2011a).

In relation to asset management, the FSB is largely taking stock of the work carried-out previously at the national and international level by IOSCO (2009), the European Commission (2009a) and the UK FSA (2005). These reports consider that while the asset management industry does not pose in itself an immediate threat to financial stability, there are a number of areas where regulatory and supervisory reform could strengthen the resilience of the industry and its contribution to stable financial markets. Five broad themes of financial stability in asset management emerge from the work carried out by these regulators: i) the overall size of the industry and its economic importance, ii) leverage and pro-cyclicality, iii) maturity and liquidity transformation, iv) transparency of the underlying exposures and v) links with the banking system. Most of these themes are already the object of supervisory oversight and regulation in the EU and the US.

i) *Overall size and economic importance.* The asset management industry is projected to experience significant growth in the medium to long-term, as tighter regulatory requirements are imposed on banks in the framework of Basel III (FSB, 2011a). The growth of asset management intermediation and capital markets is expected to have an overall positive impact on financial stability by reducing the importance of banks in the financial system and the wider economy. However, there is a reasonable likelihood that business previously undertaken by banks will move to the asset management industry, undermining the effectiveness of some of the rules under Basel III. Moreover, some areas of the asset management industry are expected to play an increasingly important role in financing the real economy. In this respect, regulators conclude that the industry should be subject to common regulatory standards and oversight from a financial stability perspective that are consistent at international level.

ii) *Leverage and pro-cyclicality.* Funds may gather leverage by borrowing directly from banks or other counterparties or using repurchase agreements (secured financing). Moreover, practices such as securities lending, re-hypothecation of collateral, short-selling and derivatives also amplify fund leverage. The average leverage in the asset management industry is low in comparison to other intermediaries but somewhat significant in some alternative investment funds (see Figure 8 above). High leverage multiplies the exposure of funds to risk. It amplifies the impact of price shocks and raises the probability of fire sales when financing withdraws under stressful market conditions. Stated otherwise, it magnifies the risks embedded in liquidity and maturity mismatches since borrowing is very sensitive to a reduction in market confidence and might suddenly dry up or not be rolled over. In this respect, supervisors have agreed to enhance their oversight capacities in order to monitor the level of leverage in the industry and its potential contribution to pro-cyclicality.

iii) *Maturity and liquidity transformation.* Investment managers can theoretically perform significant maturity and liquidity transformation, as seen for instance in some money market funds before the introduction of tighter rules on both sides of the Atlantic. In general, the degree of liquidity of investment funds depends on three aspects: a) the maturity or liquidity of the underlying positions, b) the leverage of the fund and the maturity of its financing and c) the redemption policy of the fund as represented to investors. Where these aspects are not aligned and appropriately managed, funds may incur significant asset-liability mismatches, engage in destabilising fire sales and ultimately fail to meet redemptions. Managers need therefore to manage both their underlying portfolios (using appropriate risk and liquidity management processes) and redemptions by investors (using instruments such as gates, side-pockets and suspensions). Ultimately, the liquidity of the underlying assets should be explicit for investors, as well as the possibility that redemptions may be limited in the event of exceptional market circumstances.

iv) *Transparency of the underlying exposures.* The risks embedded in investment funds depend on their underlying assets and are therefore significantly different across funds, even if they pursue similar investment strategies. Transparency is essential for financial stability – market confidence in opaque instruments is very fragile since investors cannot distinguish good from bad assets (Bank of England, 2011). At the same time, opaque instruments create contingent exposures that may only become evident during times of market stress (FSB, 2011a). Opacity in financial instruments appears directly related to their level of complexity since complex instruments are harder to value and more difficult to understand in terms of the risks they carry. As a matter of principle, investment funds need to be fully transparent about their underlying assets so that unit holders are able to determine the ultimate risk to which they are exposed (FSB, 2011b). Supervisors should also be able to monitor aggregate exposures to better understand movements in markets that may impact financial stability.

v) *Links with the banking system*. There is anecdotal evidence that banks may set up investment management activities to arbitrage the rules under Basel III. Some market intelligence suggests for instance that the limits introduced to proprietary trading by banks in the US have resulted in the transformation of some proprietary trading desks into stand-alone hedge funds (Fitch Ratings, 2011b and Strategic Insight, 2010). Similarly, supervisors are looking at the use of synthetic ETFs (exchanged traded funds) by some banks to finance their balance sheets at a lower cost than repo transactions and potentially lower requirements in terms of regulatory capital (FSB, 2011c). They are equally looking at similar practices such as securities lending. In this respect, regulators need to constantly monitor market developments and business models and be ready to act quickly to inhibit regulatory arbitrage of banking rules via the asset management industry.

Table 3. Themes of financial stability in fund management and regulatory actions

THEMES	Concerns	Actions	Instruments
Size and economic importance	- Growth propelled by tighter banking rules (medium to long-term horizon)	- Introduce minimum common rules - Enhance macro-oversight capacities	- AIFMD - UCITS
Leverage	- Magnified exposures and risks	- Introduce disclosure standards - Clarify supervisory powers	- AIFMD - UCITS
Pro-cyclicality	- Contribution to peaks in cycles - Lack of resilience to stressed market circumstances	- Mitigate reliance on risk metrics - Promote stress-testing - Oversee risk management processes	- AIFMD - UCITS

Maturity and liquidity transformation	- Risk of runs on funds	- Align redemption policies with maturity / liquidity of underlying	- AIFMD - UCITS - Rules on money market funds
Transparency of the underlying assets	- Opacity of exposures	- Strict transparency requirements - Strict look-trough to underlying	- AIFMD (sell-side) - UCITS (sell-side) - Solvency II and CRD IV (buy-side)
Links with banking system	- Arbitrage of banking rules - General interconnectedness of the financial system	- Conflict of interest rules - Aggregation of exposures - Surveillance of business models	- AIFMD - UCITS - Basel III and CRD IV - Monitoring by supervisors (e.g. synthetic ETFs)

2.3 Minimum common rules for the industry – the AIFMD

The financial crisis prompted regulators to devise a comprehensive approach to regulate and supervise all financial intermediaries from a financial stability perspective, including asset managers. Europe led the way in this respect with the enactment of the Alternative Investment Fund Managers Directive (AIFMD) in 2011. The Directive is indeed comprehensive by targeting all alternative fund managers and introducing minimum common rules to address macro-prudential risks, micro-prudential risks and the protection of professional investors. It overcomes the fragmentation of regulation and supervision in member states and introduces a single market for AIFs, providing a significant opportunity for industry development but simultaneously reducing the opportunities for regulatory arbitrage.

The AIFMD is primarily aimed at ensuring that all managers fulfil minimum standards for financial stability purposes. In line with this goal, it applies to all alternative asset managers, independently of the specific strategy, business-model or subsector. The conscious choice of a horizontal piece of legislation aims to provide consistency and avoid the risk of ill-categorising market practices and opening windows for arbitrage. Only managers that handle UCITS and no AIFs are exempted from complying with the AIFMD.[9] In effect, the UCITS Directive already goes far in ensuring the resilience of managers and funds in the interest of financial stability – and certain elements of the directive will be revised in 2012 in line with the AIFMD. Despite its all-

[9] Small managers are also exempted from the scope of the AIFMD but they may opt-in. See later in this section.

encompassing scope, the AIMFD contains elements of tailoring depending on the size and economic nature of different activities (e.g. additional obligations for funds running high leverage). Building on these common rules, secondary and other legislation is bound in the future to pay more attention to specific business models, such as private equity, real state funds and other models well established in the marketplace. For instance, legislation is due to be enacted in 2012 that will be based on the AIFMD but tailored to the specificities of venture capital and its role in the economy.[10]

The AIFMD does not regulate funds, but rather managers. It does not deal therefore with portfolio composition – it does not limit eligible assets, issuer concentration, leverage or risks. Instead, it acts at the level of the manager by setting minimum operating requirements, mandatory registration and conduct of business rules. In so doing, it levels the playing field (proportionately) with other financial intermediaries that carry out economic functions of comparable economic significance. At the same time, registration allows supervisors to identify managers and, thanks to the reporting obligations introduced by the Directive, conduct effective macro-prudential oversight. The Directive complements its approach to financial stability by mandating comprehensive disclosure to (professional) investors so that they are able to carry out meaningful due diligence. Its intention here is to take stock of one of the main lessons of the financial crisis: namely that micro-risks, such as poor due diligence, can over time result in significant threats to financial stability (Turner, 2009 and de Larosière et al., 2009). Regulating portfolio composition instead could have induced moral hazard on professional investors and undermined their incentive to carry out their own due diligence.

Small funds are exempted from complying with most of the AIFMD since they do not have a material impact on financial stability. The initial proposal of the European Commission fully exempted managers under €250 million assets under management. Under this *de minimis* threshold, the Directive would have affected around 70% of assets in hedge funds and 90% of assets in open-ended non-UCITS funds, but only 15% and 36% of managers, respectively (European Commission, 2009a, pp. 46-51).[11] The final text, however, opts for a mixed approach that exempts managers under €100 million assets under management or €500 million if investors are locked-in for five years and in the absence of leverage.[12] It also opts for a partial exemption

---

[10] Legislative proposal COM (2011) 860 final (venture capital funds).

[11] The extent to which it will apply to private equity and funds was not surveyed by the Commission.

[12] Article 3.2, Directive 2011/61/EU (AIFMD).

instead of a full exemption, since managers under the threshold are obliged to register and provide simplified reporting to authorities to enable more effective financial stability oversight. The objective is to allow supervisors to have a fuller picture of the market without imposing administrative burdens on small managers that they would not be able to bear given their size. It is however uncertain whether the obligations imposed meet the latter objective.

In the pursuit of a level playing field with comparable intermediaries, the AIFMD requires managers to provide an initial capital of €300,000 and additional capital at a ratio of 0.02% of their assets under management in excess of €250 million.[13] The sum serves as a minimum entry requirement to the industry for managers over the *de minimis* threshold. It decreases as a proportion of the total assets under management, meaning the larger the fund, the lower the capital ratio (see Table 4).

Table 4. Initial capital and own funds in the AIFMD

	€ million				
AuM	100	250	500	1,000	10,000
Capital for the first €250m AuM	0.3	0.3	0.3	0.3	0.3
AuM in excess of €250m	0	0	250	750	9,750
Additional capital (ratio = 0.02%)	-	-	0.05	0.15	1.95
Total capital	0.3	0.3	0.35	0.45	2.25
Capital ratio	0.300%	0.120%	0.070%	0.045%	0.023%

Note: On top of the initial sums of capital above, managers are required to hold additional own funds (0.01% of AuM) or professional indemnity insurance (covering 1% of AuM in excess of €250 million). See Boxes 7 and 8, ESMA Technical Advice ESMA 2011/379 (AIFMD implementation).

In effect, managers experience economies of scale in terms of regulatory capital, the more assets they manage. The former makes clear that the objective of capital requirements in the AIFMD is to ensure that the manager is financially sound and capable of performing his/her tasks rather than providing for the risk of its activities, which is in principle borne directly by investors under conditions of transparency and no government guarantees. Capital requirements are complemented by additional own funds or insurance to cover potential professional liability. It is feared however that capital requirements may jeopardise the economic viability of some subsectors of the asset management industry.

---

[13] Article 9, Directive 2011/61/EU (AIFMD).

The AIFMD addresses many of the issues of financial stability identified in fund management:

i) *Prudential oversight.* To enable effective macro-prudential oversight, the AIFMD requires managers to report detailed information about the funds they manage to supervisors. In particular, managers need to disclose the main markets and instruments in which they trade, and their principal exposures and concentrations of each fund.[14] The reporting frequency depends on the size of the manager and the fund; ESMA proposed that funds report twice a year, except funds below the *de minimis* thresholds (once a year) or more than €1.5 billion assets under management (four times a year).[15] The format of disclosure is harmonised so that supervisors can aggregate information easily. In order to allow the efficient exchange of information with supervisors outside the European Union, reporting will be standardised and will follow the model template for hedge funds provided by IOSCO (2009) with some adjustments to account for the broader scope of the AIFMD.[16] Managers are however very concerned about the costs of reporting and question the relevance of some of the information as well as the ability of supervisors to digest it.

ii) *Leverage and pro-cyclicality.* The Directive follows a commitment and monitoring approach by requiring managers to: a) set their own leverage limit, b) communicate it to investors and supervisors and c) be able to demonstrate compliance.[17] If the manager employs leverage *on a substantial basis*, it faces additional reporting requirements as to the main sources and amount of leverage. To define the use of leverage *on a substantial basis*, ESMA does not favour the use of a single threshold but instead invites supervisory authorities to consider a range of circumstances, including the nature, scale and complexity of the AIF and the markets in which it operates.[18] Reporting would extend not only to the borrowing of cash and securities but also to the leverage embedded in derivatives and the re-use of assets by the manager (e.g. re-hypothecation of collateral).[19] If any threat to financial stability emerges, supervisors are entitled to introduce limits on leverage proportional to

---

14 Article 24, Directive 2011/61/EU (AIFMD).

15 Box 110.4, ESMA Technical Advice, ESMA 2011/379 (AIFMD implementation).

16 Annex V, ESMA Technical Advice, ESMA 2011/379 (AIFMD implementation).

17 Articles 15.4, 23.1.a and 25.3, Directive 2011/61/EU (AIFMD).

18 Box 111, Technical Advice, ESMA 2011/379 (AIFMD implementation).

19 Article 24.4, Directive 2011/61/EU (AIFMD).

that threat.[20] ESMA guidance suggests that limits may be imposed to control for: a) counterparty risk to other financial institutions, b) pro-cyclical effects, c) asset-liability mismatches and d) concentration of risks in particular markets.[21] The national authority would need to notify its decision to ESMA and the ESRB but consultation is regrettably not compulsory even though financial stability is inherently a cross-border issue.[22] The AIFMD contains other provisions directed at mitigating pro-cyclicality; notably, managers are required to conduct stress tests and to report their results to supervisors in order to reduce the reliance on pro-cyclical risk metrics such as value at risk (VaR).[23] The AIFMD does not address directly the use of securities lending, repo transactions or the re-investment of collateral, even though their link to leverage and pro-cyclicality is well known. These practices are in general use throughout financial markets and therefore necessitate a horizontal approach across intermediaries, which the FSB is due to bring forward in 2012 or 2013 (FSB, 2011b).

iii) *Maturity and liquidity transformation.* The AIFMD operates at three levels: a) risk management, b) disclosure to investors and c) reporting to supervisors. Managers are required to build up liquidity management capabilities and processes, including monitoring and stress-testing.[24] The AIFMD does not impose close-ended structures for illiquid funds but follows once more a commitment and monitoring approach. In this respect, managers need to: a) set out an investment strategy, liquidity profile and redemption policy both in normal and exceptional market circumstances, b) communicate them to investors and c) ensure they are consistent.[25] Supervision should focus indeed on checking the consistency and prudency of these three items to mitigate the risk of liquidity and maturity mismatches. For prudential policy purposes, managers need to notify to supervisors the percentage of assets subject to special arrangements, such as gates or side-pockets, given their illiquid

[20] Article 25.3, Directive 2011/61/EU (AIFMD).

[21] Box 101.4, Technical Advice, ESMA 2011/379 (AIFMD implementation).

[22] Article 25.3, Directive 2011/61/EU (AIFMD).

[23] Articles 15.3.b and 24.2, Directive 2011/61/EU (AIFMD).

[24] Article 16, Directive 2011/61/EU (AIFMD).

[25] Articles 23.1.h and 16.2, Directive 2011/61/EU (AIFMD).

nature.[26] The activation of any of these arrangements should be communicated to investors immediately.[27]

iv) *Transparency of the underlying*. The AIFMD mandates extensive disclosure to supervisors in terms of instruments, markets and exposures.[28] ESMA suggests that funds disclose the main categories of assets in which they invest, including their short and long market values, turnover and performance.[29] For investors, disclosure obligations in the AIFMD do not reflect directly the underlying but more broadly the fund's investment strategy and the types of assets in which it may invest.[30] The degree of transparency of the underlying exposures of the fund is left rather to the prudential regulation of institutional investors. For instance, the Solvency II regime for insurers will apply punitive solvency charges to funds that do not provide full transparency on the underlying. The Basel Committee on Banking Supervision will be considering the capital treatment of investment funds in 2012 (FSB, 2011b).

v) *Links with the banking system*. Managers need to take all reasonable steps to avoid conflicts of interest and otherwise manage and disclose those conflicts so that they do not adversely affect the interests of investors.[31] This rule affects in particular prime brokerages, that is, the provision of financing and market-making services to funds by banks and investment firms. Notably, prime brokerage agreements need to spell out the conditions under which the assets of the AIF (alternative investment fund) may be transferred and reused by the counterparty.[32] The independence of the custody function is key to ensure that the fund assets are not transferred or reused without the explicit consent of the manager and full transparency to investors. In this regard, prime brokers are prohibited from acting as fund depositaries unless they introduce a functional and hierarchical separation of both functions.[33] Managers need to give full account to investors of the extent to which the prime broker may reuse the fund's assets.[34]

---

[26] Articles 23.4 and 25.2, Directive 2011/61/EU (AIFMD).

[27] Box 108.5, Technical Advice, ESMA 2011/379 (AIFMD implementation).

[28] Article 24, Directive 2011/61/EU (AIFMD).

[29] Box 110.3.e, Technical Advice, ESMA 2011/379 (AIFMD implementation).

[30] Article 23.1.a, Directive 2011/61/EU (AIFMD).

[31] Articles 1.d and 14, Directive 2011/61/EU (AIFMD).

[32] Article 14.3, Directive 2011/61/EU (AIFMD).

[33] Article 21.4, Directive 2011/61/EU (AIFMD).

[34] Article 23.1.o, Directive 2011/61/EU (AIFMD).

In sum, the AIFMD represents a consistent framework for the regulation of the wider asset management industry from a prudential policy perspective by introducing minimum common rules. In particular, it addresses: a) prudential oversight, b) leverage and pro-cyclicality, c) maturity and liquidity transformation and d) links with the banking system. It relies on the prudential rules applicable to institutional investors when it comes to transparency of the underlying. Despite much controversy over the enactment of the Directive, the Task Force is satisfied that the final text goes in the right direction in addressing the links between financial stability and the asset management industry. In so doing, and by introducing a single market for alternative managers and funds, it represents a significant opportunity for the industry and investors. Limits to securities lending, repo transactions and the re-hypothecation of collateral exceed the scope of the AIFMD but need to be addressed in a horizontal manner that applies (proportionately) to all intermediaries in financial markets. The challenge over the next few years will be to implement the AIFMD in a manner that limits compliance costs and avoids undermining the competitive position of EU managers at home and abroad.

Box 2. Hedge funds and financial stability

There is no commonly agreed definition of 'hedge fund' either in the industry or in regulation. In effect, the line that differentiates hedge funds from other (alternative) investment funds is sometimes difficult to draw. Regulators describe hedge funds by referring to some of their features: a) the absence of borrowing and leverage restrictions mandated by regulation, b) the presence of significant performance fees, c) limited redemption windows, d) significant participation held by the manager, e) diverse exposures, including short-selling and f) complex underlying, including derivatives (IOSCO, 2009, p. 4). In practice, however, the definition of hedge fund depends more on the legal nature of the fund than on the strategy it follows or its use of leverage. Since they do not face restrictions mandated by regulation, hedge funds may pursue an endless variety of strategies.

Hedge funds are not seen today as a major concern with respect to their effects on financial stability (de Larosière et al., 2009; Turner, 2009; IOSCO, 2009). This is because managers are relatively small in size in comparison to other intermediaries; they do not perform substantial maturity transformation; and their leverage is, on average, moderate in comparison to other intermediaries and banks in particular. Notably, hedge funds do not promise immediate redemptions to investors and can apply a variety of suspension mechanisms to manage any asset-liability mismatch, such as redemption gates, suspensions and others. Yet, in the words of Turner (2009, p. 72), hedge funds have the potential to "evolve in the future in their scale, leverage and investor promises in a way that would make them systemically relevant".

It is not because an industry is not systemically relevant today that it may not evolve in a manner that could threaten financial stability in the future, as proven by investment banking in its evolution from the 1970s and the 1980s. Regulators therefore wished with the AIFMD to set the ground today for a healthy development of the hedge fund industry tomorrow. Hedge funds are indeed recognised to benefit markets by providing liquidity, distributing risk and contributing to price discovery (BIS, 2010, p. 56 and p. 64). In effect, some alternative strategies play an important role in directing capital to productive uses and offering long-term finance and diversification to investors. In Europe in particular, some funds under the AIFMD could play an increasingly important role in improving the efficiency of capital allocation and reducing the reliance on banking intermediaries.

According to data provider HFR, the global hedge fund industry holds about $2 trillion in assets under management, roughly the same as in 2008 (see Figure 9). According to AIMA (2011), hedge funds in Europe account for about $450 billion, over 80% of which is managed by entities domiciled in the UK (FSA, 2011a). Most hedge fund managers are relatively small in size and would not therefore qualify as systemically important financial institutions (SIFIs) from this perspective. Yet, large houses may over time become systemically relevant as their size grows organically or through mergers and acquisitions. Despite the relatively limited size of the industry and its fragmentation, the presence of hedge funds in some markets is significant: they are estimated to account for 7% of the outstanding value of the global convertible bond market, 4% of the interest rate derivatives market and 6% of the global commodity derivative markets (FSA, 2011a). Unfortunately, evidence of trade volumes and the provision of liquidity by hedge funds is limited at present. The comprehensive reporting to supervisors mandated by the AIFMD, in line with IOSCO (International Organisation of Securities Commissions) standards, should bring more clarity in this respect.

Hedge funds do not appear to engage in significant liquidity or maturity transformation. The UK Financial Services Authority estimates that 60% of aggregate portfolios could be liquidated within 7 days while only 10% of investor liabilities would come due in the same period (FSA, 2011a, p. 11). Yet, these estimations are based on a voluntary survey of the industry conducted yearly by the regulator and may therefore not be fully representative.

On the side of redemptions, a survey by Deutsche Bank (2011) suggests that most professional investors are reasonably comfortable with limits to redemptions and understand the illiquid nature of hedge funds. However, the survey also reveals that investors are much less willing (or able) to accept illiquidity for longer periods in Europe than in the US. While 40% of investors in both jurisdictions would accept a one-year lock-in, only 15% of European investors would accept to block their money for 3 or more years, in contrast to 70% of US investors (DB, 2011, p. 88). Once the initial lock-in is over, most investors expect quarterly liquidity. In exceptional market circumstances, hedge funds can use 'gates' to limit the size of redemptions and 'side pockets' to separate illiquid assets. Investors in the DB survey reported that these and other similar instruments are indeed employed by managers with some frequency (DB, 2011, p. 90). The AIFMD is due to bring more clarity to managers, investors and regulators about the management of liquidity and redemptions. At international level, IOSCO is carrying out work on suspension and redemptions in collective investment schemes (IOSCO, 2011).

The exposure of prime brokers to hedge funds also raises concerns in case of failures. It appears that financing conditions offered to hedge funds by prime brokers have somewhat tightened since the financial crisis (FSA, 2011a, p. 13). Most prime brokers are banks and therefore subject to prudential rules and oversight, including standards on risk management and counterparty risk exposures. Yet, to facilitate financial stability oversight, the AIFMD mandates leveraged hedge funds to disclose their counterparty exposures.

Figure 9. Growth in global hedge fund industry

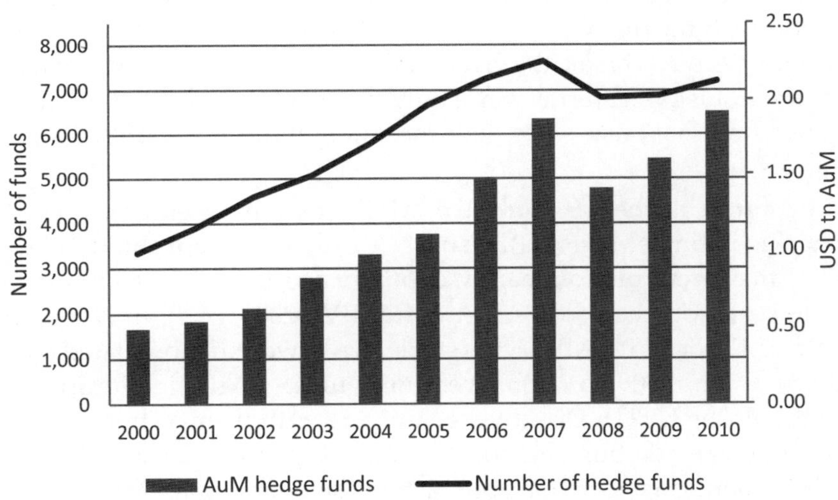

Source: Hedge Fund Research.

2.4 Problems raised by maturity transformation – money market funds

Broadly speaking, money market funds (MMFs) are open-ended investment funds that offer high liquidity to investors by holding short-term instruments. The ECB defines MMFs as "collective investment undertakings whose units are, in terms of liquidity, close substitutes for deposits, and which primarily invest in money market instruments [...] and/or pursue a rate of return that approaches the interest rates of money market instruments".[35] MMFs first originated in the US and then appeared in Europe following a more open approach to the use of the money market fund denomination. By end 2011, MMFs accounted for about $2.6 trillion assets under management in the US, according to the Investment Company Institute,[36] and €1.2 trillion in Europe under the UCITS brand, according to EFAMA (2011c, p. 5).

In the US, MMFs are mutual funds regulated under the Investment Company Act of 1940 and that comply with specific requirements on credit-quality, diversification and maturity (2a-7 rule). Notably funds are not allowed to hold more than 3% of their assets in second-tier securities or more than 5% of their assets in any single issuer and face caps as to the weighted average maturity (WAM) of their portfolios. Under the 2a-7 rule, US MMFs value their assets at amortised costs and offer a stable net asset value (NAV) to investors. Funds, however, need to monitor in parallel the mark-to-market valuation of their portfolio. If the market value falls 50 basis points below the face value, the fund would need to 'break the buck' and devalue their shares. Breaking the buck is rare in historical terms, since only two US MMFs have done so prior to the 2006-08 financial crisis since their inception in the 1970s (PWGFM, 2010, p. 8).

In contrast to the US, European MMFs may have either stable (40% of AuM) or fluctuating NAV (60%). Stable NAV funds first appeared in Europe in the 1980s; they were predominantly denominated in dollars and domiciled in Ireland to serve US clients (EFAMA & IMMFA, 2009, p. 2). In 2008 still more than half of European MMFs with stable NAV were denominated in dollars (McCauley et al., 2009, p. 68). Over time, most MMFs in Europe came to operate under the UCITS Directive, complying with its investment restrictions and enjoying its marketing passport (EFAMA & IMMFA, 2009, p. 4). However, before 2010 there was no single approach to the definition of MMFs in Europe. While some member states regulated MMFs in a manner similar to the US, others followed different approaches. In some jurisdictions, insufficient regulation opened the opportunity for managers to use the denomination 'money market' in funds with a relatively illiquid underlying. In 2010, ESMA introduced guidelines to restrict the use of the term 'money market' under the UCITS brand to funds that comply with special limits as to the eligibility,

---

[35] Annex 1 Part 3 Category 4 Regulation 2423/2001 (consolidated balance sheet of the monetary financial institutions).

[36] http://www.ici.org/research/stats/mmf/mm_02_16_12

credit-quality, diversification and maturity of their underlying, in addition to the general UCITS requirements.[37]

The challenges experienced by MMFs in 2008 showed their importance in providing short-term financing to both corporations and financial institutions, including notably banks. The run on some MMFs in 2008 was the consequence of multiple factors, including: i) inadequate portfolio composition that included complex and illiquid assets, ii) insufficient transparency towards investors on the risks embedded in some funds and iii) the use of rounded NAVs and redemptions at face value in some funds (PWGFM, 2010, pp. 8-11). In Europe, given the lack of a single regulatory definition of MMFs, these problems are more difficult to trace. On both sides of the Atlantic, however, a number of MMFs performed significant maturity transformation without appropriately managing investor expectations and aligning their redemption policies. A survey of the relevant policy documents and academic literature would explain the factors that led to the run in 2008 as follows:

i) *Inadequate portfolio composition*. In the run-up to the financial crisis some MMFs invested in complex and illiquid assets. Anecdotal evidence indicates that some MMFs had substantial holdings of subprime collateralised-debt-obligations (CDOs) in the US and in Europe (Evans, 2007; Zingales, 2008). These at the time highly-rated securities satisfied the regulatory requirements imposed on MMFs while providing attractive returns, despite embedding risks that were not at all in line with the investment policy that investors expected from MMFs.

ii) *Insufficient transparency*. Money market funds are generally perceived and sold to investors as safe investments. Some MMFs, essentially in the US, by offering immediate redemptions and even transaction services similar to cash accounts, are wrongly perceived as near-equivalents to bank deposits. Moreover, past instances of sponsor support resulted in some investors perceiving MMFs as carrying some sort of guarantee.

iii) *Rounded NAVs and redemptions at face value*. The price of units in MMFs is typically rounded to €1.00 or $1.00, fostering the expectation that it will not fluctuate. Such expectations may lead some investors to react disproportionately versus relatively small changes in the price of shares, particularly under exceptional market circumstances. Redemptions may then undermine the NAV of a fund so the manner in which such losses are distributed among investors is most relevant. To ensure shareholder equity, losses need to be borne proportionately by all shares, including the ones just being redeemed. Otherwise, investors have an incentive to

---

[37] ESMA Guidelines CESR/09-85 (common definition money market funds).

redeem their units immediately in case of market stress, which has the potential of being destabilising. Where the face value of units is lower than the market value, redemptions at face value would push the losses onto the remaining investors, as in stable NAV MMFs.

Some MMFs have historically relied on sponsor support to maintain their face value - even well-managed funds investing in high-quality securities with short maturities (PWGFM, 2010, p. 19). But sponsor support is not limited to the MMF industry. It takes multiple formats, such as capital contributions, purchases of securities or guarantees by management houses or their parent institutions. It is not explicit, since otherwise sponsors would have to account for this support in their balance sheets. Moody's (2010) identified 146 support events before 2007 in over 30 years of operation of MMFs. Yet, there is growing a consensus that sponsors are no longer able to provide support given: i) the growing size of the industry, ii) higher correlations across securities and counterparties, iii) lower maturities and more frequent turnover and iv) a more volatile institutional investor base (Moody's, 2010; PWGFM, 2010).

Regulatory reform has concentrated on portfolio composition, limiting the range of eligible instruments for MMFs. In Europe, ESMA guidelines create a two-tier system of MMFs by distinguishing between: *short-term MMFs*, which may have a constant net asset value, and *(non-short-term) MMFs*, which may use the label 'money market' but are constrained to have a floating NAV.[38] Both types of funds need to invest with the primary objective of maintaining the principal of the fund and providing a return in line with money markets. Managers are prohibited from relying exclusively on credit ratings to determine the credit quality of the instruments in which they invest and are expressly required to take into account operational and counterparty risks. The difference between *short-term* MMFs and *(non-short-term)* MMFs hangs in the maturity of the instruments in which they may invest, as reflected in Table 5.

Following the revision in 2010 of rule 2a-7 of the Investment Company Act, US MMFs are subject to the same maturity limits as European *short-term MMFs*. In addition, they have to comply with liquidity requirements so that at least 10% of assets are held in cash or cash-equivalent instruments and 30% in assets maturing in one week. The SEC also included provisions to limit the participation of MMFs in repurchase agreements and to facilitate the use of suspensions by MMFs and their orderly liquidation (PWGFM, 2010, pp. 14-15). It is also worth noting that the ESMA guidelines constitute soft law, in contrast with the SEC rules. In this respect, the Commission should consider bringing forward a legislative proposal to harmonise MMFs in Europe.

[38] ESMA Guidelines CESR/09-85 (common definition money market funds).

Table 5. ESMA guidelines on money market funds – Limits to maturity and net asset value

	Residual maturity	Weighted average maturity	Weighted average life	Net asset value
Short-term Money Market Fund	397 days	60 days	120 days	Either constant or fluctuating
(Non-short-term) Money Market Fund	2 years[39]	6 months	12 months	Fluctuating only

Notes: Residual Maturity (RM): Pending maturity until the legal redemption date.
Weighted Average Maturity (WAM): A measure of the average length of time to maturity of the underlying securities in the fund capturing its sensitivity to changing money market interest rates.
Weighted Average Life (WAL): Weighted average of the remaining life (maturity) of each security held in the fund, capturing both credit and liquidity risk.

The restrictions imposed on eligible assets are of crucial importance. But other relevant issues remain unresolved and need to be addressed by regulators, including: i) the inequitable distribution of any losses caused by redemptions, given its potential destabilising effect in exceptional market circumstances and ii) the issue of 'sponsor support' and the extent to which it may be withdrawn or factored in the capital requirements of the sponsoring entity (FSB, 2011a and 2011b). Moreover, the authorities need to deal with the effects of government intervention and sponsor support in 2008, which "distorted the incentives of managers and probably also price formation in money markets" (Zingales, 2008, p. 7; PWGFM, 2010, p. 3).[40] Any change in these respects would have to control for the possibility of reduced investor demand for MMFs and lower availability of short-term funding for corporations, financial institutions and governments, and would have to be accompanied by restrictions on unregulated substitutes where demand may shift, thereby diluting the positive effects of further reform of MMFs on financial stability.

The challenges experienced by MMFs in 2008 provide the perfect example of how maturity transformation (the lack of alignment between the fund's underlying, investor expectations and redemption policies) can pose

[39] Provided that the time remaining until the next interest rate reset date is equal to or less than 397 days.

[40] In 2008, the US Treasury introduced a temporary guarantee in favour of investors in 2a-7 MMFs. Losses in Europe were borne primarily by asset management companies and their parent undertakings - either directly or indirectly. The Federal Reserve and the ECB intervened by providing assistance to restore liquidity in interbank and money markets.

systemic risks. The SEC considered in 2010 as many as five reform options: mandating floating net asset values; mandating redemptions in kind under stressed market circumstances; providing a private emergency liquidity facility to MMFs; ensuring investments in MMFs in way similar to bank deposits; and even regulating stable NAV funds as special purpose banks (PWGFM, 2010). Ultimately, the choice boils down to two options: i) asserting the risks embedded in MMFs and clarifying their fund nature whereby the principal is not guaranteed; or ii) driving the industry and investors towards the banking system or bank-like structures based on capital requirements, deposit insurance and emergency liquidity facilities. The first choice is preferable by far: MMFs can play a significant role in diversifying the sources of financing from bank loans to securities, bringing forward disintermediation and developing capital markets, but further reform is needed to re-assert the fund nature of MMFs.

2.5 Continuous market surveillance - ETFs and bank financing

Following the experience in the financial crisis, a new approach to supervision has developed based on monitoring business models and markets continuously from a financial stability perspective and taking action at an early stage in the product life cycle (Turner, 2009; de Larosière et al., 2009). For this purpose, a range of bodies has been created at national and international level, including the Financial Stability Board (FSB) at global level, the European Systemic Risk Board (ESRB) in the EU and the Financial Stability Oversight Council (FSOC) in the US. At the same time, supervisors and regulators around the world have strengthened their expertise on financial stability. The warnings issued in the context of exchange-traded funds (ETFs) are a good example of this new approach to supervision and the way these new bodies work in practice (BIS, 2011; FSB, 2011; Bank of England, 2011; ESRB, 2011; ESMA, 2011a; AMF, 2011). The key issue from a financial stability perspective is the funding function that synthetic ETFs play for banks.

Most ETFs replicate the composition of an index, either by directly holding the securities (physical ETFs) or by entering into a derivative contract (synthetic ETFs). In the latter case, the fund manager usually contracts a total return swap with a bank that delivers the performance of the given index in exchange for the cash collected from the end investors, plus a fee. To cover the counterparty risk, the bank gives the fund manager the beneficial or direct ownership over a substitute basket of securities, whose components are generally unrelated to the underlying tracked by the fund but should have a similar market value. The advantage of synthetic ETFs for investors is their lower error in tracking the index, in comparison with physical ETFs where deviations are inevitable given physical replication. The drawback for investors is that they are not only exposed to the index but also to the substitute basket of securities, if the swap counterparty were to default. Exposure to the swap counterparty is however limited to a maximum 10% of the fund's market value for those ETFs that operate under the UCITS rules, that is, the vast majority of ETFs in Europe. Beyond counterparty risk, investors in synthetic ETFs also become exposed to the operational risks involved in managing the swap and the substitute basket. The former is not to say that counterparty and operational risks are not present in physical ETFs, in particular where they engage in securities lending to raise additional revenues.

From the point of view of financial stability, regulators are wary of the use of synthetic ETFs by banks as a source of financing. Currently, only a small number of European banks are active in the synthetic ETF market, although these banks are significant in size. They are present not as outright investors but as counterparties, frequently to their own fund management subsidiaries. In a synthetic ETF structure, banks receive the cash from end investors and use it to finance the inventory of assets they hold for market-making purposes. From this perspective, a synthetic ETF structure is a substitute for issuing commercial paper or entering into repurchase agreements. A working document from the Bank for International Settlements (BIS) estimates that using ETFs can result in substantial cost savings for banks – the higher the short-term interest rates that apply to repos, the larger the savings in using ETFs (Ramaswamy, 2011). Ultimately, managers and banks arbitrage the difference in repo rates between the assets in the basket whose return is tracked and the substitute basket transferred to the fund manager by way of guarantee. Given the incentives for banks to increase the use of ETFs to raise funding, regulators have endeavoured to better understand the possible effects that a potential over-reliance of banks on synthetic ETFs in the future could have on financial stability. Regulators are also considering the role of securities lending by investment funds (including physical ETFs) in bank funding since banks may benefit from any difference in liquidity between the securities borrowed from the fund and the collateral posted to it.

At present the ETF industry is not systemically relevant, given its size. Synthetic ETFs just account for roughly 1.5% of the investment management industry in Europe, in terms of assets under management. Their underlying swaps would therefore make up for a relatively small proportion of global derivative markets – approximately 10% of equity-linked OTC forwards and swaps and 3% of total equity-linked OTC derivatives, including options, in terms of notional amounts outstanding (Amenc et al., 2012, p. 54, based on BIS statistics). The concern of regulators is rather that growth in the industry and competition among providers could result in a reduction in the quality of the assets in the substitute basket, vulnerability of the banking system to a run on

ETFs and an increase in the complexity of ETF structures that would undermine risk-monitoring (BIS, 2011; FSB, 2011; Bank of England, 2011; ESRB, 2011; ESMA, 2011a; AMF, 2011). Complexity and doubts about collateral quality could trigger redemptions in ETFs leading to a substantial reduction in available bank funding. Bank counterparties would have contractual obligations, or otherwise reputational incentives, to service redemptions. Investors in ETFs, who expect continuous liquidity, may quickly flee from ETFs and behave adversely before any restrictions are imposed on redemptions.

The industry has responded to these objections by increasing the level of transparency on all fronts, including the components of the substitute basket and the structuring of ETFs, addressing some of the concerns raised by the regulators. Other issues cannot be addressed by asset managers but rather by their bank counterparties, such as explaining how banks replicate the returns of the given index and how they account for their funding exposures to synthetic ETFs. It is essential from this perspective that asset management and banking regulators work together to find holistic solutions to the issues raised by financial stability bodies. They should address not only ETFs under the UCITS rules but more importantly those exchange-traded products (ETPs) that behave similarly without being subject to equivalent rules in terms of counterparty risk mitigation and disclosure.

The intervention of the financial stability bodies may have resulted in significant redemptions from synthetic ETFs that may not have been in the best interest of investors. However, it has also managed to raise much-needed awareness among investors about the counterparty and operational risks embedded in derivatives and securities lending transactions, in ETF products and beyond. Higher transparency and stricter discipline will no doubt benefit the asset management industry in the long run and facilitate an adequate level of protection for investors and safeguards to financial stability. Awareness has also grown about securities lending and its role in bank financing. The case of ETFs illustrates a positive change in supervisory oversight, which has become much more proactive, open to the public and mindful of economic incentives, emerging trends and business models. The burden has been shifted to intermediaries to publicly demonstrate that their activities are socially useful, in the best interest of investors and financial stability.

3. STRENGTHENING PRODUCT INTEGRITY: WHICH WAY FOR UCITS?

This chapter will consider product integrity in retail investment funds, focusing on UCITS products (Undertakings for Collective Investment in Transferable Securities). After a short introduction to the UCITS framework, the chapter will consider recent innovations in the UCITS product range, including 'alternative' UCITS and UCITS exchange-traded funds. The core of the chapter will examine the rules on the use of derivatives and structured financial instruments in UCITS and put forward some proposals to further strengthen product integrity, which is already high in UCITS funds.

3.1 A short introduction to UCITS

Over the last 25 years, UCITS funds have enjoyed unparalleled success in Europe and abroad. Today, they account for almost a third of global assets in traditional investment funds, a quarter of which are sourced outside Western Europe. This first section considers in more detail the size and characteristics of the UCITS market. The success of UCITS is due to a large extent to its regulatory framework, which is the main focus of this chapter.

The 1985 UCITS Directive put together a new category of retail investment funds that could be marketed freely across the European Economic Area (EEA) to investors. The UCITS brand was built upon (partially) harmonised product rules based on risk spreading, liquidity requirements and the segregation of assets – a set of principles that remains valid today. Next to these rules on portfolio construction, the UCITS Directive contains a marketing passport that allows UCITS funds domiciled in one member state to be easily sold cross-border within the Union.

Figure 10. Three basic principles in UCITS

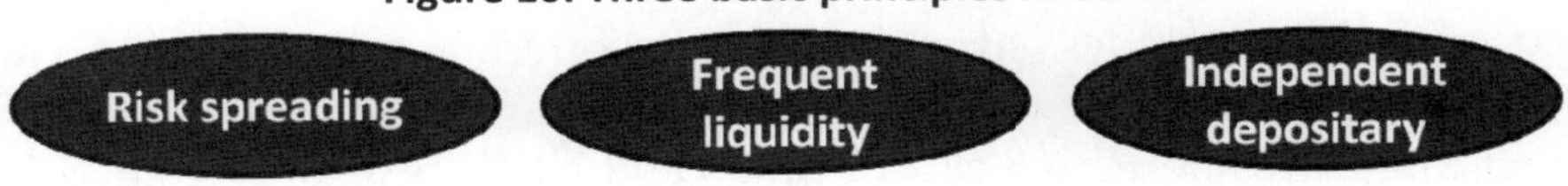

The UCITS regulatory framework was adapted and developed over the years to strengthen the single market, take stock of changes in financial markets and improve risk management. In 2003 the UCITS III Directive represented a turning point for product structuring by expanding the scope of eligible assets and permissible investment practices beyond the traditional realm of plain vanilla equities and debt securities. The 2003 Directive came to modernise the UCITS framework 17 years after its introduction. In so doing, it helped UCITS overcome some of its limitations, including the use of derivatives, within a more robust risk management framework. In 2009, the UCITS IV Directive furthered strengthened risk management, clarifying the limits to embedded leverage and exposure to market risk. Forthcoming legislation (UCITS V) is due to strengthen the management of non-market risks in UCITS in 2012.

As mentioned, portfolio structuring in UCITS is based on strict exposure limits and the liquidity of the underlying assets to allow frequent redemptions by investors (at least fortnightly). In line with these principles, more illiquid assets and strategies cannot be accessed directly but through the use of derivative financial instruments and subject to a set of conditions that will be fully discussed in the next sections. Originally, the use of derivatives in UCITS was limited to hedging risks and so-called 'efficient portfolio management'. Today however, UCITS funds are allowed to use derivatives as an integral part of their investment strategy not only to limit market risks but also to generate returns.

3.2 Product innovation under UCITS explained

The 2003 UCITS III Directive expanded the scope of eligible assets and permissible investment practices. As a result the UCITS product range has grown over the years based in particular on the use of derivatives and structured financial instruments. While long-only funds and traditional strategies remain the core of the UCITS offering still today, the use of derivatives has become commonplace both to achieve reductions in market risk and generate returns (EFAMA, 2011c). In 2008 the use of derivatives was estimated to have grown at a yearly rate of 10% since the introduction of the UCITS III Directive (PWC, 2008). Some UCITS exploit the possibilities offered by derivatives and structured financial instruments to a fuller extent, for instance to gain exposure to otherwise ineligible assets or implement alternative investment strategies. The product range within UCITS today is varied and also includes structured funds offering some sort of capital protection. Arguably the two most relevant developments in the UCITS product range are alternative UCITS funds and UCITS exchange-traded funds (ETFs). Both sorts are structured to comply in full with the requirements in the

Directive and benefit from its passport to broaden their access to investors. This section will consider the size and characteristics of these two product offerings.

3.2.1 *UCITS alternative funds*

A survey of industry participants carried out on behalf of the European Commission in 2007 concluded that UCITS III allowed the structuring of funds replicating several alternative investment strategies (PwC, 2008b). The marketplace has come up with different names to refer to UCITS that follow alternative strategies, such as newcits, UCITS III products or absolute-return UCITS. The difficulty in defining alternative strategies means that the scope and size of alternative UCITS remain unclear. EFAMA broadly defines them as "UCITS which aim to manage the risk/return trade-off by the use of a wide range of strategies and instruments" allowed under UCITS III and later UCITS IV (EFAMA, 2011c).

Each fund classification results in a different estimation of the size of this market segment. According to Strategic Insight (2010), there are about 1,000 alternative UCITS and they account for over €115 billion in assets under management. In other words just 4% of total assets under management in long-term UCITS would pursue alternative strategies.[41] If compared to the global hedge fund industry size (€1,240 billion in 2010 according to Hedge Fund Research - HFR) alternative UCITS would however account for a significant share of alternative funds in Europe. Other studies assess alternative UCITS at less than €100 billion in assets under management (Tuchschmid et al., 2010, based on data from Nara Capital).

Figure 11. Evolution of 'alternative' UCITS

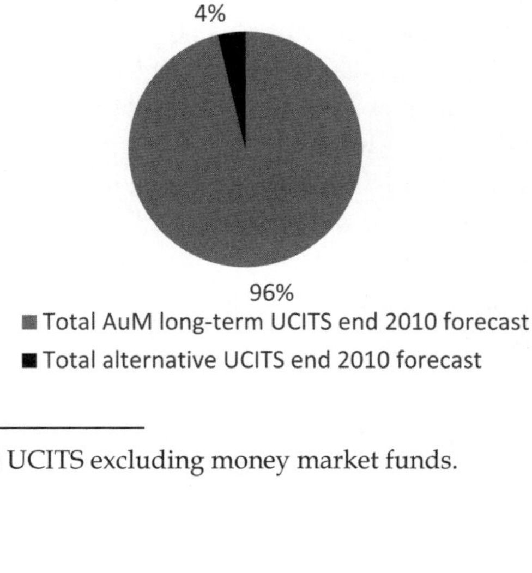

[41] Long-term UCITS are UCITS excluding money market funds.

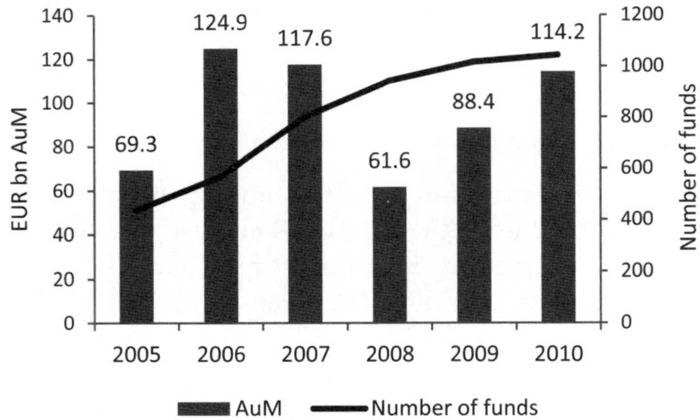

Sources: Strategic Insight (2010) and EFAMA (2011b).

Alternative UCITS have experienced rapid growth since 2005. Strategic Insight estimates that they accounted for 15% of total net flows into long-term UCITS in 2010. In absolute values, these flows were bigger than the ones experienced by similar non-UCITS products. If this trend was to continue, under reasonable assumptions, alternative UCITS could account for 10% of UCITS assets in 2020 (SI, 2010). Future growth will depend among other factors on the continued interest of high net worth individuals and institutional investors.

In the near future, alternative UCITS will compete with funds handled by managers under the AIFMD to attract professional investors. The alternative investment fund managers Directive will reduce the competitive advantage of UCITS in terms of marketing passport, transparency and regulatory seal. The interest of institutional investors in alternative strategies derives from their need to diversify their exposures and hopefully gather the returns needed to meet their liabilities. The extent to which institutional investors will prefer alternative UCITS over AIFMD funds will depend, among other factors, on their efficiency in terms of regulatory capital. To date, national authorities have frequently imposed limits on the ability of insurance companies and pension funds to access non-regulated funds (EDHEC-Risk, 2010b; PwC, 2008b). Solvency II allocates capital charges with reference to the underlying and could partially reverse this situation for managers who succeed in providing investors with a full look-through into the assets underlying the fund.[42]

---

[42] Regulatory capital requirements under Solvency II will enforce full look-through into the underlying of investment funds, whether UCITS or AIFs, and so not impact on the

Box 3. How to implement a hedge-fund strategy in UCITS?

UCITS is not just a commercial name but a comprehensive set of portfolio allocation and risk management rules. The replication of alternative strategies in UCITS faces liquidity requirements and limits on leverage, 'eligible assets' and concentration. The implementation of alternative strategies in UCITS may only be partial, given the restrictions imposed by regulation. In a study presented to this Task Force, Amenc and Sender (EDHEC-Risk, 2010b) consider the compatibility of different hedge fund strategies with the UCITS regulatory framework.[43] The main conclusions of this study are summarised below:

- Strategies that invest in a diversified pool of liquid securities, such as equity long-short, are the easiest to implement in UCITS since they comply more easily with liquidity and diversification requirements. Equity long-short strategies are directional, switching between long and short instruments on given securities, depending on the manager's view of the market. Switching from direct to synthetic shorting (using derivatives) is the main adaptation that such strategies have to undergo to comply with the UCITS rules.[a]
- Derivatives on eligible indexes are compatible with the UCITS rules and allow the partial replication of many tactical-style strategies. Most of these strategies either focus on commodities (commodity trading advisors, commodity pool operators) or invest according to the evolution of the economy expected by the manager (global-macro strategies). To comply with the UCITS framework, they need to abandon physical settlement and use derivatives, and frequently reduce their leverage. Moreover, the UCITS rules on index composition limit the implementation of strategies focused on small pools of commodities or other assets.
- Those strategies that exceed concentration limits and do not comply with liquidity requirements cannot be implemented within UCITS. Industry participants single out relative-value and event-driven strategies as the most difficult to replicate in UCITS using derivatives. The first strategy attempts to exploit the differences in the value of closely related securities, while the latter invests in companies involved in takeovers or mergers. Other hedge fund strategies, the range being almost limitless, for instance distressed securities, can hardly be reconciled with UCITS either.

---

implementation of alternative strategies into UCITS. They will, however, demand adaptation from managers to offer products that maximise expected returns while minimising regulatory capital and building the infrastructure necessary to comply with stringent transparency and reporting obligations.

43 The EDHEC-Risk Institute is part of the EDHEC Business School in Nice, France. The Institute undertakes research in finance from a theoretical and applied perspective (see www.edhec-risk.com for more information).

When it comes to leverage, the study by EDHEC-Risk finds that a large majority of hedge funds would meet UCITS leverage limits in terms of value at risk, as set under the relevant ESMA guidelines.[b] This result would indicate that some hedge funds have a level of risk comparable to some UCITS, as far as leverage provides an approximation to risk. Yet, another study presented to the Task Force members showed that alternative UCITS carry, on average, significantly less risk than hedge funds in terms of standard deviation (Tuchschmid et al., 2010). According to this later study, alternative UCITS offer in general better liquidity, lower attrition rates and lower dispersion of return than hedge funds. The lower attrition rate suggests that alternative UCITS are less likely to fail than hedge funds and are therefore more resilient (Tuchschmid et al., 2010).[c] However, the lower attrition may also be explained by the ability of hedge funds to stop their reporting to the relevant database, which is not possible under the UCITS Directive. With regard to performance, the research presented to this Task Force by Professor Tuchschmid (HEG Geneva) did not find conclusive evidence that hedge funds outperform alternative UCITS.

Product innovation in UCITS illustrates the convergence of traditional and alternative investment management. Alternative UCITS have been developed by both breeds of managers, who have gathered knowledge of each other business, regulatory framework and distribution channels.

[a] Shorting above 10% of the NaV of the fund would need to be done synthetically via derivatives, which may involve higher costs and reduce the speed of responsiveness by managers.

[b] ESMA Guidelines, CESR/10-778 (global exposure and counterparty risk, UCITS IV).

[c] The attrition rate captures the percentage of funds that have been liquidated.

3.2.2 *UCITS exchange-traded funds*

Exchange-traded funds (ETFs) are open-ended funds listed and continuously traded on a secondary market, most of which track an index. The open-ended fund structure differentiates ETFs from other exchange-traded products (ETPs), which are subject at most times to lower, if any, regulatory standards. The vast majority of European ETFs are structured to comply with the UCITS regulatory framework.[44] ETF structuring is not homogenous but may be based on directly holding a representative basket of securities (physical ETFs) or accessing the return of that same basket through a derivative contract (synthetic structures). In stylised terms, both structures rely on the participation of an authorised participant or market-maker to provide the

[44] Internal industry figures indicate that 85% to 95% of European ETFs are UCITS.

underlying securities or the derivative instruments.[45] Also common to both structures is the creation and redemption process which takes place in the primary market, between the asset manager and the market-maker. In effect, the authorised participant places the ETF units in the secondary market, where they are traded by investors (mostly institutional).

ETF units are continuously traded and settled on exchange-like stocks, offering intra-day liquidity, subject to market conditions. The units are lendable so investors may take long and short positions. Trading involves specific costs, however, such as brokerage fees and the application of related regulation, such as MiFID and the rules on short-selling. While unlisted mutual funds are redeemable at their net asset value, not all ETFs offer investors the possibility of redeeming their units at NAV. However, the UCITS Directive contains strict requirements in this respect, forcing UCITS ETFs to accept investor redemptions at NAV.

Most European ETFs are UCITS and are therefore structured to comply with the rules on portfolio construction, risk management and investor protection in the UCITS Directive. At present there are no specific UCITS rules for ETFs but, following a consultation in 2011, ESMA is expected to introduce additional requirements for listed funds in 2012.[46] The most relevant UCITS rules for ETFs are the provisions governing a) index composition and b) counterparty risks and collateral. The former are relevant for all ETFs that track and index, as for any other index-tracker UCITS. The latter are relevant for all ETFs using OTC derivatives or lending part of their securities, as for any other UCITS engaging in those practices. In effect, the specificity of ETFs from the perspective of the UCITS rules follows from their trading on secondary markets rather than from the way in which they are structured.

Index-based ETFs follow both major market indices and narrower indices focused on specific sectors, themes and styles. While most ETFs follow traditional strategies, an increasing number of them track tailored-made portfolios or indices. Investors increasingly demand ETFs offering specialised exposure to more exotic asset classes such as commodities, alternatives, currencies and credit. A small number of ETFs are even actively managed (less than 4% globally- see DB, 2011). In parallel to demand factors, the industry acknowledges a growing interest by different suppliers, in particular: a) banks

[45] In synthetic structures, the swap is provided by a counterparty, which may be an affiliate to the market-maker or authorised participant but not the same entity. Market-makers or authorised participants deal with the ETF shares, whereas the counterparty deals with the ETF assets (in practice the swap).

[46] ESMA Consultation Paper, ESMA/2012/44 (ETFs and structured UCITS).

interested in synthetic replication and b) asset managers interested in expanding their business (BlackRock, 2011).

At least 80% of assets in European ETFs are held by institutional investors (BIS, 2011; DB, 2011) who invest in these products for a variety of purposes, including managing asset allocation, taking tactical positions and increasing diversification. ETFs are often employed to hedge other exposures, instead of using futures and notes. By way of contrast, retail investors are usually interested in using ETFs to access broad market indices as core holdings. From this perspective, ETFs present fierce competition to unlisted index funds, which are progressively losing market share. Some ETFs also compete with more specialised funds and may be used by retail investors as satellite investments to access selected exposures. Buy-and-hold retail investors will not benefit, however, from the intra-day liquidity offered by ETFs.

ETFs have known success thanks to their competitive fees and liquidity, in comparison with unlisted index funds. By mid-2011, there were over 1,000 ETFs in Europe with over €240 billion assets under management (BlackRock, 2011; DB, 2011). Since 2005, the European ETF industry grew five-fold, now accounting for approximately 8% of the long-term UCITS, that is UCITS excluding money market funds, but less than 2% of the overall asset management industry in Europe.[47] The ETF industry has grown in Europe above the global average but has not yet reached the size of the US industry. Since 2000 the annual growth rate for ETF assets was 83% in Europe compared to just under 30% in the US (BlackRock, 2011). Yet the US accounts still for more than 70% of the assets managed by ETFs globally.[48] According to industry figures, yearly growth in Europe could reach 20% to 30% per annum in the next few years, led to a large extent by the growth in synthetic replication by European banks. Synthetic ETFs experienced large redemptions, however, in the third quarter of 2011 and the first quarter of 2012.

---

[47] Some ETFs invest in money-market instruments or have intra-day recommended holding periods.

[48] The US ETF market has a longer track record than the European one and is subject to different constraints and realities. In the US, ETFs are registered under the Investment Company Act of 1940 and classified as unit investment trusts or open-ended funds if they engage in securities lending. ETFs are not classified as US mutual funds, given the limited redeemability of their shares. In terms of structuring, the use of derivatives is limited by the requirement to hold at least 80% of their assets in securities matching the name of the fund (the SEC, however, is consulting on the use of derivatives). These limitations are in contrast with the use of OTC derivatives (such as total return swaps) under UCITS. US regulation, however, allows for the use of substantial leverage to deliver a multiple of the performance of the underlying index. These products are used intra-day by professional investors and may be structured to deliver inverse performance.

Figure 12. Exchange-traded funds in Europe

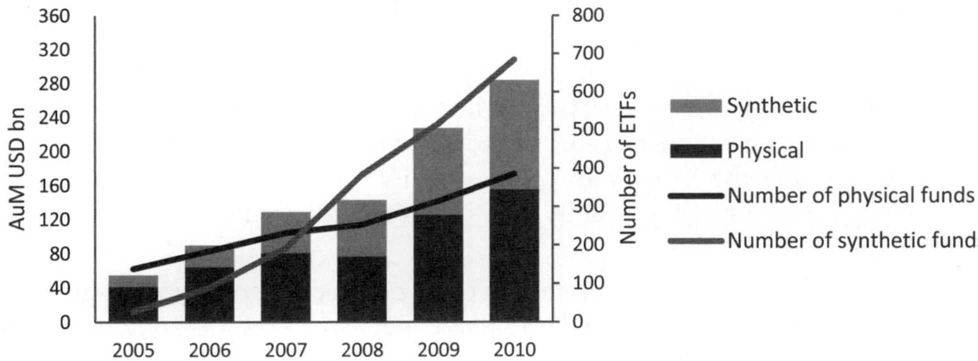

Source: BlackRock.

3.3 Three concerns about the UCITS regulatory framework

The expansion in the scope of eligible assets and investment practices under the UCITS Directives has led to significant innovation, based on the use of derivative and structured financial instruments. Arguably, regulation has not fully kept pace with the intensity of product innovation in UCITS. It is argued that the current regulatory framework raises potential concerns with regard to a) product integrity, b) investor protection and c) the single market, as described below.

i) *Product integrity.* Product innovation in UCITS has led to the use of relatively complex financial instruments and investment practices. These involve specific risks, in particular: a) operational risks when it comes to the trading, settlement, valuation and segregation of assets; b) liquidity risks in view of UCITS redemption obligations and liquidity profile as advertised to investors and c) counterparty risks including the risk related to the quality of the collateral held as way of guarantee. On the positive side, the use of some of these instruments and investment practices may smooth market risk (the volatility of returns given changes in market variables). It may also allow managers to present investors with predefined pay-outs, subject to the realisation of certain conditions in the market place - structured UCITS, as in the definition of regulation 583/2010. However, where market risks are repackaged, operational, liquidity and counterparty risks are usually affected. Frequently, market risks are transferred away to other agents generating counterparty risk (the risk of default of the counterparty in a derivative or structured financial instrument). This risk of default is mitigated via due diligence in the selection of the counterparty and the posting of collateral or other guarantees. Managing collateral, in its turn, is also subject to operational risks, particularly where collateral is re-invested or the UCITS structures most of its portfolio using derivatives. In view of these risks, managers are required to implement sophisticated risk management processes when they use complex financial instruments and investment practices. Ultimately, the responsibility falls on managers to structure their products in a manner according to their risk management capabilities. Yet, complexity may reduce the ability of supervisors to monitor compliance and the ability of investors to understand the risks embedded.

ii) *Investor protection.* From a retail investor perspective, product integrity is paramount, since most individuals do not have specific knowledge of finance. The use of some complex financial instruments and investment strategies raises questions as to a possible mismatch between UCITS liquidity requirements and the liquidity of the underlying assets, as well as to a possible mispricing or misrepresentation of operational, counterparty or liquidity risks. Most retail investors are not equipped with the knowledge and skills to discern these questions and their possible impact on their savings. UCITS rules were devised for retail investors, to allow them to access a range of investment funds under diversification, liquidity and risk limits. The existence of this set of rules entails by itself a certain guarantee of product integrity by the competent authorities, including a supervisory duty to ensure that managers adhere to the rules in practice. By way of contrast, where it comes to professional investors, the role of regulators and supervisors is more limited. Professional investors are supposed to have the specific knowledge to evaluate the risks in complex financial instruments. Chapter 4 considers investor protection at length.

iii) *The single market.* Product innovation in UCITS has taken different shapes across member states, sometimes building on the divergent transposition of the directives, highlighting that the process of harmonisation of the UCITS rules is far from achieved. From the perspective of retail investors, a plurality of national rules does not help the understanding of the risks involved in UCITS products. The differences among national bodies of legislation affect in particular the frontier of eligible assets and permissible exposures, as well as the management of heightened liquidity, operational and counterparty risks. The duties and liabilities of depositaries also vary widely across member states, but the European Commission is scheduled to put forward a legislative proposal in 2012 to harmonise the depositary rules in UCITS in line with the AIFMD. Key aspects of disclosure are affected as well by the lack of a single rule book, such as calculating total expense ratios.

3.4 Derivatives and structured financial instruments in UCITS

As a follow up to the concern about product integrity outlined above, this section aims to bring clarity to the discussions surrounding the use of derivatives and structured financial instruments under the UCITS regulatory framework. The section is structured in three parts: a) firstly, a general reflection on the use of derivatives in fund management and the role of fund regulation, b) secondly a critical analysis of the current UCITS rules governing the use of derivatives and financial indices and c) finally, a discussion on how to strengthen the UCITS regulatory framework and product integrity.

3.4.1 *Why do funds use derivatives? And the role of fund regulation*

This section provides an approximation of the use of derivative financial instruments by investment funds and the general role of fund regulation in this regard. It does not consider the provisions of the UCITS Directive, which are discussed in the section immediately after. Derivatives are contracts whose value is based upon or derived from other assets or metrics, called underlying or reference asset (Swan, 2000). Funds use derivatives both to manage certain risks and implement some investment strategies. An example of the former is the use of derivatives to increase diversification and hedge risks; for instance a currency derivative would protect holders of a fund denominated in euros against a decrease in the value of an investment in dollars due to a decline, not in the value of the investment itself but of the dollar currency (SEC, 2011). Yet derivatives may also be used by asset managers as an integral part of portfolio construction to gain or reduce exposures. This is because derivatives sometimes carry lower transaction costs than direct investments (see Deli & Varma, 2002; Koski & Pontiff, 1996). In addition, derivatives allow managers to access leverage and thereby increase the potential for future returns or losses. This leverage arises in those derivatives that require an initial outlay smaller than the potential liability (e.g. futures, swaps and options).

Derivatives are more attractive the higher the costs involved in accessing the underlying (Deli & Varma, 2002). Illiquid assets carry by definition relatively high transaction costs, which means derivatives are likely to be less expensive than investing directly in some illiquid assets. Professors Deli and Varma consider this cost advantage in the framework of open-ended funds. They observe that cash-flow shocks amplify the cost advantage of employing certain derivatives for open-ended funds. In effect, shocks induced by outflows from (and inflows to) a given fund may force the asset manager into liquidity-motivated trading. When compared to informed trading, liquidity-motivated trading carries an opportunity cost and the risk of outright losses (Grossman & Stiglitz, 1980, in Deli & Varma, 2002). Certain derivatives are useful tools to manage the liquidity of investment funds in this respect.

Derivatives involve a series of risks such as: a) leverage risk, associated with the potential liabilities embedded; b) liquidity risk, in particular for non-standardised derivatives for which no liquid market exists and c) counterparty risk, given that derivatives do not only generate exposure to the reference asset but also to the creditworthiness of a financial intermediary. Borrowing an example from the SEC (2011) in the US, when a bank and a fund enter into a total return swap on stock issued by a corporation in the pharmaceutical sector, the fund not only gains exposure to the pharmaceutical industry (the industry associated with the issuer's reference asset) but also to the banking industry (the industry associated with the fund's counterparty).

Derivatives are subject to regulatory scrutiny from various angles, including market infrastructure and financial stability. From the perspective of retail fund regulation, what matters is the impact of the use of derivatives on product integrity, as regards the protection of retail investors. Regulation needs therefore to determine the use of derivatives that is permissible in retail funds in accordance with the interest of retail investors and the frontiers of risk management. Moreover, the limitations imposed on investments in derivatives should be consistent with the ones imposed on direct investments, in order to avoid the use of derivatives to arbitrage the latter's limits.

Strict rules for direct investments by retail funds may result in distortions if not matched by similar rules for derivative exposures. It is worth noting that some of the practical advantages of using derivatives in fund management, such as lower transaction costs, are magnified by some of the operational safeguards built into fund regulation. For instance, rules requiring the segregation of client´s assets may impose a cost on some direct investments that would exceed the cost of accessing the same assets via derivatives.[49] Differences in the rules that determine which assets are eligible to be accessed directly versus via derivatives could also introduce unintended incentives to structure portfolios using derivatives rather than direct investments.

Fund regulators need to carry-out a balancing exercise with regard to the use of derivatives. In the swap example above, the fund transfers the operational risks involved in accessing directly the underlying asset but acquires some counterparty risk. Fund regulators need to balance the risks transferred to the counterparty against the risks incorporated into the fund, which are borne by the unit holders. From the perspective of fund regulators, interested in ensuring the security of retail fund investors, this counterparty

49 It is understood that derivatives may not be held in custody by the fund depositary. See discussion later in chapter 3 on non-market risks and fund depositaries.

risk can be mitigated by posting collateral or other guarantees.[50] Collateral requirements appear therefore as an essential component of fund regulation when it comes to the use of derivative instruments by investment funds.

At a theoretical level, the use of derivatives may exacerbate the agency conflicts between managers and investors (Deli & Varma, 2002). Under conditions of insufficient transparency, some derivatives could potentially be used to increase the level of risk over the one advertised to investors. This is because some derivatives require a small initial outlay in comparison to the potential gains or losses, resulting in embedded leverage that is hard to observe. It is a general agency conflict in asset management that poorly performing funds have an incentive to increase risks, hoping to raise performance and attract inflows - while good performing funds have an incentive to reduce risks to the level that allows them to avoid outflows (Koski & Pontiff, 1996). Regulation therefore needs to elicit the exposure (leverage) embedded in derivatives to mitigate the agency conflicts that exist in their use. Transparency and the appropriate measurement of leverage and risk are therefore essential parts of fund regulation.

Fund regulators therefore need a comprehensive response to address the questions surrounding the use of derivative financial instruments by retail investment funds. The figure below represents the wide range of issues that regulators need to take into account for this purpose, most of which are thoroughly addressed by the UCITS Directive, despite some room for improvement, as discussed in the next section.

Figure 13. Regulatory issues in the use of derivatives by retail investment funds

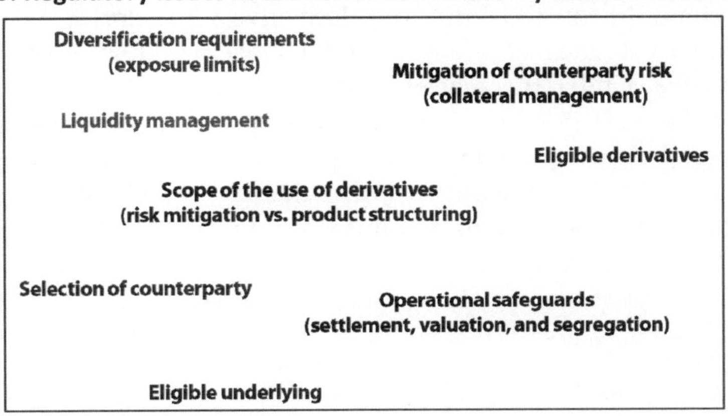

50 Other public authorities, such as the ones interested in safeguarding financial stability or promoting effective corporate governance, would, however, carry out a different balancing exercise when it comes to the use of derivatives by investment funds. For a discussion of financial stability and asset management, see chapter 2.

3.4.2 *Where are we now? The current UCITS rules on derivatives and indices*

The UCITS IV Directive contains numerous provisions that govern the use of financial derivatives and structured instruments in UCITS funds.[51] Altogether these requirements constitute probably the most advanced framework worldwide for the use of derivatives in retail investment funds. The rules comprise notably: a) limits to the global exposure of UCITS to market risk; b) limits to counterparty risk and collateral requirements; c) limits to eligible assets and diversification requirements, including specific rules for financial indices and d) related valuation and liquidity requirements. This section will consider these rules in detail explaining their strengths but also advancing some of its deficiencies.

3.4.2.1 Global exposure to market risk under UCITS IV

The exposure of UCITS to derivatives is limited in volume by national legislation depending on the approach followed to calculate this exposure. The UCITS IV Directive allows two approaches, either the calculation of the incremental exposure and leverage generated by the use of financial derivative instruments (commitment approach) or the market risk of the UCITS portfolio as a whole (market risk approach based on advanced risk metrics).[52] The methodologies to calculate these exposures are not harmonised but are codified in national legislation. ESMA guidelines propose a standard commitment approach and a standard market risk approach, which are not binding on member states, except on a comply-or-explain basis.[53]

- The commitment of a fund to a derivative represents a measure of its potential liabilities, otherwise stated, its leverage due to the use of such derivative. Under the *standard commitment approach*, each derivative is given the market value of an equivalent position in its underlying. The methodology proposed by ESMA to calculate the value of the underlying position is fairly straightforward, suitable only for simple derivative instruments. It takes into account hedging and netting, as well as the

---

[51] Relevant UCITS rules with regard to derivative financial instruments:
- Directive 2009/65/EC (UCITS IV)
- Implementing Directive 2010/43/EU (risk management, UCITS IV)
- ESMA Guidelines CESR/10-778 (global exposure and counterparty risk, UCITS IV)
- Implementing Directive 2007/16/EC (eligible assets, UCITS III)
- Commission Recommendation 2004/383/EC (use of financial derivative instruments, UCITS III)

[52] Article 41.1, Implementing Directive 2010/43/EU (risk management, UCITS IV).

[53] Article 16.3, Regulation 1095/2010/EU (ESMA).

risks involved in securities lending and repurchase agreements. The final value of the derivative exposure using the *standard commitment approach* is limited by the UCITS IV Directive to 100% of the fund's NAV, which means the total risk exposure of a UCITS fund to any instrument should be kept below 200% its NAV.[54]

- The *market risk approach* is based on the estimation of the potential loss of the UCITS due to market risk. Among the different metrics available, value at risk is the most popular (VaR). It provides an estimation of the potential decrease in value of the current UCITS portfolio based on the past performance of its components. A VaR (20 days, 99%) of €5 million means that under normal market circumstances, there is a 99% probability that the UCITS portfolio will not lose more than €5 million in value in 20 trading days. The application of the VaR depends on the type of fund. ESMA guidelines limit the VaR of funds whose objective is to outperform an (unleveraged) benchmark to twice the VaR of this benchmark, while UCITS with an absolute return objective need to keep their VaR below 20% of their net asset value. Keeping with the previous example, an absolute-return UCITS with €5 million VaR should have at least €25 million assets under management. As the VaR metric is based on past performance, managers should conduct *stress testing* on the value of their portfolio to control for the impact of exceptional market conditions. They should also *back test* their models to monitor their reliability.

The commitment approach and the risk management approach are widely different and can be arbitraged to gain additional exposure to market risk. For instance, within the risk management approach, funds may arbitrage the VaR limits set by ESMA by finding a benchmark where twice its VaR exceeds 20% the fund´s net asset value.[55] ESMA does not encourage member states to strictly regulate the circumstances under which each approach needs to be employed. It considers that the responsibility should fall on asset managers to choose, based on their investment policy and the use they make of derivatives. Yet, ESMA considers the risk measurement approach should be

---

[54] Article 51.3, Directive 2009/65/EC (UCITS IV).

[55] A fund following the absolute VaR approach (where the fund´s VaR is limited to 20% of the fund's NAV) may find it convenient to switch to the relative VaR approach (where the fund´s VaR is limited to twice the VaR of an unleveraged benchmark). By finding an appropriate benchmark (or building a tailor-made one), the fund may be able to carry on its activities increasing its leverage over 20% its NAV. To avoid this, ESMA invites member states to require UCITS to fully document their choice of VaR approach and control whether a switch is motivated by having exceeded the 20% NAV limit.

preferred whenever the UCITS has "more than a negligible exposure to exotic derivatives".[56]

The boundaries of derivative exposure are loosely harmonised in UCITS. National rules may put forward virtually any methodology to calculate the exposure to derivatives or the level of market risk in a UCITS portfolio.[57] They may also apply different limits to maximum exposure of a UCITS portfolio under the market risk approach since the limits to VaR in ESMA guidelines are not binding.[58] While member states and national supervisors converge towards the ESMA guidelines, the single market would benefit from further harmonisation in this regard.

It is important to note, however, that VaR does not measure directly the incremental exposure or leverage gathered through the use of derivatives. It is instead an estimation of the potential loss of the UCITS due to market risk based on assumptions such as normally distributed returns. It is therefore possible that a UCITS employing VaR to calculate its global exposure presents a level of leverage that exceeds 200% of its NAV. For instance, arbitrage strategies that take long and short positions may have low VaR but very high leverage - although both positions would ordinarily offset one another. No hard limits to leverage apply in practice to UCITS funds; instead ESMA guidelines require that managers disclose in the prospectus the expected level of leverage and the possibility that actual leverage may exceed the level announced (if applicable).[59] Moreover, it is widely acknowledged that VaR

---

[56] Box 1.4.a, ESMA Guidelines CESR/10-778 (global exposure and counterparty risk, UCITS IV).

[57] Articles 41.3 and 41.4, Implementing Directive 2010/43/EU (risk management, UCITS IV). The first provision allows member states to calculate global exposure by using the commitment approach, the value at risk approach or other advanced risk measurement methodologies, as may be appropriate. The second provision allows member states to permit management companies to apply calculation methods that are equivalent to the standard commitment approach described by the Directive.

[58] Only the incremental exposure to derivatives is capped at 100% NAV. There are no harmonised limits to the market risk of the UCITS portfolio other than the ones set in ESMA guidelines - Article 51.3, Directive 2009/65/EC (UCITS IV) and Article 41.1, Implementing Directive 2010/43/EU (risk management, UCITS IV). Box 1 in ESMA Guidelines, CESR/10-778 (global exposure and counterparty risk, UCITS IV) states that "a UCITS may consider appropriate for the calculation of global exposure only those methodologies on which CESR has published level 3 guidelines". However, this assertion is inconsistent with Article 16.3, Regulation 1095/2010/EU (ESMA), which provides that member states are only obliged to follow ESMA guidelines on a comply or explain basis.

[59] Box 24.2, ESMA Guidelines CESR/10-778 (global exposure and counterparty risk, UCITS IV).

does not capture all the relevant risks, and in particular the so-called 'fat-tail' risk (the risk of high loses in abnormal market circumstances). In effect, to calculate the VaR of a given portfolio, the manager has to assume a certain distribution of returns. If a normal distribution is assumed, the probability of a fat-tail event occurring may be underestimated. In addition, those funds that employ leverage magnify the impact of extreme market events in their portfolios. It follows therefore that limits in terms of VaR need to be complemented by leverage limits and rigorous stress testing.

3.4.2.2 Counterparty risk and collateral requirements under UCITS IV

The risk embedded in a derivative is composed of market risk (the risk associated with the underlying or reference asset) and counterparty risk, which depends on the credit-worthiness of the counterparty and the quantity and quality of the collateral transferred as guarantee. The UCITS IV Directive requires that counterparties to OTC derivative transactions are subject to prudential regulation and approval by member states.[60] It also limits the net counterparty exposure to 10% per OTC derivative transaction and 20% per counterparty, measured as a ratio of the UCITS assets under management.[61] This net exposure takes into account the collateral received by the UCITS, as long as it is liquid and certain.[62] A UCITS fund may therefore be structured fully synthetically based on a single derivative contract, such as a total return swap, on the condition that the counterparty posts enough collateral.

Collateral requirements are not harmonised in UCITS. ESMA guidelines set a number of high-level principles with regard to collateral quality: a) high liquidity and short-settlement cycle; b) very high grade credit rating and c) residual correlation with the counterparty.[63] Collateral of a lower quality may be employed on condition that an appropriate discount rate (haircut) is applied to its market value. The application of haircuts (over-collateralisation) is sometimes advisable also for highly rated financial instruments. The lack of harmonised rules results sometimes in divergent implementation. For instance, equities posted as collateral in Ireland are subject to a 20% haircut while in Luxembourg any haircut is agreed between the fund manager and the

---

60 Article 50.1.g.iii, Directive 2009/65/EC (UCITS IV).

61 Article 43.1, Implementing Directive 2010/43/EU (risk management, UCITS IV). Article 52, Directive 2009/65/EC (UCITS IV). Member states may raise the second limit to 35% under some circumstances.

62 Articles 43.3 and 43.4, Implementing Directive 2010/43/EU (risk management, UCITS IV).

63 ESMA Guidelines, CESR/10-778 (global exposure and counterparty risk, UCITS IV). These guidelines are scheduled to be revised later in 2012 (see ESMA/2012/44).

depositary (BIS, 2011). Collateral selection should configure a diverse basket of securities to avoid concentration in specific issuers, sectors or geographies but once more no detailed rules exist in this regard.

Establishing the quality of a given collateral basket is a complex exercise from the perspective of the fund manager. It is inherently difficult to anticipate the level of liquidity and correlation of financial instruments, particularly under the sort of stress scenario that may precede or follow the failure of a given counterparty. The derivative counterparty is usually best positioned to assess the quality of the collateral. Yet it faces a conflict of interest when it comes to selecting the composition of the given collateral basket, since higher quality may reduce the profitability of the derivative transaction. Higher costs would ultimately undermine the commercial interest of market-makers, asset managers and investors in entering into some derivative transactions.

The value of collateral needs to be constantly monitored to ensure that counterparty exposure remains within the UCITS limits. A depreciation in the market value of the financial instruments posted as collateral would require the fund to demand additional guarantees to the counterparty. ESMA guidelines only observe that collateral must be capable of being valued at least daily. Besides monitoring valuation, collateral management also requires segregating the assets to ensure the fund can access them promptly in case of a counterparty default. No specific reference is made in UCITS IV to the depositary requirements for collateral arrangements.[64] ESMA expects collateral arrangements to be fully enforceable by the UCITS at any time without reference to the counterparty. This expectation has not been technically defined in line with market practice and the relevant provisions of Directive 2002/47/EC (collateral Directive).[65] The UCITS V Directive, scheduled for 2012, is due to address these issues while the implementation of the AIMFD proposed by ESMA already advances some solutions in this respect (see section 5 in this chapter).[66]

---

[64] ESMA has however proposed a framework for the custody of collateral for alternative funds handled by managers under the AIFMD. See ESMA Technical Advice, ESMA 2011/379 (AIFMD implementation).

[65] ESMA may wish to limit collateral arrangements in UCITS to "title transfer arrangements" within the definition of Article 2 of Directive 2002/47/EC (collateral Directive). Under "title transfer collateral arrangements", the collateral provider transfers full ownership of the financial collateral to a collateral taker. They are in contrast with "security financial collateral arrangements", in which full or qualified ownership remains with the collateral provider.

[66] ESMA 2011/379 (technical advice, implementation AIFMD), pp. 158-159.

Collateral management becomes more complex when the assets are re-used. Directive 2002/47/EC states that collateral-takers have a right of use in relation to financial collateral but also a parallel obligation to provide substitute assets of an equivalent nature and value. In order to mitigate operational risks, ESMA considers that UCITS should not exercise this right of use, which means cash collateral should only be invested in risk-free assets and non-cash collateral should neither be invested nor pledged.

Given the lack of clear and detailed rules, transparency is essential to allow investors to assess the quality of the collateral and the level of diversification, among other aspects. Yet, retail investors are ill-equipped to understand these aspects. Collateral management is particularly important for those UCITS that are fully synthetic, such as swap-based UCITS funds, including synthetic ETFs. Many asset managers have gone a long way towards improving the disclosure of collateral arrangements and composition. Yet, the law does not yet impose uniform disclosure requirements in this regard. ESMA is expected to introduce guidelines in 2012 that will clarify the transparency duties of UCITS managers with regard to collateral arrangements.

Securities lending and repurchase agreements result in similar counterparty and operational risks as some derivative instruments. The Directive requires that UCITS take into account these transactions when they calculate their counterparty exposure, which cannot exceed 20% of the UCITS NAV for all transactions with the same counterparty.[67] The industry best practice is to post collateral to reduce counterparty risks in securities lending and repurchase agreements. However, the UCITS rules do not clarify whether this *collateral* can be considered when calculating the UCITS counterparty exposure to comply with the 20% limit. Moreover, the ESMA principles on collateral apply only to the collateral received by the fund in OTC derivative transactions and not to the collateral received in securities lending and repurchase agreements.[68] In contrast with these principles, the collateral received in securities lending and repo transactions (up to 100% of its value) may be reinvested by the UCITS in financial assets providing returns above the risk-free rate of return.[69] Yet, the exposure generated needs to be taken into account when calculating the UCITS global exposure.[70] In sum, securities lending and repurchase agreements are subject to the general rules on

[67] Article 41.4, Implementing Directive 2010/43/EU (risk management, UCITS IV).

[68] Box 26, ESMA Guidelines CESR/10-778 (global exposure and counterparty risk, UCITS IV). ESMA is schedule however to update these guidelines in 2012 (see ESMA 2012/44).

[69] Box 9, ESMA Guidelines CESR/10-778 (global exposure and counterparty risk, UCITS IV).

[70] Article 41.4, Implementing Directive 2010/43/EU (risk management, UCITS IV).

counterparty and global exposure in UCITS, but to different rules when it comes to the collateral received by the fund in these transactions. In addition, there is no limit on the amount of assets that a UCITS may lend, which opens the door for fully lent portfolios (at least theoretically).[71]

3.4.2.3 *Underlying assets to financial indices under UCITS IV*

Financial derivatives need to be based on assets that are eligible for direct investment by UCITS (transferable securities and money market instruments), interest rates, foreign exchange rates and currencies. Derivatives on other assets, such as commodities, are therefore not permissible. The derivative must be looked-through to factor the underlying into the general issuer concentration limits in UCITS.[72] Article 52 of the UCITS IV Directive details these limits, aimed at ensuring the diversification of the portfolio and usually referred to as the 5/10/40% rule - which is however the object of divergent interpretation across member states.

UCITS may also employ derivative instruments to access financial indices as long as the given index represents an adequate benchmark and satisfies certain transparency requirements.[73] This practice is common to some exchange traded-funds and other UCITS that replicate the performance of market indices using total return swaps. The look-through principle does not apply to the underlying of financial indices which may be composed of otherwise non-eligible assets, such as commodities, property or hedge funds.[74] There is only a requirement that the underlying components are sufficiently liquid to allow the physical replication of the index.[75] For hedge-fund indices, ESMA advises member states to set certain requirements in terms of due diligence and conflicts of interest.[76]

On the presumption that indices are representative of a relevant market, the ordinary diversification requirements in Article 52 of the UCITS IV

---

[71] To overcome some of these deficiencies, ESMA will bring forward additional guidance in 2012.

[72] Article 51.3 (third indent), Directive 2009/65/EC (UCITS IV). See also Article 43.5, Implementing Directive 2010/43/EU (risk management, UCITS IV) and Box 37.5, ESMA Guidelines CESR/10-778 (global exposure and counterparty risk, UCITS IV).

[73] Article 53, Directive 2009/65/EC (UCITS IV). See also the more detailed provisions in Article 9, Implementing Directive 2007/16/EC (eligible assets, UCITS III).

[74] Article 51.3 (third indent), Directive 2009/65/EC (UCITS IV). See also Box 37.6, ESMA Guidelines, CESR/10-778 (global exposure and counterparty risk, UCITS IV).

[75] Article 9.1.b.iii, Implementing Directive 2007/16/EC (eligible assets, UCITS III).

[76] ESMA Guidelines, CESR/07/434 (hedge fund indices).

Directive are relaxed. In principle, the index components need comply with Article 52, either considering the index on its own or within the UCITS portfolio as a whole.[77] However, the general issuer concentration limit is raised from 5% to 20%, which may be further increased by member states up to 35% in some cases.[78]

Issuer limits do not apply directly to assets other than shares and debt securities, such as commodities, which may be accessed through financial indices, given the non-application of the look-through principle. In effect, the UCITS IV Directive does not impose direct limits to the exposure gained through financial indices to individual assets or groups of assets.[79] It is therefore possible for an index to comply with the issuer concentration requirements but exceed these limits in terms of exposure. Due to the methodology followed, a component that represents less than 20% of the index could have an impact in excess of 20%, opening the opportunity for arbitrage (ESMA, 2011a).

The UCITS Directive expressly requires that financial indices represent "an adequate benchmark for the market to which they refer" but the concepts of 'benchmark' and 'market' are left largely undefined [80] From the UCITS Directive, it only transpires that financial indices need to measure the performance of a representative group of assets in an appropriate way.[81] As a result of this loose phrasing, the door is opened for the construction of tailor-made indices to underlie derivatives in UCITS. It is reported that indices are used to wrap investment strategies and arbitrage the limitations imposed to direct investments, in terms of eligible assets and issuer concentration (ESMA, 2011a). Far from representing a passive benchmark, some indices are rebalanced at very short intervals (daily or even intra-daily) and do not have a single objective but one that changes in accordance with market conditions (ESMA, 2011a).

In sum, principle-based regulation for derivatives and financial indices does not match the rule-based approach followed by the UCITS Directive with

---

[77] Article 9.1.a, Implementing Directive 2007/16/EC (eligible assets, UCITS III). See also Box 27.5 and 27.6, ESMA Guidelines CESR/10-778 (global exposure and counterparty risk, UCITS IV).

[78] Article 53, Directive 2009/65/EC (UCITS IV).

[79] It is only required that the performance of a single constituent does not 'unduly influence' the performance of the index as a whole (see Article 9.1.a.i, Implementing Directive 2007/16/EC on eligible assets, UCITS III).

[80] Article 53.1.b, Directive 2009/65/EC (UCITS IV).

[81] Article 9.b.i, Implementing Directive 2007/16/EC (eligible assets, UCITS III).

regard to direct investments. The contrast between these two approaches sets the incentives for arbitraging the hard limits imposed in terms of eligible assets and diversification for direct investments, via the use of derivatives based on financial indices.

3.4.3 Where to go from here? Revisiting the UCITS rules on derivatives and indices.

As detailed in the previous sections, the UCITS rules are fairly comprehensive when it comes to governing the use of derivative and structured financial instruments. Notably, the rules a) limit the global exposure of UCITS to market risk; b) limit counterparty exposure and require that collateral is of sufficient quality, legal certainty and liquidity and c) impose diversification requirements on the underlying, including on financial indices. The detail and sophistication of the UCITS rules are built to ensure a high level of safety for retail investors. The UCITS framework has proved over time both its resilience and its capacity to accommodate innovation. Yet, some of the provisions in the Directive may have fallen out of place with innovation by product providers. Some of the rules regarding the use of derivatives have been questioned by observers who consider they may be arbitraged easily to structure products with undisclosed or underrepresented risks such as: a) counterparty risk given inadequate collateralisation; b) liquidity risk for non-standardised derivatives and illiquid reference assets; c) operational risk present in more complex instruments and strategies and d) leverage risk that is difficult to observe and measure. Overcoming these concerns would require a targeted reform of the UCITS regulatory framework. It would not be a matter of producing a major overhaul but of closing gaps to reduce the opportunities for arbitrage and deepen harmonisation to improve consistency. The box below advances some ideas that are explained in more detail over the next few pages.

Box 4. Targeted changes to the UCITS rules regarding derivatives and indices

- Work-out a categorisation of derivatives and the use that funds make of them.
- Better delineate the circumstances under which a fund needs to follow the market-risk approach instead of the commitment approach to the calculation of its global exposure.
- Further harmonise the methodologies for the calculation of a fund's global exposure and its limits.
- Set hard limits on the leverage gathered through the use of derivatives.
- Clarify and harmonise the collateral requirements for OTC derivatives in line with the collateral Directive.
- Subject the collateral received in securities lending and repurchase transactions to equivalent rules as the collateral received in OTC derivative transactions.

- Impose stricter counterparty risk limits for total return swaps and funds that are fully synthetic in line with industry best practice.
- Define the concepts of market and benchmark for financial indices.
- Subject strategy indices to diversification requirements equivalent to direct investments.
- Devise exposure concentration limits that mitigate the arbitrage of issuer concentration limits.
- Advance towards a single rule book and simplify the structure of the regulatory framework to facilitate convergence in its implementation.

Better understand derivatives and the use that funds make of them. The UCITS IV Directive distinguishes centrally cleared from over-the-counter (OTC) derivatives and imposes additional requirements on the latter category with regard notably to the management of valuation, liquidity and counterparty risks.[82] However, beyond this straightforward distinction, derivatives and the use that funds make of them remains largely uncategorised under the UCITS framework. ESMA guidelines employ concepts such as *standard* versus *exotic* derivatives, and *negligible* versus *non-negligible* that would need to be further defined to better understand the risks involved and the regulatory approach that should be followed.[83]

Delineate the circumstances under which a fund needs to follow the market risk approach instead of the commitment approach to the calculation of its global exposure. ESMA guidelines require funds that have a 'non-negligible exposure to exotic derivatives' to follow the market risk approach instead of the commitment approach to calculate their global exposure.[84] The guidelines invite managers to use a maximum loss approach to determine whether the use of exotic derivatives represents more than a negligible exposure for the given fund.[85] ESMA should consider the feasibility of using a more straightforward definition of negligible exposure, for instance, in terms of a percentage of assets under management or further harmonising the maximum loss approach. Similarly, the guidelines provide an illustrative list of standard and non-

[82] Article 50.1.g, Directive 2009/65/EC (UCITS IV) and Article 44, Implementing Directive 2010/43/EU (risk management, UCITS IV).

[83] Box 1, ESMA Guidelines, CESR/10-778 (global exposure and counterparty risk, UCITS IV). See also Article 3.1, Commission Recommendation 2004/383/EC (UCITS III, use of financial derivative instruments).

[84] Box 1, ESMA Guidelines, CESR/10-778 (global exposure and counterparty risk, UCITS IV).

[85] Explanatory text to Box 1, ESMA Guidelines, CESR/10-778 (global exposure and counterparty risk, UCITS IV).

standard (exotic) derivatives, but the criteria used to allocate derivatives to each category are unclear. Better definitions of these concepts would be necessary to reduce the discretion of funds when it comes to choosing the market risk approach or the commitment approach to global exposure, thereby reducing the opportunity for arbitrage.

Besides global exposure, the categorisation of derivatives (and the categorisation of their use) is also relevant from the perspective of counterparty and collateral requirements. For instance, a threshold could be established over which the limits to counterparty exposure would be below the general limit of 20%, in particular for funds that are fully synthetic. Such a rule would take stock of industry best practice, such as the over-collateralisation of funds based on total return swaps.

Set hard limits on the leverage gathered through the use of derivatives. In contrast with the commitment approach, the market risk approach does not measure directly the leverage gathered through the use of derivatives. In effect, a UCITS fund that measures its global exposure using the market risk approach may have a leverage exceeding 200% of its net asset value. It follows that, even though VaR is a useful tool to measure and manage market risk in a fund, it does not fully substitute limits to leverage. In spite of this, an inner tension underlies the calculation of global exposure since exotic derivatives are precisely those where it is not feasible in practice to apply the standard approach to calculate the embedded leverage. While maintaining the 200% leverage limit would be desirable, there is a practical difficulty in devising a methodology to estimate the leverage in exotic derivatives. A possible solution would be to devise a methodology that gives a higher estimation and applies in addition to the VaR limit.

Clarify and harmonise the collateral requirements for OTC derivatives. At present, only high-level principles inform the use of collateral to reduce counterparty exposure. These principles refer to liquidity, valuation, issuer credit quality, correlation, diversification, legal certainty and the re-use of collateral. They touch on all the relevant aspects but need to be further specified, in particular with regard to diversification and correlation. In addition, these principles should be extended to the collateral received in securities lending and repurchase transactions where they currently do not apply. Detailed rules on collateral should be uniform across member states. ESMA is expected to bring forward additional guidance in this respect in 2012 but legislative action may be preferred to ensure convergence in national implementation.[86]

---

[86] ESMA Consultation Paper, ESMA/2012/44 (ETFs and structured UCITS).

The UCITS Directive relaxes the scope of eligible assets for derivatives backed by collateral of sufficient quality, liquidity and legal security. In such instances, the degree of liquidity that the underlying may lack is substituted by the liquidity of the collateral. However, the former will only work in practice if the fund can claim the collateral immediately from the depositary without recourse to the counterparty and prior to any bankruptcy proceedings.[87] To ensure legal certainty, collateral arrangements in UCITS would ideally follow the 'title transfer arrangements' defined in Article 2 of the collateral Directive.[88]

The European market infrastructure Regulation (EMIR) will re-shape the OTC derivative markets in Europe by introducing further standardisation and other measures to mitigate counterparty and operational risks. Eligible derivatives that are currently cleared bilaterally will be brought to central clearing counterparties, while derivatives that are not eligible to be centrally cleared will be subject to reviewed collateral requirements. From this perspective, any reform of UCITS rules regarding derivatives should be coherent with the changes introduced by EMIR.[89]

Revise the rules on financial indices. The UCITS Directive relaxes the issuer concentration limits for funds that track widely recognised indices that benchmark relevant markets. The idea is that market indices are by definition diversified. However, the lack of definition of 'benchmark' and 'market' has resulted in the creation of funds that track narrow tailor-made indices. Issuer concentration limits are arbitraged since principle-based regulation for financial indices does not match the hard limits imposed on direct investments. As a result, some managers use financial indices not to track a relevant market but rather to package investment strategies with more flexibility (even active strategies). To avoid arbitrage, the concepts of 'benchmark' and 'market' should be narrowly defined. Tailor-made indices that have not been designed

---

87 From the perspective of financial stability, the use of derivatives should be considered taking into account the effect of the use of derivatives in the financial system as a whole and in particular their complexity and interconnectedness.

88 Article 2.b, Directive 2002/47/EC: "Title transfer financial collateral arrangement means an arrangement, including repurchase agreements, under which a collateral provider transfers full ownership of financial collateral to a collateral taker for the purpose of securing or otherwise covering the performance of relevant financial obligations". In contrast with Article 2.c of the same directive: "Security financial collateral arrangement means an arrangement under which a collateral provider provides financial collateral by way of security in favour of, or to, a collateral taker, and where the full ownership of the financial collateral remains with the collateral provider when the security right is established". See also note 65 above.

89 Regulation on OTC derivatives, central counterparties and trade repositories, proposed by the European Commission on 15 September 2010.

to track a relevant market but to package a given investment strategy should be subject to the same limitations as direct investments. Besides, issuer concentration limits are no substitute for exposure limits in particular for financial indices where the methodology applied may result in higher exposures to a given asset (or asset class) than the limits imposed per issuer. ESMA is due to put forward additional guidance in this regard in 2012, but binding legislation should be preferred.

Advance towards a single rule book and simplify the structure of the regulatory framework to facilitate convergence in its implementation. The UCITS regulatory regime is composed of a number of directives, regulations and guidelines which are transposed and implemented by the 27 member states. At this stage in the development of the UCITS market, it is argued that the use of directives and guidelines is no longer justified to accommodate national preferences. There is a need for more detailed rules in three main areas: eligible assets, global exposure and collateral requirements. For instance, currently there is neither a uniform approach to calculate global exposure nor a uniform limit, except the ones set in ESMA guidelines. Divergent implementation ultimately undermines the single market and makes it difficult for all participants to assess the level of risks and compare funds coming from different jurisdictions.

There is also scope to clarify and simplify the structure of the UCITS rules to strengthen them. High-level principles are difficult to identify in the UCITS Directive since they are mixed in with detailed provisions. At the same time, the level of detail is not uniform, which does not help regulatory consistency either. The virtue of implementing legislation is that it can be more quickly adapted to cope with changes in market circumstances and product innovation. Improving the hierarchy and structure of the UCITS legislation would be helpful to achieve three objectives: i) clarify the high-level principles, ii) reduce the opportunities for divergent implementation and regulatory arbitrage and iii) increase the future responsiveness of regulation to product innovation.

Box 5. The role and frontiers of regulation in risk management

A recurring question in fund regulation is how to favour an effective risk management function. Managing risks is a highly specific activity that depends on the strategy followed by the fund and the instruments or markets in which it invests. It is also highly sensitive, and needs to adapt quickly, to changes in market sentiment and market structures. Risk management is in fact the core of the asset management function next to asset allocation. From this perspective, risk management may only be regulated at the level of principles.

When it comes to regulating risk management, the trade-offs between principled and detailed rules are exacerbated. Principled rules allow flexibility but are difficult to monitor and enforce, while detailed rules have mirror attributes; they facilitate supervision but may petrify the risk management function. The UCITS Directive combines both types of rules as enumerated below.

The combination of principled and detailed rules in UCITS follows a straightforward rationale: Risk *management* is regulated at the level of principles, since it is highly specific to each fund, while risk *measurement* is regulated in detail to allow supervisors to monitor that funds offered to retail investors stay under certain risk limits. This dichotomy, between risk *management* and risk *measurement*, is apparent in the UCITS rules. Exposure limits are by far the aspect that is regulated in more detail in UCITS, both in terms of calculation methodologies and thresholds.

Principle-based approach

- Managers need to have procedures in place to assess market, liquidity, counterparty and operational risks; and review this procedures periodically.[a]
- Managers need to establish a system of internal limits and carry-out stress tests and scenario analysis.[b]
- Managers need to have a liquidity risk management process in line with their redemption obligations (as prescribed by UCITS and their own redemption policies).[c]
- Managers need to measure their exposure to market risks using a methodology defined by regulation.[d]
- Managers need to keep their market, issuer and counterparty exposures within the limits fixed by regulation.[e]

Rule-based approach

[a] Articles 38 and 39 Implementing Directive 2010/43/EU (risk management, UCITS IV).

[b] Article 40.2 Implementing Directive 2010/43/EU (risk management, UCITS IV).

[c] Article 40.3 Implementing Directive 2010/43/EU (risk management, UCITS IV).

[d] Articles 41 and 42 Implementing Directive 2010/43/EU (risk management, UCITS IV) and ESMA Guidelines CESR/10-778 (global exposure and counterparty risk, UCITS IV).

[e] Article 43 Implementing Directive 2010/43/EU (risk management, UCITS IV).

A common approach to risk *measurement* has three main advantages: i) it clarifies compliance for managers and mitigates their moral hazard to choose the metric that best favours their portfolio, ii) it enables supervisors to monitor product risk easily and iii) it allows investors to compare different products and choose one that matches their level of risk aversion. Yet, it also carries two potential drawbacks: it is unlikely to capture all relevant risks and it may undermine qualitative risk management. In effect, some risks are inherently hard to measure and would pass unnoticed if the focus is placed solely on *measuring* risks instead of *managing* them.

Managers and supervisors need to bear in mind that risk metrics under-represent certain risks (such as liquidity risks in extreme market events) and are based on past performance. They should therefore give equal importance to additional mechanisms such as stress testing or scenario analysis. If compliance is focused solely on risk *measurement*, managers may neglect other areas of risk *management* that are more qualitative but equally important. Supervisors are not equipped to tell managers how to structure their internal risk management processes but can exercise a steering and monitoring role.

Another aspect worth discussing is the independency of the risk management function that is so frequently imposed upon financial intermediaries by regulation. The UCITS Directive (Article 38.1.b Implementing Directive 2010/43/EU, IV) does not require the risk management function to be separate but leaves this to the discretion of member states, in contrast with the AIFMD (Article 15), which imposes the functional and hierarchical separation. The separation of both functions derives from a mistaken conception of fund management. In effect, managing risks is an integral part of the mandate of asset managers who administer a portfolio on behalf of investors to protect their capital and generate returns. The split between the risk and portfolio management functions is artificial. What funds may need, as a safeguard, is an independent *risk control function* that has full access to review the level of risk in the fund and enforce risk limits.

Table 6 proposes an integrated approach to risk management and portfolio construction that would involve both regulators and asset managers.

Table 6. Promoting an integrated approach to risk management and portfolio construction

Regulators and supervisors	Asset managers
– Do not focus compliance solely on risk metrics	– Develop a holistic rather than simply quantitative approach to risk management; strengthen top-down resources to build and implement macro and theme views; develop risk budgeting in the form of internal limits to exposures; incorporate ESG criteria into risk management
– Make sure fat-tail events are taken into account	– Use models with full awareness of their limitations; interpret results in terms of breakdowns and trends per groups of assets, not simply in terms of overall values; implement stress testing and scenario analysis
– Steer and monitor the way asset managers implement liquidity management processes	– Monitor liquidity conditions and build internal trading capabilities; optimise trading strategy and execution

- Avoid petrifying risk management, keeping track of market, scientific and technological developments	- Constantly monitor and update risk management processes and metrics
- Do not force the strict separation of the risk and portfolio management functions	- Familiarise risk managers with trading and portfolio management functions; establish portfolio review meetings led by risk managers
- Consider risk management as an integral part of portfolio construction, different to internal risk auditing	- Establish an independent risk control function to review the level of risk and enforce risk limits; give executive functions to a chief risk officer

Source: Author's own elaboration and Fitch Ratings (2010).

3.5 Coming to terms with non-market risks and fund depositaries

This section considers non-market risks and fund depositaries by first clarifying the notion of non-market risks and then discussing the depositary rules under the AIFMD and the UCITS Directive. Particular attention is paid to the implementation of the rules in the AIFMD and the need to manage instead of insure non-market risks.

3.5.1 Rare but significant: What are non-market risks?

Non-market risks may be defined as those that do not depend on market developments such as changes in the value of underlying assets, currencies or interest rates. A similar terminology was first employed by EDHEC-Risk in its study "The European fund management industry needs a better grasp of non-financial risks", which was presented to the Task Force and discussed in-depth with the participating authorities, custodian banks and fund managers. The report considers "the security of settlement, custody and control operation outside the traditional space of securities held by central securities depositaries"(EDHEC-Risk, 2010a, p. 17). In effect, non-market risks can be defined as those that do not derive from changes in the value of an asset but from major operational risks or counterparty failures. Operational risks comprise internal or external failures in trading, settlement and valuation processes, as well as legal risks and failures in the segregation of client assets.

Non-market risks have a low frequency but on average higher impact than market risks. In effect, the occurrence of a non-market event may completely wipe out the value of a portfolio or entail its physical disappearance, e.g. in case of a loss of assets that might be unrecoverable. By way of contrast, market risks are defined with reference to "changes in market variables, such as interest rates, foreign exchange rates, equity and commodity prices or an issuer's credit worthiness".[90] Market risks materialise constantly and have on average a small impact on the value of the portfolio.

Non-market risks are more difficult to measure and represent than market risks. While value-at-risk indicates the exposure of a fund to market risk, at present there is no synthetic indicator of the level of non-market risks present in an investment fund. The focus on risk measurement over risk management has meant that non-market risks have not been sufficiently accounted for until some of them materialised dramatically in the 2008 financial crisis. Lack of awareness affected not only investors but also supervisors and even parts of the fund management industry.

Figure 14. Frequency and impact of different risk events

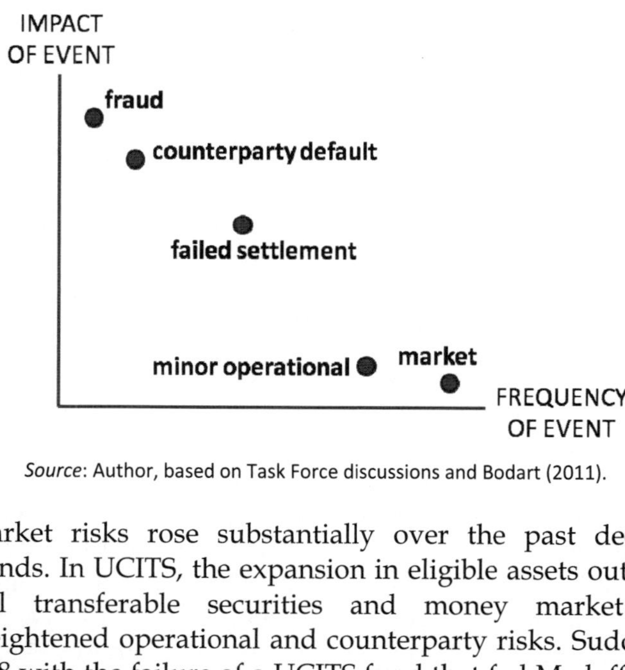

Source: Author, based on Task Force discussions and Bodart (2011).

Non-market risks rose substantially over the past decade in retail investment funds. In UCITS, the expansion in eligible assets outside the range of traditional transferable securities and money market instruments, introduced heightened operational and counterparty risks. Sudden awareness arrived in 2008 with the failure of a UCITS fund that fed Madoff, and Lehman, a large sub-custodian. Both events resulted in the temporary unavailability or outright loss of assets in several investment funds in Europe.

Non-market risks can be managed and effectively mitigated. Regulation has a triple role to play in this respect: i) mitigate legal risks from the start by ensuring the uniformity and clarity of the law, ii) consider the specific methods

[90] Article 3.9, Implementing Directive 2010/43/EU (risk management, UCITS IV).

that help manage and mitigate non-market risks and iii) establish the maximum level of non-market risks that is tolerable for investor protection purposes and ultimately financial stability. The regulation of funds for retail investors has to pay particular attention to the two last elements: risk mitigation and risk limits. In addition, it needs to provide for the effective disclosure of non-market risks that should allow investors to make informed decisions.

Custody and operational risks are an integral part of the risk management function. To mitigate these risks, a fund manager needs to put in place a number of processes, including: i) segregating client assets to avoid the loss of assets held under custody and instances of fraud, ii) managing legal risks in trading and settlement; including in particular controlling the legal title over the assets and collateral held by the fund and iii) establishing strong valuation processes. To minimise conflicts of interests and ensure the integrity of the segregation of assets, the depositary function should not be carried out by the manager itself but by an independent third party.

3.5.2 *A matter of principles: The depositaries rules under the AIFMD (and forthcoming UCITS V)*

A depositary is an agent whose primary role is keeping securities and other financial instruments on behalf of others (BIS, 2003). They should be independent, that is, depositaries should not act as counterparties to the fund except if their depositary and counterparty functions are functionally and hierarchically separated.[91] For most securities listed in regulated markets, central securities depositaries (CSDs) perform the so-called 'notary function' by keeping a central register of a particular issue of securities for the purpose of enabling the settlement of transactions.[92] Fund depositaries hold securities

---

[91] Prime brokers act as counterparties by providing finance to fund managers, fulfilling an essential role for investors. Their financing is used both for leverage purposes, suitable to some investment strategies, and for bridge financing, allowing managers to swiftly seize investment opportunities. Prime brokers have frequently performed the role of custodians facing a clear conflict of interest. Article 21.4 of Directive 2011/61/EU (AIFMD) requires the functional and hierarchical separation of the depositary and prime brokerage functions. By separating prime brokerage and custody, depositary costs will become more explicit. It is thought that prime brokers subsidised depositary services through the revenues obtained by financing funds. Part of these revenues came from re-using the collateral posted by the funds by way of guarantee (Article 14.3 of Directive 2011/61/EU requires any re-use of assets to be explicitly agreed and disclosed).

[92] In Europe, despite liberalisation efforts, CSDs remain largely national. MiFID gives issuer the freedom to designate any EU CSD to settle its transactions. However, there remain barriers in national legislation.

on behalf of their clients via participation arrangements with CSDs and independently hold those other assets for which no CSD exists.

The segregation of client assets has been an integral part of UCITS since its inception. In effect, depositaries were regulated by the original 1985 Directive but only at the level of principles.[93] These principles worked well for over 25 years, until the Madoff affair and the default of Lehman made it apparent that they had not been kept up to date. Drafted with plain-vanilla bonds and equities in mind, they were not adequate for the exotic assets and strategies allowed by UCITS III. Moreover, insufficient harmonisation resulted in different levels of protection for investors across member states. A mapping exercise by ESMA revealed scattered transpositions and widely different interpretations of the depositary rules, despite UCITS being marketed under a European passport.[94]

Following the mapping by ESMA, the revision of the depositary rules should naturally have taken place in UCITS. However, due to the legislative agenda, the rules were revised to be first inserted in the AIFMD. The switch immersed depositaries into a highly political discussion on hedge funds which somewhat distorted the process. The UCITS principles on depositaries were incorporated into the AIFMD and developed in great detail. The AIFMD rules on depositaries are scheduled to be incorporated (with minor changes) into the UCITS framework in 2012.

The concept of deposit is simple and refers to keeping an object in a vault on behalf of someone else. Civil law countries apply an obligation of restitution, which may only be exonerated in exceptional circumstances, while common law countries apply a more flexible standard (duty of care). Deposit involves a simple separation of ownership and possession of a given object. It becomes complicated for dematerialised securities where possession and sometimes ownership are represented by one or several notations in securities accounts.

The duties of fund depositaries in EU regulation may be boiled down to three: i) control the title of any assets received by the fund, ii) keep assets in custody or, where this is not possible, keep their records and iii) monitor cash flows and other oversight functions. The difference between *custody* and *record-keeping* is the fundamental one in the discussion. Custody involves holding a security, either physically or electronically while record-keeping only concerns taking note of an ownership right without holding the asset. The AIFMD

---

93 Article 14, Directive 85/611/CEE (UCITS I).

94 ESMA Paper, CESR/09-175 (mapping of duties and liabilities of UCITS depositaries).

imposes strict liability for the loss of an asset kept in custody while liability in record-keeping arises in case of negligence or intentional failure (see below).[95]

Strict liability means a depositary is liable except in very rare circumstances. The AIFMD refers to "an *external event* beyond the reasonable control of the depositary".[96] Strict liability is coupled with a reversal of the burden of proof, which means the depositary is liable unless it can prove the above event occurred in practice.[97] Strict liability only applies in case of the loss in assets held in custody. Yet, determining which assets can be *kept in custody* instead of *kept in record* is not self-evident. The difference between property and contractual rights has been advanced in this regard, but it is not satisfactory since the content and form of these rights are not harmonised across jurisdictions. Lack of harmonisation of securities law suggests that any formal criterion would be inadequate and that a functional approach is preferable.

Table 7. Depositary duties and liabilities in stylised terms

Type of damage	Depositary duty infringed	Standard of liability	Conditions for exoneration	Burden of proof	Obligation under liability
Loss of financial instrument	Custody	Strict	Cause: external not controllable Consequence: not avoidable	Reversed (depositary)	Restitution without undue delay
Any other damage	Record-keeping Monitoring Others	Intent or negligence	Lack of intent or negligence (standard?)	Ordinary (plaintiff)	Adequate compensation

In addition to the safekeeping of assets, depositaries are required to oversee compliance by the manager in a number of areas. Most notably, depositaries need to ensure that any instruction by the manager, operation with fund units or their valuation is in accordance with national law and the fund rules. They are also required to monitor all cash flows involved in fund transactions (no account may exist without the overview of the depositary to

95 Articles 21.7, 21.8, 21.9 and 21.12, Directive 2011/61/EU (AIFMD).

96 Article 21.12, Directive 2011/61/EU (AIFMD).

97 The burden is reversed because it does not fall on the plaintiff (the manager or the investor) to prove there is no *external event*, so that the defendant (the depositary) is liable. Instead, the burden falls on the depositary to prove there is an *external event* and it is not liable. Still, the manager or the investor will have to prove *prima facie* (indicative proof) that the asset was held under custody by the depositary and has been lost. Article 21.13, Directive 2011/61/EU (AIFMD).

avoid any fraudulent cash transfer). By entrusting these functions, regulation takes stock of the trend to externalise back office functions to custodian banks and formally gives an auditing role to depositaries. The only risk is to raise costs for managers and investors by duplicating the tasks carried out elsewhere, particularly where it comes to the valuation of the fund units.[98] In their oversight capacity (as in their record-keeping capacity), depositaries face liability only in case of intent or negligence. The liability in these instances refers to the compensation of the damage caused by not performing a duty properly and in principle not to the restitution of a lost asset.[99]

3.5.3 *The challenge of implementation: Managing versus insuring non-market risks*

It is a general principle that risks should be managed and only secondarily insured. The opposite may result in perverse incentives such as the ones present in the originate-to-distribute models that led to the 2008 financial crisis. With regard to depositaries, the former principle entails that the level of liability imposed needs to match their ability to effectively fulfil their duties. Avoiding insuring non-market risks is ultimately the objective of the AIFMD where it excludes liability in case of *external events*. In effect, if strict liability would fall on depositaries in circumstances that are outside their control, the outcome would be in stark contrast with the objective of the rules themselves and the lessons learned from the financial crisis. The devil however is in the detail and the balance between managing and insuring non-market risks in the fund industry depends on multiple factors:

- Determining the instruments to which the duty of custody (instead of record-keeping) applies
- Defining external event
- Defining loss of assets, as opposed to their temporal unavailability
- Defining immediate restitution (restitution without undue delay)
- Clarifying the role of CSDs
- Allocating responsibilities between fund depositaries and managers
- Improving the legal certainty of securities holding transactions

---

[98] The list of oversight functions in the AIFMD (Article 21.9) has been copied from UCITS IV (Article 22). However, the scope of these duties remains to be defined by ESMA in both cases.

[99] For instance, if a manager diverts cash, the depositary would be liable if it negligently failed to monitor this cash transaction. A depositary would also be liable for any loss caused by carrying out instructions in conflict with national law or the fund rules. For other functions, such as overseeing the valuation of units, the liability of the depositary will depend on how these duties are defined by ESMA.

In sum, the extent to which non-market risks are managed instead of insured depends on: i) the precise content of the duties and standards imposed on depositaries, ii) the ability of depositaries to fulfil those duties within the legal framework of securities holding transactions and iii) the distribution of responsibility between fund managers and depositaries.

To avoid insurance, liability for the loss of financial instruments should only fall on depositaries where they have effective control over these instruments. This means that the duty of custody should be restricted to those financial instruments over which the depositary controls their transfer (the transfer of the legal title). In effect, the difference between managing and insuring the loss of financial assets depends on determining which instruments are apt to be held in custody (instead of record-keeping) and in which circumstances. A functional approach based on the notion of control over those instruments is preferable to a formal approach, given the fragmentation of securities law.

In its advice to the European Commission to implement the AIFMD, ESMA proposes to restrict the custody function to transferable securities, money-market instruments and units of collective investment undertakings.[100] It does however consider that the list may be revised in the future to include other instruments over which the depositary would have control, defined as the ability to instruct the transfer of an instrument and retrieve it if ever lost.[101] ESMA rightly considers that the forthcoming securities law Directive (SLD), by harmonising the law that applies to securities holding transactions in the European Union, may invite a revision of the list of financial instruments eligible to be held in custody.

The advice highlights that holding derivatives in custody is not feasible in practice (except those embedded in securities) and limits the role of depositaries to ownership verification and record-keeping. The former may change when the forthcoming European market infrastructure Regulation (EMIR) introduces central clearing for certain types of derivative instruments and harmonises other aspects that affect derivatives transactions. Besides derivatives, ESMA also excludes from the custody function any financial instrument held by the issuer or its agent, unless it is held in an account in the

---

100 Transferable securities [including those that embed derivatives in accordance with Article 51.3, final sub-paragraph of Directive 2009/65/EC (UCITS IV) and Article 10 of Directive 2007/16/EC (eligible assets, UCITS III)], money market instruments or units of collective investment undertakings [as listed in Annex I, Section C of Directive 2004/39/EC (MiFID)]. Box 79.1 ESMA 2011/379 (technical advice, implementation AIFMD).

101 ESMA 2011/379 (technical advice, implementation AIFMD), p. 157.

name of the depositary.[102] The role of CSDs is not clarified further from this perspective, pending the adoption of a forthcoming legislative piece on the matter (see below).

Any transferable securities, money-market instruments or units of a collective investment undertaking received by the fund as collateral should be held in custody.[103] The former however applies only to collateral arrangements under Directive 2002/47/EC (collateral directive).[104] As a corollary, any instrument's collateral pledged by the fund falls outside of the custody function since the depositary does not retain control over it.[105] Similarly, assets that are subject to a repurchase agreement, are lent or reused abandon the custody books of the depositary.[106]

Beyond the list of assets to which the custody duty applies, the liability of depositaries depends on the concept of damage (loss of an asset) and the conditions for exoneration. The AIFMD only exonerates depositaries if they can prove that the loss is attributable to "an external event beyond their reasonable control".[107] The advice of ESMA in this regard contains three separate elements which the depositary would need to prove: i) that there was no error or omission on its part, ii) that it could not have prevented the event or the loss and iii) that it had the appropriate due diligence processes in place. The third element is the most important since it requires depositaries have comprehensive processes in place to monitor, identify and mitigate potential risks.[108]

The concept of *loss* is defined by ESMA so as to exclude the temporal unavailability of assets, during for instance liquidation or bankruptcy proceedings. The distinction between temporal and permanent loss mitigates substantially the principle of strict liability and the obligation of immediate restitution. ESMA places on each depositary the responsibility to determine

---

[102] Box 79 and p. 157, ESMA 2011/379 (technical advice, implementation AIFMD).

[103] ESMA 2011/379 (technical advice, implementation AIFMD), pp. 158-159.

[104] This report proposes to formally restrict the available collateral arrangements in UCITS to those allowed under Directive 2002/47/EC (collateral Directive).

[105] Box 79, ESMA 2011/379 (technical advice, implementation AIFMD).

[106] Any asset that was held in custody will cease to be held in custody if subject to a repurchase or lending agreement during the effective duration of the agreement. The same applies to the re-hypothecation of collateral received by the fund. ESMA 2011/379 (technical advice, implementation AIFMD), p. 158.

[107] Article 21.12, Directive 2011/61/EU (AIFMD).

[108] Box 92, ESMA 2011/379 (technical advice, implementation AIFMD).

when there is no scope to recover the given asset.[109] The lack of a time frame (which, once exceeded, would entail the immediate restitution) means that managers and depositaries will negotiate a solution to the given loss or bring the matter to adjudication.

A high standard of liability increases the incentives of depositaries to effectively manage non-market risks but may reduce these same incentives for asset managers who see their liabilities transferred away. Fund managers are responsible for certain non-market risks such as the ones embedded in derivatives and other instruments that are not held in custody by the depositary. Managing non-financial risks is therefore a shared responsibility. Yet, the AIFMD alters the duty of depositaries towards managers by allowing investors to present direct claims against the depositary.[110] To avoid setting perverse incentives on managers, this possibility should only be offered where the fund manager has defaulted from its obligation to recover the lost assets from the depositary.

Overall, the implementation proposed by ESMA strikes a good balance between duties and liabilities to ensure that non-market risks are managed by asset managers instead of insured by depositaries: i) it restricts the custody function to those instruments over which the depositary has control, ii) it distinguishes permanent from temporary loss and iii) it puts the stress on comprehensive risk management. By insisting on risk management (both as a duty on its own and as a condition for depositaries to avoid liability where an external event results in the loss of an asset), ESMA has succeeded in reconciling strict liability with the managing of non-market risks, avoiding perverse incentives for both asset managers and depositaries. Supervision will however play a key role in ensuring effective risk management takes place in practice. At the time of writing, the process of implementation is not completed, and the final result will depend on the will of the European Commission to follow the advice of ESMA and the absence of opposition from the European Parliament and the Council.

3.5.4 *The wider challenge: Future regulatory reform and the role of depositaries*

The Task Force agreed that the AIFMD rules on depositaries are overall a step in the right direction by clarifying the duties and liabilities of depositaries and fund managers with respect to non-market risks. Previously, the nature of the custody obligation and the standard of liability were given by the law of the

---

[109] Box 91, ESMA 2011/379 (technical advice, implementation AIFMD).

[110] Article 21.15, Directive 2011/61/EU (AIFMD).

home member state of each fund where divergent rules applied. Following the introduction of the new depositary rules in the AIFMD and UCITS, a uniform regime will exist in Europe affording an equivalent level of protection to investors, independently of the home country of the investment fund. In addition, the AIFMD rules ensure the independence of the depositary function by introducing the functional and hierarchical separation of the prime brokerage function and requiring consent and transparency for the fund assets to be reused by prime brokers.[111]

While the rules in the AIFMD are an important step forward, some issues remain to be tackled. Several regulatory initiatives are in the pipeline that will directly impact the management of non-market risks by fund managers and depositaries:

- The securities law Directive (SLD) that will clarify and harmonise the law that applies to securities holding transactions in the European Union.
- The legislation on central securities depositaries (CSDs) that will harmonise the functioning of CSDs and certain aspects of securities settlement in the European Union.
- The European market infrastructure Regulation (EMIR) that will address OTC derivatives, central counterparties and trade repositories in the European Union.

Beyond the European Union, additional efforts are needed to achieve more consistency in the law that applies to securities holding transactions and CSDs. However, the same standards cannot be expected in emerging countries, which lack the infrastructure and legal rules present in advanced jurisdictions. The former should not result in professional investors being denied the possibility of accessing investments in emerging markets, as long as appropriate safeguards are put in place, both in terms of risk management and disclosure. This principle is in the spirit of the AIFMD, which permits under certain conditions the transfer of liability to sub-custodians in emerging economies so that professional investors can access investment opportunities in countries where depositaries are not subject to standards equivalent to the ones in the AIFMD.[112] Chapter 4 (Box 10) considers this issue in more detail.

---

[111] Article 14.3, Directive 2011/61/EU (AIFMD).

[112] Where the local entity does not satisfy the general requirements for delegation, the depositary may still delegate safekeeping to a local entity, as long as the law of the third country requires local custody, the AIF manager authorises it and investors are duly informed. Additional conditions apply to the transfer of liability to this local entity, namely

To the extent that the harmonisation of depositary rules would be successful and effective across all member states, it may become possible to introduce a depositary passport in the future. The single market for financial services has been strengthened by the new depositary regime in the AIFMD and the UCITS Directive. However, in order to realise the full potential of the single market, the full harmonisation of depositary duties and liabilities should be followed by the introduction of a depositary passport. The European Commission could commit to consider in the medium run the convenience of introducing a depositary passport by introducing a review clause in its UCITS V proposal scheduled for 2012.

The Madoff affair and the default of Lehman Brothers in 2008 brought regulators to step up their efforts to improve the oversight of non-market risks and clarify the duties and liabilities of fund depositaries. Awareness of these risks among investors has increased, particularly among professional and institutional investors, which is most welcomed. However, most retail investors remain unaware of the non-market risks and how they may impact their savings. The Task Force considered that more action is needed to improve the knowledge and visibility of non-market risks among investors.

---

the fund rules need to allow for such a transfer and investors need to be informed prior to their investment (see Article 21.11, Directive 2011/61/EU – AIFMD).

4. DISTRIBUTION: THE SINGLE MARKET, INVESTOR PROTECTION AND CHOICE

This chapter aims to present a complete picture of fund distribution and related aspects from a regulatory perspective and advance proposals to complete the single market and improve investor protection. The first section will introduce the regulatory framework for fund distribution in Europe and the main changes introduced by the AIFMD. The second section will consider regulatory reform and in particular how to exploit the single market potential, improve retail investor protection and enhance investor choice.

4.1 How does distribution work in Europe?

From a regulatory perspective, the distribution of investment funds in the EU follows a two-step approach that differentiates market access from marketing requirements. As a first step, any fund manager has to comply with a number of conditions in order to be granted the possibility of placing its products in the marketplace (market access). As a second step, the sale process is itself regulated to protect investors (marketing rules). The functioning of this framework is characterised by the distribution of powers between Brussels and national capitals, as defined in the EU treaties. Market access is primarily an EU competence, which means member states may limit market access only where no EU rules exist, while investor protection is clearly a shared competence so member states may easily 'goldplate' marketing rules established at EU level.[113] Figure 15 represents this difference graphically.

---

[113] Article 4.2 of the Treaty on the Functioning of the European Union establishes that shared competence between the Union and the member states applies in several areas, including consumer protection. Article 169.4 establishes that measures adopted by the Union in the field of consumer protection cannot prevent any member state from maintaining or introducing more stringent protective measures.

Figure 15. Single market aspects of distribution

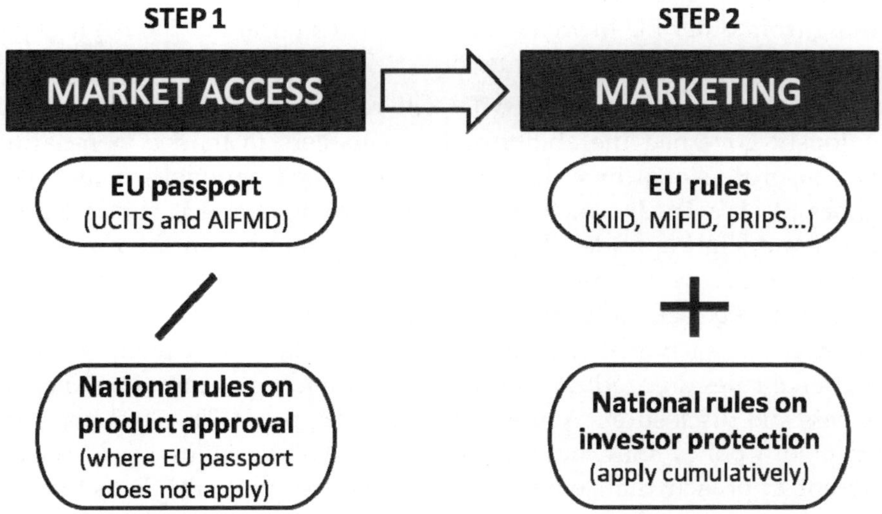

As a general EU principle, market access is based on two pillars: mutual recognition and minimum harmonisation. Member states commit to give access to equivalent products from other member states under a condition of reciprocity as they mutually recognise each other's regulation as equivalent. In practice, however, harmonised rules are needed to establish which products are deemed equivalent and the breath of access. Harmonisation may cover for instance prudential and operating requirements, product structuring or the scope of access to retail or professional investors.

The 1985 UCITS Directive introduced a harmonised category of investment funds that enjoy access to retail investors. Access is gained by virtue of the so-called *passport*, an instrument that allows a fund to market its units in all member states upon notice to each local supervisor. Based on harmonised rules, the passport is granted only to funds that comply in full with the requirements in the UCITS Directive. Compliance is supervised by the member state where the fund is domiciled, except for issues related to investor protection, including marketing and advertising, which belong to the member state of destination. The passport works by setting a common framework for authorisations and disabling any national rules that may restrict market access to locally authorised funds.

The AIFMD is also built around the notion of passport to allow an AIF authorised or registered in one member state to market its units to professional investors in all other member states. While the UCITS passport applies to retail investors and effectively extends to all investors alike, the AIFMD passport is limited to the marketing of funds to professional investors. Member states may extend the AIFMD passport to allow the marketing of certain AIFs to retail investors as long as they do not discriminate between local AIFs and AIFs coming from other EU member states.[114] The extension of the AIFMD passport to retail investors is discussed later on.

The passport in the AIFMD will replace the national rules that had previously governed the ability of EU managers to market non-harmonised funds to professional investors (sometimes called national private placement regimes).[115] It will do so, however, only for investment funds handled by managers operating under the Directive. The harmonisation of national rules on market access for professional investors was declared an EU policy objective in 2006 (EC, 2006, p. 13). At the time, the idea was to remove national barriers to transactions between designated market participants by getting rid of national rules on product approval and providing exemptions to conduct of business and disclosure requirements (EC, 2006, p. 13). The 2008 financial crisis prompted a policy shift that resulted in the AIFMD following a substantially different approach than envisaged in 2006. In effect, the Directive disables national rules on product approval in its field of action but it goes much further than originally anticipated in terms of harmonisation. The biggest policy change affects conduct of business and disclosure requirements which have not disappeared but have been rethought and codified in detail to ensure that the ultimate beneficiaries are sufficiently protected and professional investors have access to the information they need to conduct meaningful due diligence. Table 8 presents this policy shift by comparing the policy in 2006 with the AIFMD.

---

[114] Article 43, Directive 2011/61/EU (AIFMD).

[115] Private placement regimes were defined in 2008 by the European Commission as "a distribution method through which authorised market participants can buy and sell financial instruments to each other without having to comply with the rules that would usually apply when the same instruments are offered to the public or to retail investors" (EC, 2008, p. 1).

Table 8. Policy shift in the distribution of non-harmonised funds

Before the 2008 financial crisis (2006 White Paper)*		**After the 2008 financial crisis** (2011 AIFMD)**
Emphasis on *freeing up* transactions between designated counterparties (p. 13)	→	Introduction of comprehensive requirements on managers of non-harmonised investment funds
"No compelling investor protection reasons for national regulators to interfere in financial transactions involving professional investors" (p. 13)	→	"Inadequacies have been exposed in the due diligence applied by professional investors" (p. 20)
No consideration of macro-prudential risks	→	Main focus on macro-prudential risks
Proposal to introduce a retail passport for certain non-UCITS funds such as open-ended real estate funds (p. 11)	→	Proposal abandoned (the AIFMD expressly leaves to member states the extension of its passport to retail investors)

* COM (2006) 686 final (White Paper on investment funds).

** SEC (2009) 576 (Impact assessment AIFMD).

Once funds are granted market access (first step), they may actively sell their units to investors as long as they respect a set of marketing rules (second step). Investors are subject to different levels of protection at the point of sale in accordance with their level of expertise. Marketing rules cover two main areas: pre-contractual disclosure and selling practices. Pre-contractual disclosure refers to the information that should be made available to investors before a purchase is concluded. The UCITS Directive requires the publication of a fully harmonised key investor information document (KIID) aimed at retail investors.[116] The AIFMD also contains requirements on pre-contractual disclosure but with a different scope given the professional nature of investors in AIFs. As for selling practices, these are mainly regulated by the markets in financial instruments Directive (MiFID, under review in 2012) and national implementing legislation. The main conduct of business rules in MiFID I refer to:

- o Client categorisation (retail investors, professional investors and eligible counterparties)[117]
- o Conflicts of interest and inducements[118]

[116] Regulation 583/2010 (UCITS IV implementation, KIID).

[117] Article 4.1.12, Directive 2004/39/CE (MiFID).

- General disclosure to clients (complementary to the principles in UCITS and AIFMD)[119]
- Order handling (advised and non-advised sales, suitability and appropriateness tests)[120]
- Marketing rules[121]

Beyond market access and marketing, the distribution of investment funds also hangs on efficient and compatible processing. Fund distributors need in practice to handle orders, deliver units and receive payments. In Europe, there is no single model to process the distribution of fund units or shares, which represents a major obstacle to efficient cross-border distribution. Beyond national peculiarities, distribution either employs transfer agents (TAs) or central securities depositaries (CSDs). Each model presents its own strengths but the main concern is fragmentation itself. A hybrid model would ideally combine the settlement security of CSDs with the ability to identify orders present in TAs, both of which are essential for secure and efficient distribution. Standardisation proposals have been put forward by market participants that foster convergence between both models (CACEIS, 2011). Cross-border distribution is also helped by international CSDs and global transfer agents, which are an alternative to national systems.

The EU regulatory framework for fund distribution is currently at an advanced but still incomplete state of development. Progress has been achieved slowly and recently in a number of areas, such as: market access for non-UCITS funds under the AIFMD, conduct of business and transparency obligations for funds marketed to professional investors also under the AIFMD and standardised pre-contractual disclosure for retail investors under UCITS IV. Yet more progress is needed still to overcome difficulties in a number of areas, including i) the definition of professional and eligible investors, ii) marketing rules and selling practices, such as the definition of advice, independence and professional standards for advisers, iii) the level-playing field among retail investment products and iv) the convergence of fund processing models. The following sections will consider these latter issues in great detail.

---

118 Articles 13.3, 18.1 and 18.2, Directive 2004/39/CE (MiFID) and Article 26, Directive 2006/73/CE (MiFID implementation).

119 Articles 19.2, 19.3 and 19.8, Directive 2004/39/CE (MiFID).

120 Articles 19.4 and 19.5, Directive 2004/39/CE (MiFID).

121 Article 19.2, Directive 2004/39/CE (MiFID) and Articles 24 and 27, Directive 2006/73/CE (MiFID implementation).

Box 6. Market access for non-EU funds under the AIFMD

The introduction of the AIFMD raised the question of market access for funds handled by managers domiciled outside Europe, who would ordinarily fall outside the scope of the Directive. Regulators had to strike a complex balance to avoid the legislation being circumvented and still allow foreign managers to sell their funds in Europe. If foreign managers would not have to comply with the Directive and professional investors were allowed to invest in offshore vehicles, large-scale relocation of management activities would lead to the Directive not being applied in practice. Banning offshore products or other blanket limitations to market access would amount to market foreclosure, and face challenge by trading partners as it happened with early drafts of the Directive. Despite much controversy, the AIFMD strikes a reasonably good balance although one that will require clever implementation and strong commitment by stakeholders for it to work well in practice. In the future, non-EU managers will need to comply with the Directive (albeit not fully) to be able to market the funds under its passport. Their jurisdictions of origin will need to satisfy three basic requirements: i) effective prudential supervision, ii) exchange of tax information, iii) close supervisory cooperation. A fourth principle requiring the reciprocity of market access was dropped in the final text.

Given the inherent difficulties in applying the Directive to non-EU managers marketing their funds in the EU, three phases are foreseen: i) in the first three years the passport will not be available for offshore funds so they will continue to be marketed in each member state under the existing national private placement regimes; ii) from 2015, the passport will most probably be introduced but co-exist for some years with national private placements and iii) ultimately national private placement regimes are expected to disappear, meaning non-EU managers will have to comply with the AIFMD to market their funds in Europe. There is however no fixed date for the disappearance of private placements which will depend on the results of an assessment that will be carried out by ESMA and the Commission in 2017.[a] In the meantime, offshore managers will have to comply with the some parts of the Directive, notably those on disclosure to investors and reporting to authorities.[b] Figure 16 represents these three phases leading to the extension of the AIFMD rules and passport to offshore managers. Annex 2 presents in tabular form the third country rules in the AIFMD.

Figure 16. Phased approach to the introduction of the AIFMD for non-EU managers

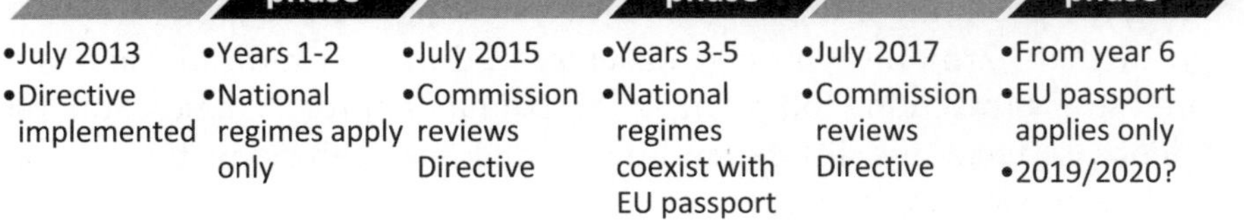

Funds handled by managers that do not comply with the AIFMD may still be accessed by investors on their own initiative. This process is called reverse solicitation, in contrast with the active marketing of funds in a given jurisdiction. Foreign funds handled by managers who do not comply with the AIFMD may not be marketed in Europe actively through the AIFMD passport, but since the Directive does not prohibit reverse solicitation, member states may allow professional investors to purchase these funds on their own initiative.[c] Additional due diligence requirements are expected to apply to these investments in the future however.[d]

The question of reciprocal market access remains controversial for EU managers who would like to see more of a level playing field among non-EU jurisdictions, including notably the US but also emerging markets such as China or Brazil. Non-EU managers offering their funds in Europe bring positive competition to the marketplace but EU managers would like to benefit from the same opportunity to market their funds and services in non-EU jurisdictions. It is argued that European authorities should engage more with other jurisdictions to achieve this objective.

[a] Articles 67-69 Directive 2011/61/EU (AIFMD).

[b] Article 42 Directive 2011/61/EU (AIFMD). Non-EU managers will have to comply only with Articles 22-24 and 26-30 Directive 2011/61/EU (AIFMD) under the national placement regimes.

[c] Preamble 70 and Article 4.1.x Directive 2011/61/EU (AIFMD).

[d] Preamble 92 Directive 2011/61/EU (AIFMD).

4.2 An agenda for regulatory reform: Which goals?

"Confidence in European financial markets is the main driver encouraging retail and institutional investment flows, thus boosting integration."

EIWG – European Investors Working Group, 2010

Several legislative reforms are impacting the picture of distribution in Europe, including the UCITS IV Directive, the AIFMD, the review of MiFID and the insurance mediation directive (IMD), and the initiative on packaged retail investment products (PRIPs). This section will consider these reforms with reference to three overarching objectives: completing the single market, improving retail investor protection and expanding the choice of investors. In effect, the Task Force considers that regulatory reform should focus on: i) leveraging the potential of the single market, making it work better in practice through further harmonisation and faster procedures, ii) radically improving retail investor protection, following a horizontal approach across all retail investment products and iii) expanding or at least preserving the choice of retail and professional investors.

4.2.1 *Leveraging the single market potential*

Completing the single market is essential to foster growth and competitiveness in Europe. Advancing the single market is an inexpensive policy but progress remains slow. In 2011 the European Commission put forward its strategy to advance the single market with several concrete proposals.[122] However, more progress is needed and the single market "must be must be brought to its next stage of development, by reinforcing governance and raising standards of implementation".[123] Advancing the single market for asset management products and services is of particular importance, given notably their importance for the financing of businesses and governments and the provision of retirement income to European citizens (see chapter 5). In this regard, action is needed at several levels, including market access, pre-contractual disclosure, selling practices and fund processing. The following paragraphs consider the progress achieved so far in each of these fields and highlight those areas where more action is needed.

Market access

The experience gathered in UCITS shows that national barriers that frustrate pan-European market access are not easy to overcome. The UCITS passport took years to work reasonably well in practice, given the notification procedure foreseen to market funds in other member states. National supervisors applied overly comprehensive and divergent requirements to validate notifications. A recent survey revealed the persistence of many hurdles to fund distribution at the notification stage just before the introduction of UCITS IV in July 2011 (CACEIS, 2011). The top seven target countries for fund distribution required submission of up to 10 different documents in varying formats; in most instances they also required these documents to be locally certified and transmitted by a local agent (CACEIS, 2011). UCITS IV has put an end to most of these issues by introducing a simplified notification procedure and prohibiting member states from requiring additional documents at this stage.[124] Documents are now transmitted between supervisors, avoiding certification requirements and the participation of local agents, and bringing the overall time spent in this procedure down to 10 working days instead of 2 months. The harmonisation of authorisation requirements in UCITS IV

---

122 European Commission Communication COM(2011) 206 final (Single Market Act).

123 Joint Letter to President Van Rompuy and President Barroso of 20 February 2012.

124 The list of documents is limited to the fund rules or instruments of incorporation, latest annual report and any subsequent half-yearly reports, and the key investor information document - Article 93, Directive 2009/65/EC (UCITS IV).

however may not stop member states from demanding additional documents at a later stage, as long as marketing rules remain loosely harmonised.

The passport introduced by the AIFMD takes good account of the best practice established by UCITS IV, including the transmission of the notification by the home supervisor, a closed list of documents and a maximum delay, which is fixed at 20 working days.[125] In effect, all non-UCITS funds which had so far not enjoyed cross-border market access may from July 2013 benefit from the AIFMD passport to market their units to professional investors if they comply with the Directive. With the AIFMD being a novel piece of legislation, ESMA will have to play a pivotal role in ensuring supervisory cooperation and procedural convergence.

The AIFMD passport affects the marketing to professional investors of funds handled by managers who comply with the Directive. There are however several national examples of alternative funds being successfully marketed to retail investors, such as open-ended real estate funds. The European Commission envisaged the introduction of a passport for some of these products in 2006 but has so far not proposed legislation in this respect. The introduction of the AIFMD may in fact operate against the pan-European marketing of retail AIFs. The Directive formally allows member states to extend its passport to retail funds but is however unlikely to lead to the development of a pan-European market for retail AIFs. The AIFMD does not match the UCITS approach to product regulation that most member states would require to grant access to retail investors.[126] Moreover, the Directive prohibits member states from discriminating between national and other EU AIFs in their ability to access retail investors. Member states are permitted by the Directive to impose *additional requirements* on specific categories of AIFs marketed to retail investors but are expressly prohibited from imposing different *requirements* on AIFs coming from fellow EU member states. The problem in practice will be in determining when these *additional requirements* apply to the same or a distinct category of AIFs, on which the presence of

---

125 Article 32, Directive 2011/61/EU (AIFMD). See also Annex IV of the same directive.

126 In effect, non-UCITS funds marketed to retail investors, such as open-ended real estate funds, are backed by product regulation. See for instance the Expert Group Report on Open-Ended Real Estate Funds published in 2008 by the European Commission. The report details the depth and types of requirements set in national rules to protect retail investors (eligible assets, risk-spreading, borrowing, frequency of redemptions, liquidity requirements, independent valuation, depositary, conflicts of interest and others). They effectively amount to product regulation, in contrast with the AIFMD. In some respects however, the AIFMD provides for stricter requirements than national rules for retail AIFs, in which case the latter will need to adapt to comply.

discrimination will hang. Besides, member states are not expressly prohibited from discriminating against non-EU funds wishing to access retail investors.[127]

Pre-contractual disclosure

In terms of pre-contractual disclosure, the level of harmonisation is different for professional and retail investors, in line with the different level of standardisation required by these groups. The UCITS IV Directive introduces full harmonisation of the key investor information document (KIID) with an implementing regulation on its objectives, elements and format.[128] In addition, ESMA guidelines provide a standard template, instructions to maintain clear language and layout and harmonised methodologies to calculate the charges and 'risk-reward' indicators.[129] The UCITS Directive expressly states that member states may not impose additional requirements on the content or format of the KIID.[130] Each fund produces a single KIID document valid for all member states, save for its translation into the national languages of the countries where it is marketed.[131] In spite of this substantial progress, some member states are reported to still demand additional documents to funds marketed in their jurisdictions. Further harmonisation is therefore necessary to overcome market fragmentation.

Disclosure requirements for alternative funds follow a different approach since they are directed to professional investors. They aim at enabling i) due diligence by these investors and ii) supervisory monitoring for financial stability purposes. The former means that while the AIFMD provides for significant pre-contractual disclosure, this is mostly not standardised, in contrast with the UCITS KIID.[132] One notable exception refers to the disclosure of leverage where a harmonised calculation methodology is proposed by ESMA in its advice to the European Commission, given the relevance of this ratio for macro-prudential oversight.[133] From a single market perspective, the

---

127 Article 43, Directive 2011/61/EU (AIFMD).

128 Regulation 583/2010 (UCITS IV implementation, KIID)

129 ESMA Guidelines, CESR/10-1321, CESR/10-1320, CESR/10-674 and CESR/10-673, respectively.

130 "Key investor information shall be used without alterations or supplements, except translation, in all Member States where the UCITS is notified to market its units in accordance with Article 93" – Article 78.6 Directive 2009/65/EC (UCITS IV).

131 Article 94.1.b, Directive 2009/65/EC (UCITS IV).

132 Article 23, Directive 2011/61/EU (AIFMD). See also Chapter VIII.II in ESMA/2011/379 (AIFMD, implementation, advice).

133 Box 109.1.a, ESMA/2011/379 (AIFMD, implementation, advice).

goal should be to avoid the divergent implementation of the disclosure requirements in the Directive that would undermine cross-border marketing.

Selling practices

As for selling practices, MiFID provides partial harmonisation in a number of areas including in particular how to distinguish retail from professional clients, how to establish that a given fund is adequate for an investors and how to manage conflicts of interest in distribution. The substance of these rules is discussed later on with reference to investor protection. From a single market perspective the level of harmonisation of selling practices in Europe remains insufficient. Different implementation of the rules in MiFID I by member states has raised the barriers to market certain products in some countries (Valiante, 2011). Distinct national rules are partially justified by the differences in the distribution models that prevail in national markets (the bank-insurer model in most of continental Europe versus third-party financial advisors in the UK). Yet, further harmonisation would be positive to consolidate national best practices and promote convergence. Fragmentation represents also a significant regulatory and supervisory cost since similar gains in investor protection may be realised by common rules. The review of MiFID in 2012 is an opportunity to advance in this respect.

Fund processing

The convergence of fund processing is also a crucial element to achieve a truly single market. The European Commission highlighted in 2006 that message routing, order-processing and settlement had not kept pace with market growth and changes in distribution (European Commission, 2006, p. 9). These inefficiencies persist due to industry inertia and coordination difficulties, despite efforts led by industry associations. In effect, solutions to standardise and facilitate cross-border distribution are currently available, offered mostly by international CSDs and financial messaging firms, but have not yet been widely adopted. Regulators should monitor and stimulate convergence in close contact with the industry, removing any regulatory barriers. If coordination difficulties persist, the use of standards could be envisaged to correct market failures.

4.2.2 *Regulatory reform: Revisiting retail investor protection*

This section examines the reasons that justify investor protection, the achievements of EU regulation and its shortcomings with a view to proposing a comprehensive agenda directed at radically improving retail investor protection in the Europe. The section is structured in four parts. The first one considers the fundamentals of investor protection by both referring to selected empirical evidence and the theory underpinning investor protection and introducing the EU regulatory framework, including the proposals tabled by the European Commission in the past few years to improve retail investor protection. The other three parts of this section will propose a reform agenda based on three objectives: ii) fostering disclosure and comparability so that investors can make informed decisions, ii) awarding a level of protection that takes into account the degree of complexity of each product and iii) ensuring investors can access transparent, independent and quality advice.

4.2.2.1 *Fundamentals of retail investor protection and its regulation in the EU*

Retail and professional investors need a different standard of protection. Traditionally, investor protection has been reserved for retail investors when they access financial instruments directly. The 2008 financial crisis prompted a change in approach by revisiting the protection afforded by regulation to professional investors, including institutional ones. The protection of professional investors is based on two pillars: minimum disclosure to enable the conduct of meaningful due diligence processes and conduct of business rules to enforce the fiduciary duty of product providers against their clients. The AIFMD follows this approach with a double objective: reduce systemic risk and protect the ultimate beneficiaries of pension funds, insurers and other institutional investors in alternative funds.

Retail investors are subject to a different standard of protection. For professional investors the focus is on enforcing disclosure to enable meaningful due diligence while for retail investors the focus is on assisting (and in the margin substituting) them in their investment decisions. Table 9 summarises the two different approaches to investor protection which run in fact through the whole product cycle and are not limited to the marketing stage.

Table 9. Investor protection for professional and retail investors

	Professional investors	Retail investors
At the level of the product provider	- Conduct of business rules	- Conduct of business rules
At the level of the product structuring	- Restrictions for financial stability purposes	- Restrictions for investor protection purposes
At the time of investing / during the investment life	- Minimum disclosure obligations	- Standardised and comparable disclosure - Intermediation and advice - Distributor responsibility

Multiple reasons justify retail investor protection, proportional to the characteristics of investors, products and sale processes. Retail investors lack specific knowledge in finance and the ability to understand the risks involved in financial products. These products are to a large extent so-called 'experience' or 'credence' goods (i.e. their performance cannot be fully ascertained until their life cycle has ended). The market is therefore characterised by asymmetries of information between manufacturers, distributors and investors. Some products exhibit complex risk and pricing structures that are difficult to apprehend even by individuals with a reasonable degree of expertise in finance. Moreover, most individuals purchase so infrequently that any experience gathered is likely to be lost at the time of buying again. It is worth mentioning that the market for investments, pensions and securities is the worst perceived by consumers in the European Union in terms of ease to compare products, trust in suppliers and consumer satisfaction (European Commission, 2011a).

Empirical evidence also calls for investor protection. The behaviour of investors in retail markets has been abundantly researched, including for policy purposes.[134] Two recent experiments revealed that retail investors i) have difficulties to choose the optimal product, even within simple alternatives; ii) make worse decisions where fees are framed as percentages or returns not compounded and iii) rely heavily on advice, basing many of their decisions on trust and are vulnerable to persuasion by the adviser (Charter et al., 2010). Behavioural economics has demonstrated that investors have limited rationality and are easily influenced. Ordinary biases in decision-making are exacerbated by the specific characteristics of financial products but some of these biases persist even in financially literate individuals since they are closely related to psychological factors (de Meza et al., 2008).

Investors would benefit from uniform rules. So far, however, EU regulation has largely followed a sectoral approach, applying different requirements to substitutable investment products according to their legal form and the sales channel. The divergences in the rules exceed the measure of the particular characteristics of each product and result plainly in an uneven level of protection. UCITS is the most tightly regulated product range both in terms of pre-contractual disclosure (KIID) and selling practices (MiFID). Non-UCITS funds and unit-linked insurance policies marketed to retail investors are not subject to the KIID but to national rules. The rules in MiFID I apply to all investment funds and structured securities but not to unit-linked life insurance

134 For a comprehensive review of the literature, see chapter 2 in Charter et al. (2010).

policies (sold under the IMD) and structured term deposits (no rules at EU level).

Progress has been achieved on standardising disclosure. Empirical evidence suggests that standard and simple product information can improve retail investment decisions significantly (Charter et al., 2010). Based on extensive research and consumer testing, UCITS IV introduced a standard key investor information document (KIID) in July 2011. The document overcomes the deficiencies found in the simplified prospectus in terms of length, content and ease of comparison.[135] The KIID is composed of no more than two pages using a standard template and clear language. It presents in a concise manner the investment objectives and policy of the fund, past-performance, a charges figure and a synthetic risk-reward indicator. The calculation methodologies are fully harmonised to ensure these figures are comparable. The content of the document is tailored to the specificities of some products, such as funds of funds and structured UCITS.

But standardised disclosure is no panacea. Consumer testing has shown that the KIID, while significantly facilitating investor understanding, has some limitations (IFF Research et al., 2009). Most customers did not read the whole document and focused selectively on particular sections, both when reading alone and when guided by advisers. Investors have difficulties understanding the concepts behind some of the strategies, risks and assets mentioned in the documents. They also had difficulties understanding the application of charges and their effect on returns. In practice, the effectiveness of disclosure is closely correlated to the degree of literacy and experience of each investor.

Many retail clients need professional advice. Investment advice may help investors to overcome some of their limitations in making optimal investment decisions. The use of advice is indeed widespread among retail investors. There is evidence that 80% of retail investments are undertaken in a face-to-face setting where intermediaries influence investor decisions (Charter et al., 2010). MiFID regulates investor protection at the time of purchase. It provides rules on conduct of business, conflicts of interest and inducements based on the principle that investment firms need to act honestly, fairly and in the best interest of their clients.[136] This principle results in different practical obligations depending on the nature of the service. Where providing advice or portfolio management, the intermediary is required to assess the *suitability* of the

---

[135] The simplified prospectus was the standard of pre-contractual disclosure fixed by UCITS III.

[136] Article 19.1, Directive 2004/39/CE (MiFID).

product for the investor.[137] Where it provides non-advised sales, it has to assess the *appropriateness* of the product for the investor.[138] Both tests are similar and essentially demand the firm to consider the characteristics of the investor and the product (for further reference, see Valiante, 2011 and Casey & Lannoo, 2009).

But advice may be waived for simple instruments. As an exception for non-complex financial instruments, investors may ask the distributor to execute their orders directly without any intermediate assessment of their *appropriateness* (so-called execution-only service). UCITS are under MiFID I considered non-complex financial instruments, which means retail clients may access UCITS without any assessment of their profile.[139] This exception represents a significant commercial opportunity for management houses and distributors which are able to sell UCITS to retail investors using multiple channels, including in particular online platforms. It is estimated that in some member states execution-only services account for two-thirds of retail investment transactions in shares, money market instruments, bonds, securitised debt and UCITS instruments (European Commission, 2011b).

Conflicts of interest and inducements also need to be addressed by regulation. MiFID I prescribes that conflicts of interest are prevented or otherwise managed and disclosed in accordance with the Directive.[140] It is however revealing that inducements are not considered in the text of MiFID I but in secondary legislation. In principle, the Directive prohibits investment firms to provide or receive any inducements (monetary or otherwise). However, inducements are allowed if they satisfy three requirements: i) they are designed to improve the quality of the service to the client, ii) they do not impair the ability of the firm to comply with its duty act honestly, fairly and in the best interest of their clients and iii) they are appropriately disclosed.[141] This test puts the weight on the individual self-assessment by firms of each inducement on a case-by-case basis.[142] While it is correct in substance, it is loosely framed and therefore not operational for firms and supervisors. The European Commission (2011b) has recognised that it is not well articulated for investors. Implementation at EU level has followed a soft-approach based on interpretative guidelines and a market survey for firms to "benchmark

---

137 Article 19.4, Directive 2004/39/CE (MiFID).

138 Article 19.5, Directive 2004/39/CE (MiFID).

139 Article 19.6, Directive 2004/39/CE (MiFID).

140 Article 18, Directive 2004/39/CE (MiFID).

141 Article 26, Directive 2006/73/EC (MiFID implementation).

142 ESMA Report, CESR/10-295 (inducements, MiFID), p. 18.

themselves against industry compliance practices".[143] ESMA concedes that the test is not easy to apply in practice (therefore also difficult to supervise) and that a large number of firms have not substantially changed their behaviour following its introduction.[144] Moreover, the rules in MiFID I refer to inducements across all investment services and do not cater specifically for retail investor protection. Despite the different models of distribution in member states, the types of inducements employed by originators are similar.[145] Most distributors receive one-off rebates of entry fees and ongoing rebates of management or performance fees from fund managers. They also receive non-monetary benefits such as training, marketing material, research and IT products.[146] Some of these inducements may distort incentives in the application of the *suitability* and *appropriateness* tests or result in biased advice or recommendations that reflect more the economic incentives of the distributor than the interest of investors.[147] The remuneration policy fixed by the distributor for its sales staff is the major transmission mechanism for these incentives.

Gaps in the application of MiFID undermine investor protection. Concerns have been expressed about gaps in the application of selling rules to originators engaging directly with end investors (European Commission, 2009, p. 23). Relevant exceptions in MiFID I concern i) collective investment undertakings and pension funds, their depositaries and managers and ii) persons providing non-remunerated investment advice in the course of providing another professional activity not covered by MiFID I. Similarly in the market for unit-linked insurance products, the IMD does not cover the sales by the employees of insurance companies. These provisions should be revisited from the point of view of their effects on investor protection and the opportunities they may offer for regulatory arbitrage.

The distribution of responsibilities between originators and distributors remains unclear. It is estimated that 40 to 60% of fees collected by asset managers are

---

143 ESMA Recommendation, CESR/07-228b (inducements, MiFID) and ESMA Report, CESR/10-295 (inducements, MiFID), p. 5.

144 "CESR [ESMA] acknowledges that the application of the test might not always be straightforward" – ESMA Report, CESR/10-295 (inducements, MiFID), p. 22. "Most of the investment firms sampled said that they assess payments and non-monetary benefits they provide or receive for compliance with the MiFID inducements rules" – ESMA Report, CESR/10-295 (inducements, MiFID), p. 8.

145 ESMA Report, CESR/10-295 (inducements, MiFID), p. 18.

146 ESMA Report, CESR/10-295 (inducements, MiFID), p. 18.

147 Inducements may provide an incentive to push the products of those providers that pay the highest commissions to distributors.

paid back to distributors (CACEIS & PwC, 2011). A report by Cerulli Associates (2012) suggests that €32 billion were paid to distributors out of the total €60 billion revenues generated by the European asset management industry in 2011. Distributors face the responsibility of complying with the duties imposed on them by MiFID. This involves notably the application of the suitability and appropriateness tests in advised and non-advised sales, respectively. For this purpose distributors need to have the ability to effectively understand the characteristics of the product and the needs of the investors. Manufacturers also bear some responsibility with regard to the general suitability of the products they offer in the retail market. The distribution of responsibilities in the production and distribution chain should, however, be clarified to ensure investor protection - notwithstanding the fact that the legal framework for contractual and tort liability is mostly given by national law.

It follows that regulatory reform is needed to strengthen retail investor protection in Europe. To overcome some of the problems highlighted above, the European Commission proposed in 2011 changes to MiFID in the context of a full recast of the legislative text.[148] The Commission proposes to award the label *independent advice* where the distributor accepts no monetary inducements from the originator and to remove certain UCITS funds from the non-complex product category so that they cannot longer be sold on an execution-only basis. It also puts forward additional measures to strengthen retail investor protection that are summarised in Table 12. The proposed changes are in line with a broader initiative to improve EU legislation on retail products, strengthen its coherence and enhance investor protection after the financial crisis.[149] This initiative was outlined in the Communication on packaged retail investment products (PRIPs) in 2009.[150] The PRIPs initiative is expected to propose the harmonisation of selling practices and conduct of business requirements across all packaged retail investment products, in a first stage, and to all retail investment products (packaged or not) in the long term. It represents the most comprehensive EU strategy formulated to date on retail investor protection (see below). Under this strategy: i) MiFID rules will be reformed as detailed above and extended to structure deposits where no EU legislation previously applied, ii) selling practices for unit-linked insurance products will be regulated in the insurance mediation Directive (IMD) in a manner equivalent to MiFID but preserving the strengths of the IMD with regard for instance to conflicts of interest and iii) the standard of pre-

---

148 Legislative Proposal COM (2011) 656 final (MiFID recast).

149 Press Release, 2798th Council Meeting, Economic and Financial Affairs, Brussels, 8 May 2007.

150 European Commission, Communication COM (2009) 204 final (PRIPs).

contractual disclosure set by the UCITS KIID will be extended to other retail investment products. In sum the proposal aims at harmonising selling practices and disclosure for retail investors across investment funds (UCITS and AIFs), unit-linked insurance policies, structured securities and structured term deposits.[151] Beyond the changes proposed by the European Commission, the responsibility ultimately will fall on the European Parliament and member states to bring reform forward and improve investor protection.

The next sections will consider the reform of distribution from a triple perspective, following the priorities identified by the Task Force to improve investor protection: i) fostering disclosure and comparability so that investors can make informed decisions, ii) awarding a level of protection that takes into account the degree of complexity of each product and iii) ensuring investors can access transparent, independent and quality advice.

Box 7. Commission Proposals to strengthen retail investor protection in MiFID II

- MiFID requirements (conduct of business and conflicts of interest rules) are extended to the sale of structured deposits.[a]
- The safe-keeping of financial instruments on behalf of clients is classified as an investment service (instead of ancillary service).[b]
- The power of member states to exempt certain investment firms is narrowed down by imposing member states to apply analogous requirements to the directive in some respects.[c]
- Senior management is explicitly given the responsibility to approve the policy governing the services and products offered by the firm, with reference to the characteristics and needs of its clients.[d]
- The quality of best execution is promoted by imposing transparency obligations on firms (notably, firms will be required to publish the top five venues where they executed client orders in the preceding year for each class of financial instruments).[e]
- Improve the transparency of advice services by requiring firms to disclose if the advice is independent, considers a broad range of instruments and considers ongoing suitability.[f]
- A new category of advice called 'independent' has to meet two conditions: i) assess a broad range of instruments and ii) do not receive any monetary inducements provided by a third party.[g]
- Monetary inducements are banned for portfolio management services.[h]

[151] The detailed scope remains subject to discussions. The European Commission is scheduled to table a legislative proposal in this regard in 2012.

- Complex UCITS may no longer be sold on an execution-only basis (the appropriateness test will apply for the non-advised sales of some UCITS).[i]
- Suitability in investment advice will need to be reviewed, to some extent depending on the complexity of the financial instrument and the service offered to the client, periodically.[j]
- Local authorities and municipalities are reclassified as retail investors.[k]
- The provision of services to retail clients will require the establishment of a branch in the Union.[l]

[a] Article 1.3, Legislative Proposal COM (2011) 656 final (MiFID recast).
[b] Annex 1, Legislative Proposal COM (2011) 656 final (MiFID recast).
[c] Article 3, Legislative Proposal COM (2011) 656 final (MiFID recast).
[d] Article 9.6.c, Legislative Proposal COM (2011) 656 final (MiFID recast).
[e] Article 27.5, Legislative Proposal COM (2011) 656 final (MiFID recast).
[f] Article 24.3, Legislative Proposal COM (2011) 656 final (MiFID recast).
[g] Article 24.5, Legislative Proposal COM (2011) 656 final (MiFID recast).
[h] Article 24.6, Legislative Proposal COM (2011) 656 final (MiFID recast).
[i] Article 25.3.iv, Legislative Proposal COM (2011) 656 final (MiFID recast). The definition of complex UCITS in the original proposal of the Commission is limited to structured UCITS as defined by Regulation 583/2010 (implementation UCITS IV, KIID).
[j] Article25.5, Legislative Proposal COM (2011) 656 final (MiFID recast).
[k] Article30 and Annex II, Legislative Proposal COM (2011) 656 final (MiFID recast).
[l] Article42.1, Legislative Proposal COM (2011) 656 final (MiFID recast).

4.2.2.2 *Fostering disclosure and comparability*

As noted above, empirical evidence suggests that standard disclosure helps investors identify the optimal choice when confronted with similar investment options (Charter et al., 2010). One of the main features of the KIID is that it allows retail investors to compare different UCITS and shop around for the best product according to their needs and aspirations. Building on the experience gathered in UCITS, the European Commission proposed to extend the standard of pre-contractual disclosure in the KIID to other retail investment products (European Commission, 2009c). The goal is to improve investor protection by enabling investors to compare options across different product categories and raising the standards of disclosure for retail investment products other than UCITS in order to mitigate the incentives for regulatory arbitrage. The creation of a level playing field in pre-contractual disclosure should not be understood to benefit some originators over others but to benefit retail investors as a whole.

The KIID standard is based on three pillars: i) selective content, short length and clear language to get the key information across; ii) standardised risk, cost and performance metrics to facilitate comparison and iii) a single document valid in all member states where the marketing of the product is allowed. Of course the KIID standard will need to be tailored to the specific characteristics of each product category. The challenge is to ensure both the comparability of products within the same product category and the comparability of different product categories. The existence of a key investor information document should not mislead investors about the nature of each product category. It is important that investors understand not only the market risk present in each product but also the nature of the product itself, e.g. whether the underlying assets are owned by the investor.

The extension of the KIID standard should be ambitious in scope. Ultimately, the KIID standard should be extended to all retail investment products, including plain-vanilla financial instruments such as shares and bonds. The principle of proportionality should, however, be applied in order to reflect the level of complexity of each product category. The European Commission has proposed to initially limit the extension of the KIID to packaged retail investment products (PRIPs): retail AIFs, unit-linked insurance products and retail structured products. In the future however, the European Commission should consider specific KIID standards for long-term saving products including pensions and plain-vanilla instruments, such as shares and bonds. It is acknowledged that the breath of the task does not allow for the immediate extension of the KIID standard to these later product categories. However, it is felt that the Commission should set a calendar to put forward legislative proposals in these areas in due time.

Table 10. Scope of the PRIPs approach in the framework of current rules

	AIFs	UCITS	INSURANCE PRODUCTS	LISTED SECURITY	Un-listed security/structured products	
Selling Practices	AIFMD + local rules	MiFID UCITS Local rules	IMD + local rules	Prospectus Directive	MiFID	PRIPs APPROACH
	Distance Marketing of Financial Services Directive					PRIPs APPROACH
Pre-contractual disclosure	AIFMD + local rules	UCITS IV (KID)	IMD + local rules	Prospectus Directive		PRIPs APPROACH
Asset Allocation	Local rules	UCITS	Solvency II			
Prudential	AIFMD MiFID CRD	UCITS MiFID CRD	Solvency II			

The UCITS KIID was introduced for new funds in July 2011 and will need to be rolled out for all existing funds before July 2012. The document is no doubt a big step forward in pre-contractual disclosure. It could however be improved further by giving more relevance to certain aspects, namely non-market risks (such as counterparty and operational risks) and recommended holding periods, as follows:

- When it comes to non-market risks, the UCITS rules require managers to disclose any material counterparty and operational risks in the KIID.[152] They also need to disclose the impact on risk of the use of derivatives and other practices such as securities lending.[153] Additional regulatory and supervisory guidance would be helpful to strengthen the adherence of funds to these provisions. The Commission could also explore the feasibility of introducing a synthetic indicator of counterparty, operational and other non-market risks (EDHEC-Risk, 2010a).
- Nor are 'Recommended holding periods' part of the information that should be consistently disclosed in the KIID. Managers are only obliged to insert the mention "this fund may not be appropriate to investors who plan to withdraw their money within [period of time]" if they consider a minimum holding period is an essential element of the investment strategy.[154] It is felt however that this phrasing is negative and may misrepresent to investors the importance of investment horizons and the nature of 'recommended holding periods'. Disclosure of this essential element should rather be phrased proactively in all instances.

Finding a coherent approach to the disclosure counterparty, operational risks and holding periods is important not only with regard to UCITS but also in view of the extension of the KIID standard to other packaged retail investment products, in order to foster comparability.

Last but not least, the approach followed in the UCITS KIID could also be useful to address the disclosure of the services offered at the point of sale. Investors would benefit from a short standard document to compare the services offered by different intermediaries in advised and non-advised sales. Among the key aspects to disclose: the breath of instruments and providers considered by the intermediary and the presence and level of inducements or up-front charges. Disclosure could be extended to the services offered in addition to the initial recommendation, such as the periodic survey of product performance, information on substantial changes to the product, and the

[152] Article 8.5, Regulation 583/2010 (UCITS IV implementation, KIID).

[153] Article 8.5.e, Regulation 583/2010 (UCITS IV implementation, KIID).

[154] Article 7.2.f, Regulation 583/2010 (UCITS IV implementation, KIID).

ongoing assessment of suitability for the investor (disclosing both the content of these services and any costs involved). Investors should be empowered to shop around not only for products but also for advice services. In this regard, promoting the comparability of the service provided by different intermediaries is essential.

4.2.2.3 *Addressing complexity in its various forms*

The level of protection awarded to investors in the sale process should be in line with the nature of the product. In this respect, MiFID I allows investors to access some products directly without requiring the investment firm to assess the appropriateness of the product for the client. This exception is awarded in view of the non-complex nature of the following instruments: shares admitted to trading, money market instruments, bonds and other securitised debt and UCITS funds.[155] In view of financial innovation in some of these products, the European Commission proposes to exclude instruments that embed a derivative or incorporate a structure that makes it difficult for the client to understand the risk involved.[156]

The Task Force considered that a holistic approach to product complexity is missing in the overall regulatory framework for retail investment products in Europe. Policy-makers and regulators should engage in a broader discussion to define product complexity at different levels and the nature of the measures to best protect retail investors. It would be important to determine both the characteristics that make a product complex and their impact on investor protection. In effect, complexity may be approached from at least three perspectives:

i) *Complexity in the product structuring,* due for instance to the use of derivatives or structured financial instruments.

ii) *Complexity in the risk-reward profile,* due for instance to the use of algorithms linked to the performance of certain reference assets or the realisation of specific conditions.

iii) *Subjective complexity,* from the perspective of the lack familiarity of investors with certain types of instruments and risks. For instance, investors are usually less familiar with the investment risk present in exotic securities, or the counterparty and other operational risks in derivatives.

---

155 Article 19.6, Directive 2004/39/EC (MiFID).

156 Article 25.3, Legislative Proposal COM (2011) 656 final (MiFID recast).

Limits to the complexity of financial instruments may be introduced for *macro-prudential* purposes (to ensure financial stability and in particular reduce the interconnectedness of the financial system) and *micro-prudential* purposes (to ensure product integrity and in particular the ability of product originators to manage counterparty and operational risks). Limits may also be introduced in the sale process of complex instruments for *investor protection* purposes (to mitigate the risk of misselling).

One of the core principles of MiFID is that investors should understand what they purchase in order to avoid the risk of misselling. In effect, firms are required to check whether the investor has the knowledge and experience to understand the risks involved in the product purchased (suitability and appropriateness tests).[157] So far regulators have focused on improving the awareness of investors about the level of market risk in each product rather than the level of counterparty and operational risks embedded in complex structures. Complex product structuring is frequently employed by originators to respond to investor demand and reduce market risk, for instance by introducing capital guarantees or otherwise mitigating the risk of capital losses due to movements in markets. The paradox is therefore that complex structured products may present a risk-reward profile that is simpler and offers more certainty to the investor than plain vanilla securities.[158] Investors however should not be misled about the importance of counterparty and operational risks and their potential impact on their investments. Market risk has on average low impact but high frequency while generally counterparty and some operational risks materialise more rarely but may completely wipe out the value of an investment. Retail investors cannot be expected to understand product structuring but should be made aware of the existence and level of counterparty, operational and other risks that are different from market risks. Targeted pre-contractual disclosure should be the first step in response to this concern (see above).

Beyond pre-contractual disclosure, complexity in the *product structuring* should be addressed in the context of product rules where they exist. In the case of UCITS, the Directive imposes requirements to limit counterparty and operational risks and ensure they are appropriately managed. If there are concerns about the level of non-market risks in some UCITS, these should first be addressed by clarifying the rules on eligible assets, use of derivatives,

---

157 Articles 35.1.c and 36, Directive 2006/73/EC (MiFID implementation).

158 For instance in the framework of UCITS, the industry recognises that funds that use derivatives systematically or extensively may provide a more linear market exposure to investors but at the expense of higher counterparty risks and operational risks derived from the instruments and strategies employed (EFAMA, 2011c).

depositary responsibility and management of collateral. Only then may residual issues at the point of sale be addressed at the level of MiFID.

Complexity in the *risk-reward profile* should be addressed at the level of selling practices. Structured UCITS whose risk-reward profile is too complex to be understood by an average retail investor should require the participation of an adviser in the sale process. It is important however that equivalent limits are applied to all retail structured products, whether in a fund format or otherwise. Notably, if a risk return profile is so complex that there is a high risk of misselling (because the investor is unlikely to understand it even with the help of an adviser), the product should not be made available to retail clients in the first place.

In conclusion, policy-makers and regulators should consider that complexity is not an unequivocal concept and may therefore need a regulatory response at different levels. Complexity in the *product structuring* should be addressed separately from complexity in the *risk-reward profile* of retail investment products. The former should be tackled by product regulation to the extent that it is deemed necessary to ensure product integrity (see chapter 2). By way of contrast, the latter should be addressed via the rules on distribution to the extent that it is deemed necessary to protect investors at the point of sale. Finally, regulators and industry should make an effort to improve the disclosure of non-market risks to investors so that products that reduce market risk at the expense of higher counterparty and operational risks are fairly represented to investors. It is fundamental that the same rules apply across Europe since divergent initiatives by member states would reverse the progress achieved in the single market.

4.2.2.4 Reshaping advice services and sale procedures

Advice plays an essential role to promote the participation of retail investors in financial markets. As noted above, the use of advice is commonplace in retail markets. Most retail clients lack the knowledge to understand the risks involved in financial products and to make optimal investment decisions – which illustrates the cause for a pan-European initiative on financial education Advice is meant to help investors identify those financial instruments that best fit their needs and their ability to bear the risk of possible losses. In practice, however, advice may be given that does not result from a professional and fair assessment of the investor's needs and the characteristics of the different products available in the marketplace. Advisers may profit from information asymmetries to push products that are not in the best interest of investors.

Regulation intervenes in investment advice to protect retail investors. The standard of protection afforded depends crucially on the definition of advice from three perspectives: i) the circumstances under which an intermediary is understood to be giving advice, as opposed to merely executing an order received from the investor; ii) the conditions the intermediary should meet and the process it should follow to be able to deliver advice and iii) the characteristics that the advice (final recommendation) should have to be deemed in the best interest of the investor. Table 11 elaborates on the determinants of retail protection in the provision advice.

Table 11. Determinants of the level of investor protection in the provision of investment advice

Scope	- Differentiating advised from non-advised sales (defining advice) - Definition of independence in advice services
Intermediary	- Professional qualifications (entry requirements) - Continuous professional development (ongoing requirements) - Ethics - Accreditation
Nature of service	- Range of products and providers considered - Remuneration by providers (inducements) or clients (up-front charges)
Advice process	- Level of transparency on the nature and costs of the service - Depth of the information to be gathered from the client - Recording of the process
Final recommendation	- Form of the communication (for instance, oral or written) - Definition of suitability (the standard that applies for a financial instrument to be in the best interest of the investor) - Circumstances under which a final recommendation should be refused

Research has found important failures in the provision of advice to retail investors. Advisers have been found to generate ambiguity and confusion in investors about the process of advice and the responsibility of advisers (ESMA, 2011, p. 7). In the context of face-to-face intermediation, it is difficult to differentiate the provision of advice from the execution of client orders. This circumstance may be exploited by firms to avoid complying with the requirements imposed by regulation on the provision of advice. Poor recording of the process of providing advice exacerbates this problem. Unfortunately, most advisers have been found to follow poor recording practices (Synovate, 2011, p. 7). Research has also shown that:

- Many advisers do not understand the risks involved in the products they sell (FSA, 2007).

- Most advisers do not collect sufficient information on the knowledge, investment experience and financial situation of the investor (Synovate, 2011, p. 6).
- Most clients are not asked for their risk-return preference and less for their ability to deal with investment risk (Synovate, 2011, p. 8).
- Most final recommendations do not meet investor needs in terms of liquidity and risk (Synovate, 2011; FSA, 2011a; FSA, 2010a).

The widespread failures listed above may not be present in all national markets to the same extent but nevertheless call for a profound reform of the rules governing the provision of advice by investment firms. The content of such reform could be the object of a separate report. Yet, in line with the areas where failures have been detected, the reform should consider: i) the definition of advice and the nature of the service provided, ii) the transparency about the nature and costs of the service provided, iii) the process of delivering advice; iv) the definition of suitability and v) the professional standards of advisers. Each of these areas is discussed in more detail below.

i) The definition of advice and the nature of the service provided

The distinction between advised and non-advised sales is vague in practice. MiFID I prohibits investment firms from issuing personal recommendations to clients without carrying out an assessment of the suitability of the recommendation for the client.[159] The Directive therefore does not distinguish the context of the recommendation – for instance whether the advice is issued by an independent third-party (who may consider a broad range of products and providers and charges the client up-front) or by the sales staff of a bank (who may only consider a restricted sample of products and accept inducements from product providers). Research has shown that face-to-face

[159] See the following pieces of legislation:

- Article 19.4, Directive 2004/39/EC (MiFID): "When providing investment advice [...] the investment firm shall obtain the necessary information [...] so as to enable the firm to recommend to the client or potential client the investment services and financial instruments that are suitable for him." [emphasis added]
- Article 4.1.4, Directive 2004/39/EC (MiFID): "Investment advice means the provision of personal recommendations to a client, either upon its request or at the initiative of the investment firm, in respect of one or more transactions relating to financial instruments."
- Article 52, Directive 2006/73/EC (MiFID implementation): "That recommendation must be presented as suitable for that person, or must be based on a consideration of the circumstances of that person." [emphasis added] It is suggested that it should read instead: "That recommendation must be based on an 'assessment of suitability', as provided in Article 35 of this Directive."

intermediation induces in investors a high level of trust, which may be exploited by the intermediary if there is no regulatory or supervisory intervention (Charter et al., 2010). The intention of MiFID I is to mitigate the risk of misselling by imposing on all sorts of intermediaries the same obligation to assess suitability. It is argued here that the approach of MiFID I is right but should be strengthened to avoid circumvention. As noted above, intermediaries may arbitrage their obligations to conduct a suitability assessment by inducing confusion in the advisee as to their responsibility in the process of delivering advice, attempting to reclassify advised sales as non-advised sales.

It is important that all sorts of intermediaries are subject to the same minimum standards when dealing with retail investors (assessment of suitability). These standards are meant to avoid products being recommended to investors that do not match their risk aversion or their financial ability to sustain possible losses. They should be therefore understood as a minimum common denominator that every personal recommendation to a retail investor should fulfil. However, these standards should not be used as an excuse to hide from clients the nature of the service provided. It is possible to distinguish different types of intermediaries in accordance with two criteria: i) the range of product types and providers considered when delivering advice and ii) whether the intermediary charges up-front for providing advice or is financed by the product provider. The figure below summarises the four main combinations that are possible.

Figure 17. Mapping of advice services

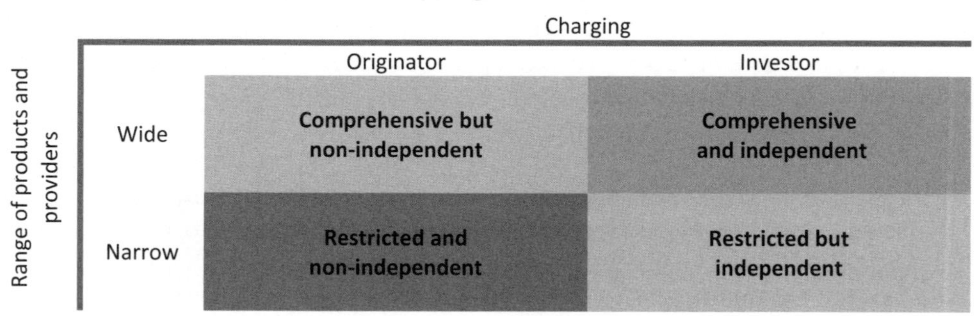

- *Comprehensive and independent* advice has the potential to be the ideal standard for all investors. Individuals with a limited amount of money to invest would also benefit from comprehensive and independent advice, as far as it is made accessible to them in practice.
- *Restricted but independent* advice is adequate for investors looking for targeted expertise in a specific type of products and who are aware of the

restrictions placed in the scope of the service. For instance, an adviser may be solely specialised in UCITS funds or in retail structured products.

- *Non-independent advice* presents a higher risk of bias in the recommendation given to investors. In particular, the adviser may be inclined to advise those products for which the product provider pays higher inducements. Yet, firms may negotiate inducements in a way that reduces their conflicts of interest. If the advice is comprehensive, investors are more likely to get a better service. Restricted and non-independent advice is offered most frequently by originators who distribute their own products.

ii) Addressing the different kinds of advice services provided

To address the different kinds of services provided, there are two distinct policy alternatives: restrictions and disclosure obligations. The approach followed by MiFID I combines both. On the one hand, firms are required to act in the best interest of investors – a principle that justifies restrictions to certain practices.[160] On the other hand, firms are required to communicate to clients any risk of damage to their interests that the firm cannot fully control for – a principle that justifies disclosure obligations.[161] Yet, implementation of these principles in respect of the provision of advice services is incomplete. There are three major shortcomings in MiFID I from this perspective:

- The rules are partial in scope and only address certain characteristics of the service provided. In effect, MiFID I only imposes specific restrictions and disclosure obligations for inducements.[162] Firms are not expressly required to inform investors about the range of products and providers they consider when delivering advice.
- The rules are poorly applied in practice. Research has shown that a very small number of advisers discloses inducements and other conflicts of interest to clients (Synovate, 2011, p. 9). Regulators have conceded that the restrictions imposed on inducements by MiFID I are difficult to apply and supervise in practice and have not led to substantial changes in the behaviour of firms in most member states (ESMA, 2010).
- The rules do not apply across all intermediaries and financial products.

In effect, partial restrictions on inducements need to be specific enough to avoid arbitrage by investment firms and product originators. They also

[160] Article 19.1, Directive 2004/39/CE (MiFID).

[161] Article 18, Directive 2004/39/CE (MiFID).

[162] Article 26, Directive 2006/73/EC (MiFID implementation).

necessitate intense supervisory monitoring to ensure firm compliance and adapt the rules in line with market practices. From this point of view, the behaviour of national authorities is crucial. The problems to make partial restrictions work in practice speak in favour of two alternative policy options: enforcing stricter disclosure of inducements or banning inducements completely, as in the UK (FSA, 2010b, Box 8). The table below compares both approaches.

Table 12. Disclosure versus banning of inducements

Disclosure of inducements		Banning of inducements
Soft approach (alter competition dynamics among advice providers)	←→	Hard approach (alters the market structure of advice providers)
Medium- to long-term horizon to realise changes in market structure	←→	Short- to medium-term horizon to realise changes in market structure
Relies on investors to look for providers who offer independent advice	←→	Considers investors should only access independent advice

A complete ban of inducements would eliminate the risk of bias induced by originators and probably bring more transparency to investors about the real costs of distribution. However, it may introduce significant side-effects that would need to be controlled for:

- Up-front charging may not be understood by less-sophisticated retail investors. Research suggests that between 20 to 30% of investors are disproportionately averse to paying an up-front fee for advice (Charter et al., 2010, p. 10). The former is a credible threat to the level of participation of some retail investors in financial markets – it is uncertain however whether banks and other originators would start to demand a fee to advise investors about their own product ranges.
- The lack of inducements may discourage banks and other originators from offering products from competing providers, narrowing the scope of their services to the detriment of small investors.
- Independent advisers may not find sufficient economic incentives to serve individuals with few resources available to invest. Regulators would have to stimulate competition and the emergence of independent advice services for small investors, which may not be easy in practice. Moreover, it may not be economically viable to offer independent advice in certain geographical locations, such as rural areas.
- Adviser-charging would introduce other biases; for instance advisers may be inclined to sell more complex instruments, sell products that

require ongoing services, or rotate portfolios to generate additional fees. These incentives may be addressed at least partially via suitability requirements and the unbundling of services.

- Given the current market structure of distribution in continental Europe, dominated by banks instead of third-party financial advisers, a sudden ban on inducements could result in disruptions to their service - as illustrated by the effects of recent reform in Australia. If regulators would wish to ban inducements, they should rather set a medium- to long-term horizon, and design a (publicly available) road map structured in several phases for all players and all products.

Disclosure is arguably a better policy alternative than banning inducements, at least in the short to medium term. The content and the form of the disclosure are however highly relevant to ensure it is effective in practice:

- Empirical research has shown that investors have difficulties to understand how inducements may affect the independence of the service they are being provided (Charter et al., 2010, p. 9). Simply disclosing the existence of inducements is not sufficient to protect investors; they many need a short explanation of their potential impact on their interests.
- The presence of inducements is only one of the aspects that determine the nature of the advice. For disclosure to be complete, investors should also be informed about the range of products and providers considered by the adviser.
- Experience gathered in the fund management sector highlights that the format of the disclosure is important and that the content should be selective to get the key message across. Standardised disclosure in maximum two pages (similar to the KIID) should allow investors to understand the nature of the service provided more easily. It should also allow investors to compare different providers of advice. Ideally, the document would place the intermediary in a matrix according to its degree of independence and the comprehensiveness of its service, so that investors are made aware of the existence of services of a different nature.
- Hard disclosure would see investors being periodically informed about the costs of the services provided by distributors, whether paid up-front by the investor or in the form of inducements by the product originator.

It is worth mentioning however that the impact of disclosing conflicts of interest is not straightforward. Empirical research has found that disclosure tends to result in better investment decisions when the interests of the advisor and the advisee are misaligned but to worse decisions when their interests are aligned (Charter et al., 2010, p. 9).

iii) Revisiting the duty to assess suitability

Beyond the nature of the service and its disclosure, the structure of the advice process also determines its quality. As noted above, MiFID requires advisers to carry-out an assessment of suitability before issuing a personal recommendation to a client. The recommendation issued needs to be suitable to the needs and characteristics of the client. To conduct this assessment, the firm has to gather information from the client. MiFID I requires firms to gather information in two respects: his or her financial situation – income, assets, and regular financial commitments and his or her investment objectives – investment horizon, risk profile and purposes of the investment. There is empirical evidence showing that advisers do not collect sufficient information (Synovate, 2011; FSA, 2011a). There is also a great concern among supervisors that firms rely on poorly designed risk-profiling and allocation tools (ESMA, 2011b). Most worryingly, a risk of misselling is derived from two aspects: i) a significant share of advisers does not record the process of gathering information and assigning a profile to the investor and ii) most advisers do not inquire the ability of investors to financially bear the possible losses derived from the investment risk of the product recommended (Synovate, 2011; FSA, 2011a; ESMA, 2011). Supervisors should endeavour to raise the standards of information collection and recording.

MiFID I defines suitable investment as one which (a) meets the investment objectives of the investor; (b) is such that the client is able financially to bear any related investment risks; and (c) is such that the client has the necessary experience and knowledge to understand the risks involved.[163] As argued before, the assessment of suitability is meant to avoid the risk of (gross) misselling – that is selling a product to the investor that may put his financial situation at risk. By way of contrast, it is argued that the current definition of suitability in MiFID I does not require the adviser to select the best product of its class for the investor. Otherwise advisers would be explicitly required to: (a) consider a wide range of product types and originators; and (b) compare the fees and costs embedded in each product to select the less expensive alternative to the investor. Therefore, the current definition of suitability would allow advisers to recommend the product that is most suitable for the investor among the range of products offered by the firm (as long as there is no misselling), even if the adviser is aware that other firms offer products that are more suitable for the client. It follows that informing the client about the nature and the scope of the advice (independent and

---

[163] Article 35, Directive 2006/73/EC (MiFID implementation).

comprehensive or non-independent and restricted) would significantly increase investor protection.

iv) Addressing the professional aptitudes of advisers

As a final element in this discussion, it is worth noting that the quality of advice also depends on the professional aptitudes of advisers. In effect, advisers need to be trained in the process of providing advice and be able to understand and respond to the needs and characteristics of the client. Even more relevant is their ability to fully understand the risks embedded in the financial products they sell, given the increasing level of complexity of financial innovation. Unfortunately, research has shown that many financial advisers do not understand the risks embedded even in relatively non-complex products (FSA, 2011b). In the framework of its retail distribution review (RDR), the UK has introduced continuous professional development programs and raised the level of the professional qualifications advisers should hold to enter the profession (see Box 8). The European Commission should consider whether EU rules would be an appropriate incentive for other national authorities to follow a similar approach. Lax supervisory cooperation of the kind proposed by ESMA may not work in practice (ESMA, 2011b). An integrated market demands closer approximation of the training and competences required from investment advisers.

Conclusion

The failures found in the market for advice demand a comprehensive reform of the regulatory framework. Investors cannot rely on suitability alone to ensure they purchase best-in-class products. Policy-makers and regulators should not only concentrate their attention on inducements but also on the scope, transparency and quality of the advice. Intermediaries who only consider a narrow range of products are unlikely to select the best solution for the investor. Acting at the level of inducements would not on its own broaden the scope of advice, which should in any event be disclosed to investors. The standard of disclosure needs to be sufficiently high so that investors understand the nature of the advice given and the availability of alternative solutions that may suit their needs better. Investors should also be informed about the costs of the services provided by distributors, whether paid up-front or in the form of inducements by product originators. Moreover, regulators should reduce the opportunities to arbitrage the assessment of suitability and find a common EU approach to raise the professional aptitude of advisers.

Box 8. The reform of investment advice proposed by the European Commission

In 2011, the Commission proposed a reform of MiFID. With regard to investment advice, the Commission proposed to introduce a new legal category of adviser called 'independent' that would need to fulfil two conditions: i) he or she assesses a sufficiently large number of financial instruments available on the market and ii) does not accept or receive any monetary benefits paid or provided by any third party other than the investor.* In addition, firms would have to inform clients about the nature of the advice provided: i) whether the advice is provided on an independent basis, ii) whether it is based on a broad or on a more restricted analysis of the market and iii) whether the investment firm will provide the client with an ongoing assessment of the suitability of the financial instruments recommended.** The Commission therefore favours disclosing the nature of advice over banning inducements outright for all investment advisers. The main risk to the success of the current proposal is that third party advisers would cease to describe themselves as independent in order to avoid complying with the new provisions of the Directive – there is a 'significant possibility' that this would occur according to the impact assessment accompanying the proposal (European Commission, 2011c, p. 68, 193 and 258). There is also a risk that banning inducements for 'independent' advice would undermine the competitive position of third party advisers in favour of banks and insurers. To avoid these perverse effects, which would completely cancel the objectives of the reform, the emphasis should be placed on the effective disclosure to investors of the nature and scope of advice, as well as its costs, whether paid up-front by the investor or in the form of inducements by the product provider. Investors should be made aware of the advantages of 'independent' advice and its availability in the marketplace.

*Article 24.5, Legislative Proposal COM (2011) 656 final (MiFID recast).
**Article 43.3, Legislative Proposal COM (2011) 656 final (MiFID recast).

Box 9. The Retail Distribution Review in the UK

The Financial Services Authority (FSA) undertook between 2006 and 2010 an in-depth review of the regulatory framework for the distribution of retail investment products in the United Kingdom, the so-called 'retail distribution review' (RDR). The review covered five areas: the sustainability of the distribution sector, the impact of incentives, professionalism and reputation, consumer access to financial products and services and regulatory barriers and enablers (FSA, 2007, p. 13). Based on consultation with stakeholders, the FSA identified three priorities in 2009: improve the clarity with which firms describe their services to consumers, address the potential for adviser remuneration to distort consumer outcomes and increase the professional standards of advisers (FSA, 2009, p. 3). Most of the rules will enter into force by 2013.

Distributors offering advice will not be able to accept any benefits (monetary or otherwise) from product originators (FSA, 2010b). Instead, charges will be agreed with clients and paid by them upfront (*adviser-charging*). Adviser firms will have to design their own pricing structure to reflect the service offered to the client and not the particular product or product provider advised. For instance, advisers may charge per service, per volume of assets invested or per hour. The FSA does not prefer one charging structure over another as long as they are product neutral. Firms will have to decide for instance whether they charge for a first meeting where no actual advice is provided and whether they charge differently to clients who accept the advice and clients who decide not to pursue the recommendation given by the adviser. In any case, clients will need to be informed in advance of the service offered by the adviser and its price. Ongoing charges however may only be requested where an ongoing service is provided. The FSA supports the unbundling of advice from ongoing services, which should be separately presented to clients. In practice, clients should not be forced to contract ongoing services when receiving advice and if they do, they should be able to cancel them in the future.

Advice services will be divided between *independent* and *restricted* and disclosed to clients as such. The difference does not depend on the presence of inducements, prohibited in either case, but on the range of financial instruments considered. *Independent* advice will therefore be required to consider as relevant market "all categories of retail investment products that are capable of meeting the investment needs and objectives of a retail client" (FSA, 2010, p. 14). The FSA limits the range of circumstances that would allow a firm to exclude certain products and still label its advice as *independent*. Firms are effectively deterred from specialising in a relevant market; specialised firms presenting themselves as *independent* will be required to assess whether a client would be better served by a non-specialised independent adviser. Advisers will have to label their services as independent or restricted but also explain the nature of any restrictions; for instance "XX only provides advice on the restricted range of instruments that we have either selected or developed for our customers" (FSA, 2010, p. 15). Disclosure will be provided both in writing and orally. The use of the word *restricted* to label non-independent advice is the result of consumer research carried out on behalf of the FSA to find the most effective alternative to communicate to customers the nature of the advice given.

The FSA also provides some clarity as to how the suitability and appropriateness tests fit within the framework of *independent* and *restricted* advice by stating that "it is not acceptable for a firm to recommend a product that most closely matches the needs of the customer, from the restricted range offered, when that product is not suitable" (FSA, 2010, p. 15). The FSA brings this observation even further by considering that "if a stakeholder pension is suitable for a customer, we would not expect to see a more expensive SIPP (self-invested personal pension) being sold to that customer because it is the closest product that the adviser has to meet the customer's needs"(FSA, 2010, p. 16). Firms should also consider whether the advice offered is likely to be of value to the client once charges are taken into account.

Where disclosing to clients the nature and costs of their services, the FSA puts forward two standard documents that adviser firms may use (the services and cost disclosure document and the combined initial disclosure document). However, the FSA does not make the use of these documents compulsory. It considers that such standards, in being additional to the disclosure requirements in MiFID I, would be incompatible with the Directive.

The RDR does not alter the regulation of non-advised sales. However, it revisits the MiFID I test on inducements by specifying the circumstances under which an inducement may be deemed to enhance the quality of the service provided to the client.[a] The FSA will also monitor if non-advised sales are used to circumvent the prohibition of inducements imposed for advised sales.

The RDR also sets professional standards for individuals selling retail investment products (FSA, 2011c). Advisers will be required to hold a statement of professional standing (SPS) awarded by an accredited body. The SPS will be renewed annually and will notably identify the adviser and verify its qualifications. The RDR improves the robustness of the qualifications that advisers need to hold to be admitted into the profession and also obliges adviser to follow at least 35 hours of accredited continuing professional development (CPD) per year. Individuals working in advised and non-advised sales will have to meet the same professional requirements. Accredited bodies will fulfil an essential role in guiding advisers and verify their adherence to professional standards.

The UK has a large population of third-party financial advisers in comparison with continental Europe where the role of banks and insurers in distributing retail financial products is more pronounced. The number of independent financial advisers (IFAs) in the UK is estimated to be 16,000 (Oxera, 2009).[b] In the short term, 25% of firms in the UK are estimated to leave the market following the introduction of the RDR, resulting in an 11% reduction in the number of clients advised (FSA, 2010). In the medium term, however, the gap is expected to be filled by new players and the expansion of incumbents (Oxera, 2009).

Beyond the pros and cons of banning inducements, which are discussed below, the key concern is that divergent rules on investor protection at member state level may reverse the progress achieved in the single market for investment products.

Table 13. Comparison of the MiFID II proposal and the UK RDR

	MiFID II PROPOSAL[c]	**UK RDR**
***Independent* label for advice**	Reserved for advice that is not biased by monetary inducements and considers a wide range of financial instruments	Reserved for advice that considers a wide range of financial instruments
***Restricted* label for advice**	Not considered	Obligatory for advice that does not consider a wide range of financial instruments

Monetary inducements	Forbidden for *independent* advice only	Forbidden for all advice services
Non-monetary inducements	Not forbidden[d]	Forbidden for all advice services
Ongoing suitability	Recommended for advised sales	Ongoing services should in principle be unbundled
Structured term deposits	Within the scope of MiFID II	Outside the scope of the RDR
Insurance products	Outside the scope of MiFID II	Within the scope of the RDR
Professional qualifications	Outside the scope of MiFID II	Within the scope of the RDR

[a] Article 26, Directive 2006/73/EC (MiFID implementation).

[b] By way of contrast, the number of third-party financial advisors in continental Europe nears just 20,000 (European Commission, 2011c, p. 257).

[c] Original Legislative Proposal COM (2011) 656 final (MiFID recast).

[d] See, however, Article 26, Directive 2006/73/EC (MiFID implementation) and discussion of limits to inducements in MiFID above.

4.2.3 *Regulatory reform: Preserving and enhancing investor choice*

Investor choice is an element of investor protection that does not receive sufficient attention, in spite of its importance. Investors need to have the ability to access the range of products they need to channel their savings in the most propitious and effective way to meet their investment objectives. Under strained economic conditions, falling wages and contracting public finances, the importance of investor choice cannot be sufficiently stressed in particular where it comes to long-term savings. Regulators should endeavour to better understand investor choice under appropriate safeguards. This section will consider first retail investors and later professional investors.

4.2.3.1 *Enhancing investor choice: Retail investors*

Regulation pays a pivotal role in fostering the participation of retail investors in financial markets. In the field of asset management, EU rule-making has focused so far almost exclusively on a subset of open-ended funds under the UCITS regulatory framework. Other fund categories have not been harmonised, despite their track record in some member states. This section considers four broad categories of investment funds that may merit regulatory action to foster access by retail investors:

a) Illiquid funds

UCITS rules impose strict liquidity requirements to allow investors to exit the fund at any given point in time. For this purpose, eligible assets are limited to liquid instruments, which have low transactions costs and bid-ask spreads assets, and can therefore can be sold with low friction. A stream of academic literature finds evidence that liquid instruments involve an opportunity cost for those investing to satisfy consumption needs in the long-term. In a 2010 study presented to this Task Force, Amenc & Sender (2010) review the literature on the premium associated with illiquidity and find evidence of its significance (EDHEC-Risk, 2010b).[164] While most UCITS funds can be used in long-term investing, investors may benefit from combining UCITS with investments in less liquid asset classes. Chapter 5 considers long-term investing in greater detail and proposes the introduction of a new category of illiquid retail investment funds in Europe.

The level of liquidity of a given investment fund depends both on its underlying assets and the redemption policy applicable to its units, as advertised to investors. To avoid mismatches, redemption policies should be broadly in line with the liquidity of the underlying assets and strategies. In this respect, some industry participants fear that a small number of UCITS may not be as liquid as investors would expect. Illiquid products are legitimate but they need to be marketed to investors under correct assumptions. The introduction of a harmonised category of illiquid funds would probably help preserve the UCITS brand from such intrusions.

b) Real estate funds

Open-ended real estate funds (OERE funds) are an interesting example of alternative funds with a track record in being sold to retail investors. Over ten member states have national rules for OERE funds, but no harmonised regime exists in Europe. Despite the absence of EU-wide market access, assets under management in OERE funds exceed €1 trillion (BVI Investment Statistics). These funds offer retail investors the possibility to access illiquid investments in real estate assets under risk-spreading rules, borrowing limits, liquidity and redemption requirements. They can serve retail investors to diversify their portfolios and to channel part of their long-term savings. Some concerns are raised about liquidity transformation by these funds which can render redemptions difficult under stressed market circumstances – as shown by past experiences (Bannier et al., 2007). Concerns have brought national regulators to limit redemptions by imposing mandatory holding periods and notice

---

164 Amihud (2009), Mendelson et al. (2005), Aragon (2004) and Loderer et al. (2003) in Amenc & Sender/EDHEC-Risk (2010b).

requirements.[165] The national markets for open-ended retail funds are mature, which points in favour of their harmonisation via a single product regulation, possibly within a broader framework that would also cover other retail illiquid funds, for example.

c) Hedge funds

As with open-ended real state funds, retail investor may benefit from accessing other alternative assets and strategies. Access to hedge-fund-style vehicles is subject to different national approaches. Member states usually require hedge funds to be nationally registered in order to be sold to retail investors, and impose minimum 'entry' tickets and investor wealth thresholds (PwC, 2008b). However, the use of wrappers to arbitrage national limits to the marketing of hedge funds to retail investors is widely acknowledged.[166] The most popular way of accessing hedge funds by retail investors is through funds of funds, listed close-ended funds and structured notes or delta one certificates (AIEG – Alternative Investment Expert Group, 2006). Diversification in funds of funds may reduce the risk of investing in individual hedge funds. However, some subsectors of the industry still need to improve their transparency and governance – both offshore and via nationally-regulated vehicles.[167] The AIFMD is expected to improve transparency and governance substantially but its standards are aimed at professional investors. Retail investors would need a further layer of protection in some regards, such as standardised and comparable disclosure. In effect, the lack of investor education and selling expertise remain key obstacles since they result in a high risk of misunderstanding by investors or outright misselling. The KIID represents a good benchmark for pre-contractual disclosure but may be difficult to adapt to

---

165 See for instance as in the German Investors Protection and Functionality Improvement Act of 11 February 2011. It imposes a 12-month notice period for existing and new investors and a 24-month holding period for new investors for withdrawals of more than €30,000 per calendar half-year. The Act also puts forward stricter leverage limits and valuation requirements.

166 According to the Alternative Investment Expert Group – AIEG (2006), "Well-intentioned national measures merely succeed in pushing investors to obtain hedge fund access through other means, such as acquiring hedge fund exposure through structured products, shares in closed-end funds or investing offshore".

167 See for instance the case of the Arch Cru hedge funds in the UK. According to the Financial Times, the funds raised around £422 million from over 10,000 retail investors via 900 financial advisors in the UK. The funds were suspended in 2009 and it became clear they had failed in late 2011. The funds were UK domiciled and regulated, although they were invested in cells listed offshore and managed in this way to arbitrage UK rules (see "Call for inquiry after losses at Arch Cru", Financial Times Fund Management (FTfm), 15 January 2012.

represent the risks embedded in more exotic assets and strategies. It is hoped the PRIPs initiative would bring progress in this regard. The lack of selling expertise in its turn may only be tackled by raising professional standards and qualifications. It appears therefore that, while retail investors may benefit from hedge-fund-like vehicles, important barriers to an adequate level of investor protection remain.

d) Responsible funds

Socially responsible funds satisfy specific investor demand for investing in specific sectors, such as green power, or in companies respecting employment, social and environmental standards. Currently, retail investors directly hold less than 10% of the assets under management by SRI (socially responsible investment) funds in Europe (Eurosif, 2010). Yet, the potential for growth is elicited by the participation shares of retail investors in countries such as France and Germany - over 35 and 40% respectively (Eurosif, 2010). Contrary to some perceptions, SRI returns appear to be broadly in line with markets (Mercer, 2009). The challenge is instead to ensure the integrity of SRI funds with regard to the goals they purport to achieve, while fostering the single market. The current approach based sometimes on national rules but mostly on self-regulation may be insufficient in this respect. Retail investors may therefore benefit from regulatory action at European level. Chapter 5 considers responsible investing in greater detail.

4.2.3.2 Preserving investor choice: Professional investors

Subject to prudential rules, professional investors face fewer restrictions to access alternative investment funds than retail investors. The AIFMD will create a pan-European market for non-UCITS funds, thereby expanding substantially the choice of professional investors. National rules limiting the access of institutional investors to locally-regulated funds[168] will need to be removed to the extent that the AIFMD prohibits any discrimination against fellow AIFs coming from other member states. By advancing the convergence between traditional and alternative asset managers, the AIFMD discredits the use of nominal distinctions in prudential regulation. Capital and solvency charges should apply instead according to the underlying of each fund, as long as the manager complies with the AIFMD or equivalent standards. This is the principle followed for instance by Solvency II when it withdraws punitive capital charges for funds offering full look-through into their underlying.[169]

---

[168] See EDHEC-Risk (2010b) and Alternative Investment Expert Group - AIEG (2006).

[169] See section on Solvency II in Chapter 2.

A crucial question for investor choice is the limits that should be imposed on non-EU funds handled by managers who do not comply with the standards in the AIFMD. To avoid the risk of significantly curtailing investor choice, national private placement regimes for offshore funds will not be superseded by the AIFMD immediately but will co-exist for some time. The Directive will allow offshore funds to be marketed to professional investors under existing national rules at least until 2018. During this transition period, non-EU managers will not be bound by the Directive unless they wish to be granted its passport, in which case they will need to comply with most of its provisions.[170] However, from 2013 any manager marketing its funds in Europe will have to abide by the transparency provisions in the AIFMD, given their importance to enable effective due diligence and monitoring by investors.[171]

In the case of reverse solicitation, managers will not even have to comply with the transparency obligations in the AIMFD. Where foreign funds offer a degree of transparency comparable to EU funds, reverse solicitation is a useful instrument to protect investor choice. The responsibility falls on the investor not to access opaque funds where meaningful due diligence is impracticable. In this respect, policy-makers should speed-up its work to heighten the due diligence requirements where funds are accessed through reverse solicitation, as proposed in the preamble of the AIFMD. Moreover, prudential rules may be a useful instrument to limit the ability of institutional investors to access opaque funds, for instance through the application of punitive capital charges in a fashion similar to Solvency II but mindful of investor choice. A future review of the AIFMD should consider the extent to which reverse solicitation is used (if at all) to circumvent the transparency requirements in the Directive, given their importance for investor protection and ultimately for financial stability.

Limits to the choice of professional investors are also imposed to ensure financial stability oversight. The Directive prescribes that no AIF may be marketed in the European Union unless the home supervisor signs a memorandum of understanding (MoU) that allows the host member state to receive all information material to monitor macro-prudential risks.[172] This provision will apply even for AIFs marketed under national placement regimes. While the Directive dictates that the agreement is entered between national supervisors, for practical reasons ESMA should lead the negotiations so that a single model is simultaneously signed by all member states with each

---

170 Articles 37-40, Directive 2011/61/EU (AIFMD).

171 Article 42, Directive 2011/61/EU (AIFMD).

172 Article 42, Directive 2011/61/EU (AIFMD).

relevant third country.[173] Ultimately, the EU would need a single supervisor with exclusive powers to deal with third-country issues such as these.

A related threat to investor choice is the international fragmentation of asset management regulation. Despite the fact that the AIFMD implements a G20 consensus, it is not fully in line with legislation adopted elsewhere, such as in the US under the Dodd-Frank Act. More worryingly, many other jurisdictions have not taken any steps to regulate alternative investment managers so far. The Directive would nevertheless need to apply to all funds marketed in the EU regardless of their geographical origin if it is to attain its objectives. In a world of free capital flows, managers will otherwise move jurisdictions to avoid complying with the Directive. Attempting to apply the AIFMD to offshore managers may however reduce investor choice dramatically so the process should be handled with care. The AIFMD foresees that ESMA undertakes, before phasing-out national private placement regimes, an in-depth review on the possible effects of this change on investor choice in the EU.[174]

Offshore managers will only be granted the AIFMD passport if they comply with most of the provisions in the Directive and if their jurisdictions of origin engage in supervisory and tax cooperation to a very high standard – including for instance the possibility of on-site inspections at the request of the EU authorities.[175] Poor levels of commitment by foreign supervisors would make the full application of the AIFMD to non-EU managers impracticable, with substantial limitations in terms of investor choice. In such circumstances two alternative options would emerge: i) keeping national private placement regimes alive together with the passport, which would limit the single market but afford some protection to local managers or ii) substitute private placement regimes by a workable passport for offshore funds. The latter option would consolidate the single market but, if the rules are too lenient, would remove one of the few incentives for managers to stay or come back onshore. Ultimately, investor choice will determine the success of the passport as investor demand may shift from unregulated to AIFMD-compliant funds.

In sum, the AIFMD passport will greatly expand the choice of professional investors by creating a single market for the EU AIFs and AIF managers. Where it comes to non-EU funds, the situation will be somewhat different. In a first phase (from July 2013), the Directive will limit investor choice to managers who comply with its transparency obligations and are

---

[173] Box 122, ESMA 2011/379 (technical advice, implementation, AIMFD)

[174] Article 68, Directive 2011/61/EU (AIFMD).

[175] Article 37.7, Directive 2011/61/EU (AIFMD).

domiciled in a jurisdiction willing to commit to supervisory cooperation for the purpose of prudential oversight. In a final phase (probably from 2018), investor choice would be limited to managers who comply with most of the provisions in the AIFMD and are domiciled in jurisdictions that engage in broad supervisory and tax cooperation with the EU. This final phase has not fixed a date of entry into force and is still full of uncertainties. The success of the EU passport will depend on the willingness of offshore funds to comply with the directive to gain direct access to European investors. The process will be mostly demand driven and has a chance of being successful if institutional investors continue to favour regulated over unregulated investments. The success or failure will also depend on the ability of EU authorities to speak with one voice in the negotiation of supervisory and tax agreements with third countries. Overall, the process should be carefully managed to protect (informed) investor choice. Reverse solicitation will allow marginal relief but should be carefully monitored to avoid the arbitrage of the transparency obligations in the Directive. At the time of writing, the process of implementing the AIFMD is not over and the advice of ESMA reflected in this section may be modified by the European Commission.

Box 10. Limits to investor choice imposed by depositary rules in the AIFMD

Depositary requirements in the AIFMD may also curtail the choice of professional investors in Europe. Limitations to the delegation of depositary tasks and the transfer of depositary liability may represent a significant hurdle for investors wishing to access emerging economies. There is a balance to be struck between heightened custody and other operational risks, on the one hand, and the opportunities for attractive returns outside OECD jurisdictions, on the other. The bottom line is that professional investors should not be denied opportunities in emerging economies on the condition that the former risks are appropriately disclosed and managed. This principle informs the AIFMD when it requires investors to be informed about the delegation of custody tasks and the transfer of liability to local sub-custodians in third countries but allows both practices under certain conditions, including due diligence and monitoring by the main depositary and the fund manager.[a]

As a general rule, the local (third-country) sub-custodian needs to i) be subject to prudential regulation, minimum capital requirements, supervision and periodic audit and ii) segregate the assets of its clients from its own assets in a manner equivalent to the safe-keeping duties in the Directive.[b] These requisites would however truncate investor access to emerging economies where local custody is imperative but local entities are unlikely to satisfy the standards in the Directive. To avoid this outcome and where the former conditions are met, the AIFMD exceptionally allows safekeeping to be delegated to such local entities as long as investors are duly informed.[c] It is worth noting that no transfer of liability will be effective in practice unless the conditions for delegation are not fulfilled to begin with (see Figure 18).

Figure 18. Delegation of depositary tasks and transfer of liability under the AIFMD

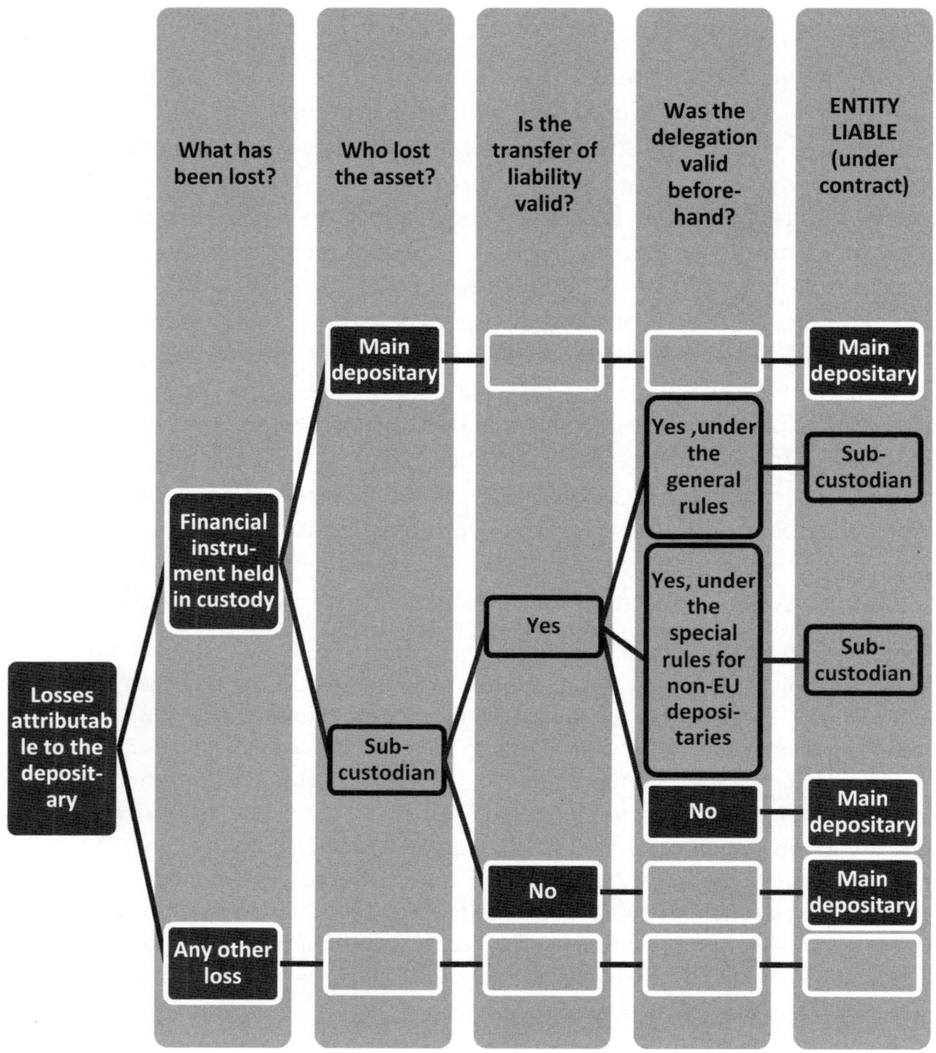

A further obstacle to accessing emerging economies could be found in the objective reason that depositaries and managers will need to put forward in order to justify the delegation of custody functions and the transfer of liability. However, in its advice to the European Commission, ESMA stretches the concept of objective reason to encompass process optimisation and cost savings.[d] Broad interpretation by ESMA will therefore most probably facilitate delegation as long as the liability stays with the main depositary and due diligence, monitoring and all other requirements are met.

When it comes to the transfer of liability and in contrast to the delegation of tasks, the Directive places the duty on the manager rather than on the depositary to weigh the pros and cons of such transfer. In effect, the manager shall balance the interest of investors in maintaining a given investment wherever related custody risks bring the main depositary to object to servicing such assets. If the manager understands that it is in the best interest of investors to maintain the given investment, he may authorise the transfer of liability to the local sub-custodian. Crucially, investors will need to be duly notified of the manager's decision and his or her assessment. By allowing liability to be transferred under these conditions, the Directive is likely to preserve investor choice while ensuring transparency so that investors can make informed decisions. Yet, if any of the required conditions in the Directive is not met, the transfer of liability will not be effective in practice.

---

[a] Articles 21.11 and 21.12, Directive 2011/61/EU (AIFMD).

[b] Article 21.11.d, Directive 2011/61/EU (AIFMD).

[c] Article 21.11 second paragraph, Directive 2011/61/EU (AIFMD). To transfer liability, there needs to be valid delegation of tasks as a pre-condition. Only the custody of financial instruments and the safekeeping of other assets may be delegated (monitoring of cash flows and ancillary tasks may not). The main depositary will have to demonstrate the existence of an objective reason for this delegation. Liability is transferred via a written contract that needs to expressly allow direct action by the manager against the sub-custodian. The main depositary will also have to demonstrate the existence of an objective reason for this transfer. Where the local entity does not satisfy the general requirements for delegation, the depositary may still delegate safekeeping to a local entity, as long as the law of the third country requires local custody, the AIF manager authorises it and investors are duly informed. Additional conditions apply to the transfer of liability to this local entity, namely the fund rules need to allow for such a transfer and investors need to be informed prior to their investment.

[d] Box 65, ESMA 2011/379 (technical advice, implementation, AIMFD). Article 21.11.b, Directive 2011/61/EU (AIFMD).

5. Nourishing the Real Economy: Today and Tomorrow

The asset management industry accounts for about €14 trillion in assets under management in Europe (EFAMA, 2011a). Beyond the sheer size of this number lies a significant contribution to the financing of companies and governments in Europe that is not immediately apparent and is seldom acknowledged. This final chapter will consider the participation of investment funds and investment mandates in equity and debt securities, compared to the share of other intermediaries, to better illustrate the position of asset managers. In addition, the chapter will explore the role of *long-term* investing, *responsible* investing and venture capital in fostering economic growth and prosperity in Europe. In the pursuit of deeper and broader capital markets in Europe, the asset management industry has an increasingly important role to play in providing finance to the real economy.

5.1 The contribution of asset management to the economy

The European asset management industry plays a significant role in financing the European economy. Investment funds are estimated to hold approximately 13% of debt securities issues by residents in the euro area, and over 16% of listed shares. If investment mandates are taken into account, a large majority of which are managed on behalf of institutional investors such as insurance companies or pension funds, the participation of European asset managers would probably account for 25% in debt securities and 30% of listed shares in the euro area (EFAMA, 2011a, p. 40, based on ECB data).

The relative size of asset management intermediation, in comparison to pension funds and insurance companies, has increased dramatically over the past two decades. Investment funds accounted for 40% of the assets under management of these three intermediaries globally in 2009, up from 25% in 1995 (IMF, 2011, p. 5). This sizeable increase in the importance of the asset management industry (up by 40%) was accompanied by a reduction in the assets under management by pension funds and insurance companies by 19% and 11%, respectively, over the same period. The change may be attributed at least partly to the move from defined benefit to defined contribution pension schemes, initially in the US and later in Europe. While these data refer solely to investment funds and do not include investment mandates, they also reflect, albeit partially, the increasing externalisation of portfolio management by some insurers and pension funds.

Figure 19. Assets under management by type of intermediation (% of total)

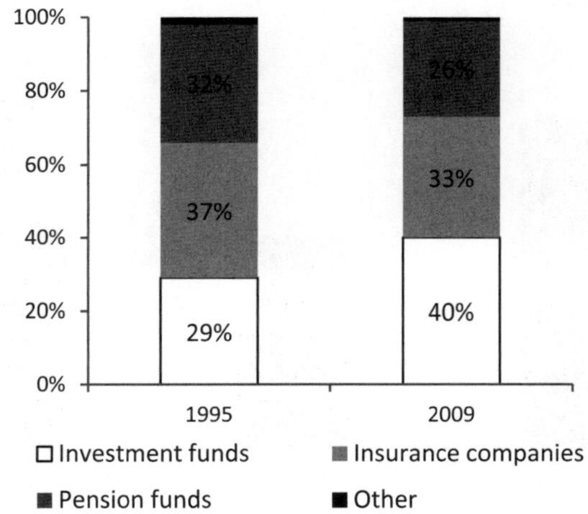

Source: IMF (2011, p. 5).

A study by Fitch Ratings in 2011 offers the most complete picture so far of asset allocation in Europe. According to this study, assets under management by long-term investment funds amounted in 2010 to approximately 43% of GDP in Europe. In effect, the economic significance of investment funds ranks above that of insurance companies in Europe, whose total investments amounted in 2010 to 37% of GDP (48% including unit-linked insurance products). The size of investment funds is also well above that of pension funds in Europe, whose total investments amounted to just 24% of European GDP in 2010, although the differences among member states are very significant - pension funds account for 134% of GDP in the Netherlands but only 14% in Germany (Fitch Ratings, 2011b, p. 4).

In terms of asset allocation, the study by Fitch shows that asset managers are the largest investors in non-debt securities, including listed equity. In absolute terms, long-term investment funds held €3.6 trillion in non-debt securities in 2010, well above pension funds and insurers.[176] Approximately 63% of this figure is estimated to be invested in listed securities (€2.3 trillion) (OEE, 2011, p. 36). In relative terms, investment funds allocate 60% of their assets to non-debt securities, similarly to pension funds (55%) but well above insurers (25%). Conversely, insurers are the biggest investors in debt securities, in particular corporate debt (Fitch Ratings, 2011b, p. 5).

Figure 20. Asset allocation to debt and other securities in Europe by type of intermediary (€ trillion)

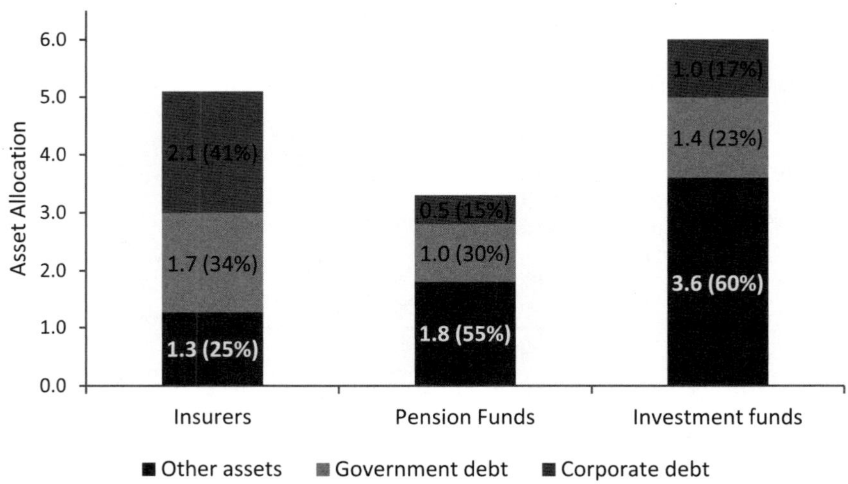

Notes: Estimation of asset allocation at end 2010 (€ trillion). Insurance excludes unit-linked products. Mutual funds exclude money market funds not considered long-term investments.

Source: Fitch Ratings (2011b, p. 5).

The picture for investment mandates is similar to that of investment funds. European asset managers were estimated to hold €1.9 trillion in equity and €3.3 trillion in debt instruments under discretionary mandates in 2009, most of which was managed on behalf of institutional investors (OEE, 2011, p. 36). The sheer size of these figures is revealed by comparing them to the total investments by insurers and pension funds in Figure 20 (€8.4 trillion).

What is then the direct share of participation of the asset management industry in securities issued by corporations and governments in Europe? A recent study by the Observatoire de l'Epargne Européenne (OEE, 2011) shows

176 Long-term investment funds include UCITS and other open-ended investment funds, therefore excluding money market funds.

that approximately 49% of investment funds allocation to equity in Europe goes to shares issued by European companies, in contrast to 64% in investment mandates. The difference may well be explained by the higher allocation to emerging markets in investment funds and the conservative risk profile of the institutional investors in most investment mandates. An IMF study on the factors determining private asset allocation reveals that the long-term growth prospects in destination countries is the main pull factor for investors (IMF, 2011, p. 13). In this respect, faltering growth prospects in Europe may well lead to a decrease in the allocation to local issuers in the next few years. In effect, investors increasingly see emerging market securities as a potential source of higher returns and are giving them more weight in their portfolios (IMF, 2011, p. 20). Unresolved liquidity and policy risks, however, continue to discourage investors wishing to invest outside the OECD. In contrast with equity, there are no differences in the weight of European debt securities between investment funds and investment mandates (just above 70% in both instances).

Figure 21. Asset allocation by investment funds and mandates in Europe, end 2009 (€ billion)

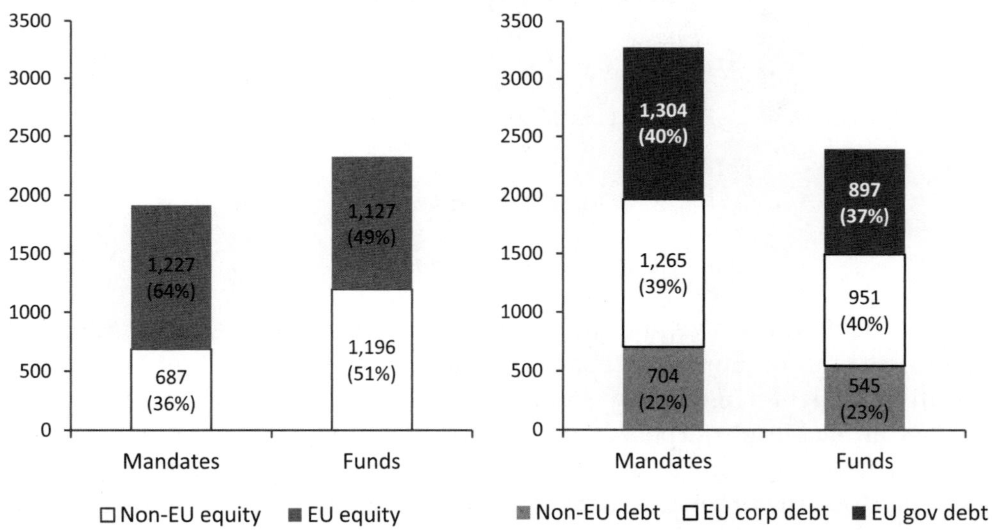

Source: OEE (2011, pp. 36-37).

Other subsectors of the asset management industry also contribute significantly to the financing of the European economy. The collection of data outside harmonised investment funds in Europe has so far not followed a consistent approach. The introduction of the AIFMD, given the extensive reporting obligations imposed on managers, will resolve this situation and bring to light the contribution of the whole asset management industry to the economy. Alternative managers frequently invest in assets that are less correlated to traditional equity and debt securities. One area in which sufficient data collection exists is the private equity and venture capital industry. Despite the industry having very much suffered from the financial crisis, after having grown significantly in the years immediately before, in 2010 it represented €43 billion in investments in non-listed equity. According to industry statistics, over 70% of this amount was invested in European businesses and almost 50% in small and mid-sized companies (EVCA, 2011).

Figure 22. Funds raised and investment by private equity managers in Europe (€ billion)

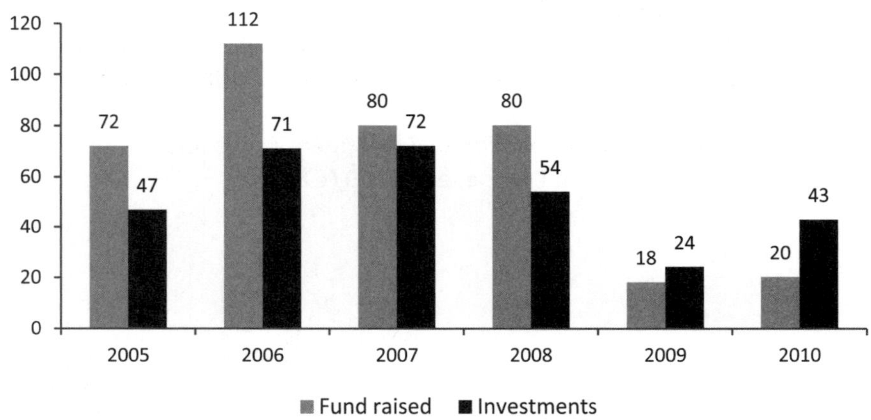

Source: EVCA (2011).

Taken as a whole, the contribution of the asset management industry to the financing of European businesses and governments is very significant. Moreover, tighter regulatory standards imposed on other intermediaries for financial stability purposes mean that asset management will play an increasingly important role in the future to finance the economy and channel savings towards productive activities. Yet, the asset management industry still needs to address concerns, including the impact of management and performance fees on the returns that are ultimately delivered to investors and the potential contribution to volatility and pro-cyclicality of some investment practices.

The positive impact of asset management is magnified by best practices, such as long-term and sustainable investing, which will be considered in the next sections. In addition, certain subsectors of the industry such as venture capital play a key role in fostering entrepreneurship and innovation in knowledge-based economies.

5.2 Long-term investment

> *Long-term investors have the ability to create investments, rather than look for assets in the market and invest in them* (WEF, 2011, p. 44).

The asset management industry offers products that can be employed in long-term investing. The World Economic Forum defines *long-term investing* as "investing with the expectation of holding an asset through an entire business cycle by an investor with the capability to do so" (WEF, 2011, p. 11). It is not so much an investment style as an approach that may employ a variety of strategies based on both liquid and illiquid instruments. Asset classes such as unlisted equity, real estate or infrastructure require a long-term approach to investing, given their illiquid nature. Yet, relatively liquid instruments may also be an integral part of *long-term investing* strategies, typically in combination with more illiquid asset classes (see Figure 23). The asset management industry offers a choice of products with different levels of liquidity, from the less liquid (private equity, venture capital or infrastructure funds) to the more liquid (hedge, commodity or mutual funds).

Long-term investing is essential for the economy since it directs resources towards those activities whose pattern of returns is more skewed towards the long-term and therefore cannot be undertaken under short-term financing constraints. Activities such as innovation, research and development or infrastructure development are frequently characterised by the uncertainty of their short-term profitability but also by their potential to generate outsized returns in the long-run and their many positive externalities. Investing long-term is in line with the horizon of the liabilities borne by some investors, such as the provision of retirement income and others. However, its positive externalities benefit society in general by driving supporting economic growth and competitiveness (OECD, 2011). Moreover, long-term investors are supposed to contribute positively to financial stability to the extent that they behave counter-cyclically in times of market stress, by holding onto their investments, avoiding fire sales and profiting from falling prices to increase their strategic stakes (WEF, 2011).

The potential benefits of *long-term investing* do not impinge on the importance of short-term investors for the effective functioning of financial markets. In effect, short-term investors fulfil an essential role in providing market liquidity and monitoring corporate performance at ever-shorter frequencies. They also contribute to price formation by immediately feeding the constant flow of information into asset prices. However, given the horizon of their investment positions, short-term investors will naturally give more weight to information referring to short-term rather than long-term performance. Long-term investors provide a counterweight by focusing on the developments that affect performance in the long-term - yet they remain sensitive to short-term drops in asset prices given constraints such as mark-to-market accounting. The divide between short and long-term investing is more a question of balance than anything else.

Beyond macro-considerations, investing long-term also carries potential benefits for the individual investors. As mentioned above, long-term investment strategies are usually the best fit for investors facing liabilities in the long-term. But investors may derive additional benefits from *long-term investing* such as: i) accessing structural risk premia associated with the illiquidity, market risk or complexity of long-term investment opportunities; ii) taking advantage of emerging trends that will materialise in the future; iii) engaging with corporations to improve long-term performance or iv) minimising the costs associated with transactions and market disturbances (WEF, 2011, p. 35). For all these reasons, both retail and institutional investors should be able to access long-term investment opportunities.

The asset management industry offers a range of products with a long-term orientation, both in the form of funds and tailored solutions for institutional investors. Direct investments in infrastructure, private equity and venture capital may be administered by independent asset managers on behalf of institutional investors under investment mandates. These investments (given their size, illiquidity and return pattern) may only be undertaken by investors with sufficient resources both to fund the initial outlay and maintain their position over many years. Investors who are unable or unwilling to make this sort of commitment may access illiquid asset classes via fund products, offering more liquidity and the opportunity to pool resources with other investors. Funds investing in unlisted equity, infrastructure and real estate are instruments that fit well in a long-term investment strategy (WEF, 2011, p. 14). Traditional open-ended investment funds (such as UCITS and mutual funds) may also be employed by investors in the framework of long-term investing. These latter funds invest in liquid instruments such as public equity and debt securities, allowing investors to redeem their units frequently and on short notice. Despite their liquidity, traditional open-ended investment funds may be held over the long-term to access some of the benefits of *long-term investing* described above. Yet, fund instruments investing in more illiquid asset classes are better positioned to capture these benefits. The optimal combination of liquid and illiquid instruments in a given portfolio is specific to each investor.

Figure 23. Asset class liquidity versus time horizon and long-term investing

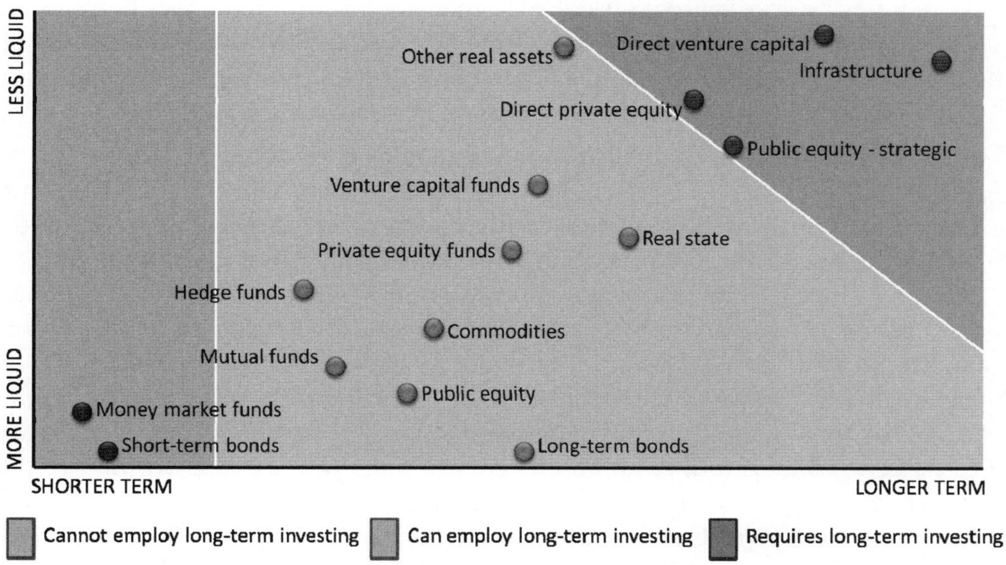

Source: Adapted from WEF (2011, p. 14).

Despite the proven ability of the asset management industry to offer *long-term investing* solutions to retail and professional clients, a number of barriers have been indentified that may lessen the long-term orientation of investment funds and mandates or hamper the access of retail and professional clients to long-term investment opportunities:

- *Principal-agent concerns.* Investment managers may pursue a shorter-term investment horizon than optimal for the unit holders or ultimate beneficiaries given for instance the use of: variable compensation based on short-term performance, benchmarks such as market indices which discourage investments with a divergent pattern of returns or risk metrics that discourage investments with high short-term volatility, even if expected returns are superior in the long-run. Staff turnover in senior and junior positions may also generate a short-term bias (WEF, 2011, p. 44).
- *Retail investor access.* Regulation restricts the access of retail investors to funds invested in illiquid assets such as real estate or unlisted equity. In Europe, harmonised product rules only exist for open-ended investment funds under the UCITS Directive. There are no product rules that would facilitate the access of retail investors to illiquid asset classes with a distinct long-term orientation.
- *Institutional investor access.* Prudential regulation discourages *long-term investing* by imposing higher capital requirements on certain asset

classes, coupled with heavier compliance burdens - for instance, risk-adjusted capital charges are higher for equity than for high-grade corporate bonds under the Solvency II framework. Mark-to-market accounting also undermines the ability of institutional investors to hold on to their investments in stressful market circumstances.

In order to address these concerns, action is required both at industry and regulatory level. Asset managers and trade associations should endeavour to better understand how agency conflicts affect their fiduciary duty towards long-term investors. Remuneration, benchmarks and risk metrics should be revised to better factor the interests of investors. To avoid clients fleeing long-term funds in times of market stress, the strategy of the fund should be better communicated, as well as any exceptional limits to redemptions. When it comes to retail investors, regulators should facilitate their access to illiquid funds for their long-term and retirement savings. Harmonised product rules could be used to introduce a new category of retail funds in the EU that would invest in long-term financial instruments and real assets. Standardised disclosure and investment advice should give more relevance to investment horizons, while suitability requirements should be reinforced for illiquid products. With regard to institutional investors, regulators should re-consider prudential and accounting rules to ensure that they promote rather than hinder *long-term investing*. Ideally, every legislative initiative would be screened from this perspective, in isolation and in terms of its cumulative impact.

Box 11. A proposal to introduce long-term retail funds

Strengthening the long-term orientation of savings and fund investments should be viewed as one of the main challenges (and opportunities) faced by the asset management industry and regulatory authorities in Europe. UCITS rules impose strict liquidity requirements to allow investors to exit the fund at any point in time. For this purpose, eligible assets are limited to liquid instruments (transferable securities), which given their low transaction costs and bid-ask spreads, can be easily sold to meet redemptions. Proponents of regulated long-term retail funds (LTRFs) consider that retail investors should be given the opportunity of investing in long-term financial instruments (including unlisted instruments) and real assets, in line with their investment horizon.

LTRFs would be regulated at EU level based on the experience gathered in the UCITS and AIFMD frameworks. Harmonised management and product rules would allow LTRFs to be marketed cross-border to retail investors. The objective should be to offer investors access to the structural premium embedded in illiquid assets while avoiding the risk of suspensions. Moreover, as a vehicle for *long-term investing*, LTRFs could have a positive impact on the European economy in line with the Europe 2020 Agenda.

LTRFs would be based on the following principles:

- An explicit objective to channel private savings with a long-term horizon into long-term assets
- A broad scope of eligible assets, including non-listed financial instruments and real assets
- Strong diversification and issuer concentration limits, similar to the UCITS Directive
- Careful attention to operational, valuation and other risks embedded in illiquid asset classes
- Management company and governance standards equivalent to the AIFM and UCITS frameworks
- Depositary standards equivalent to the AIFM and UCITS frameworks
- A fully fledged marketing passport for retail investors, as in the UCITS Directive
- Limits to redemptions in terms of frequency, size and advanced notice
- Adequate instruments to manage redemptions in exceptional market circumstances

Management and product provisions should be complemented with specific marketing rules aimed at expressly communicating to investors the long-term orientation of LTRFs and the pros and cons of illiquidity and limits to redemptions. Suitability requirements in investment advice would need to be revised to ensure LTRFs are sold to investors where they are in line with their individual profile, investment objectives, horizon and financial ability to bear lock-in periods or any other conditions attached to the illiquid nature of the investment. Multiple voices in the industry support the introduction of some sort of LTRFs in Europe and highlight in particular their importance in the context of defined-contribution second and third pillar pensions.

5.3 Sustainable investing

The asset management industry has the ability to offer products and services that cater for specific environmental, social and governance (ESG) goals. *Sustainable* or *responsible* investing may be broadly defined as any investment process that combines financial objectives with the consideration of environmental, social and/or governance criteria (Eurosif, 2010, p. 8). ESG considerations may be implemented in investment processes and in the exercise of voting rights attached to securities in the pursuit of different objectives that, despite their diverse nature, are frequently complementary in practice, such as:

i) Promoting ethical objectives (e.g. excluding the defence industry)

ii) Promoting international standards and conventions (e.g. human and children rights, international labour standards)

iii) Minimising certain risks (e.g. liability arising from environmental damage)

iv) Profiting from macro-trends in specific subsectors (e.g. investing in renewable energies)

v) Proactively seeking to translate ESG factors into financial gains (e.g. building stable relationships with stakeholders to raise productivity and gain a competitive advantage).

Investors may employ ESG criteria to screen and select investment opportunities, either negatively or positively. Negative screening is used to exclude companies or sectors that do not comply with selected ESG requirements, while positive screening is used to find the companies that exhibit the best performance with regard to a set of ESG parameters (best-in-class and best-of-sector approaches). Financial analysis increasingly considers ESG performance indicators next to traditional financial indicators to gain a better understanding of the risk-return profile in equity and debt securities issued by profit-oriented companies.[177] Once an investment commitment has been made, *responsible* investors will engage in corporate decision-making to promote ESG criteria in line with their goals, whether ethical or profit-oriented.

Ethics aside, the World Economic Forum defines *sustainable investing* as "an investment approach that integrates ESG criteria into investment and ownership decision-making with the objective of generating superior risk-adjusted financial returns" (WEF, 2011b, p. 10). The word *sustainable* is preferred to *responsible* to emphasise that ESG factors are not only ethical considerations but can be translated into business practices with the potential to deliver higher returns to investors, at least over the longer-term. Several studies have shown that *sustainable* investment performs in line with traditional benchmarks, if not better, and shows better resilience in periods of crisis. The consultancy firm Mercer surveyed in 2007 and 2009 the academic literature studying the performance of *responsible* investment strategies and

---

[177] See for instance the Key Performance Indicators (KPIs) for ESG 3.0 developed in 2010 by the European Federation of Financial Analysts Societies (EFFAS) and the Society of Investment Professionals in Germany (DVFA). KPIs are standardised sets of quantitative indicators for ESG in 114 subsectors based on the Dow Jones Industry Classification Benchmark (ICB). They are used to measure the ESG performance of profit-oriented companies, facilitating comparable reporting by corporates and investors, and the integration of ESG data into mainstream investment analysis.

found that 20 out of 36 studies showed clear evidence of a positive relationship between ESG criteria and financial performance, while only three studies found a clearly negative relationship (Mercer, 2009).

According to Eurosif (2010, p. 8), *responsible* investment may have reached €5 trillion assets under management in Europe in 2009. Yet, this figure includes investment funds and investment mandates with very different approaches to ESG criteria. One of the key challenges is to identify and clarify these different approaches and measure the performance of funds and mandates not only in financial terms but also with reference to the ESG goals they purport to support. Better defining the many different approaches to *responsible* investment would require considering both the goals pursued and the processes followed in selecting investments and exercising voting rights. Moreover, increasing investor participation would require better tools to measure the success of managers in applying *responsible* investing processes to generate positive financial returns (through the pursuit of ESG objectives). In other words, better reporting is needed to allow more effective monitoring and increase the confidence of investors in the integrity of *responsible* investing. While much has been achieved in this respect, the progress so far has not led to the emergence of universally acceptable standards. In this regard, it is worth noting the ongoing work of the International Integrated Reporting Council (IIRC) to develop a global framework for integrated reporting. And the work of other private organisations, such as Novethic and Luxflag, to create quality labels for *responsible* funds that go well beyond assessing the level of transparency of the given fund.

Institutional investors are estimated to hold over 90% of the assets under management in *responsible* investment schemes in Europe (Eurosif, 2010, p. 16). The weight of institutional investors is very much explained by the importance given to ESG criteria by pension funds, to which several member states apply regulatory requirements in this respect. By way of contrast, retail investors hold directly less than 10% of *responsible* assets in Europe. Yet, the small overall figure should not hide the latent retail demand for *responsible* investment funds proven by the success they have gathered in some member states such as Germany, France or Belgium (Eurosif, 2010, p. 18). In this respect, a harmonised approach to responsible investment funds for retail investors would be greatly beneficial in Europe.

The European Commission has not scheduled a broad legislative action in the area of *responsible* or *sustainable* investing, but it has put forward an agenda to modernise company law and the framework of corporate governance in Europe (European Commission, 2010, 2011 and 2012). While these initiatives do not relate directly to *responsible* investing, they may however have a material impact in the way institutional investors and asset managers interact with the companies they invest in. Fostering the consideration of ESG criteria by institutional investors has the potential to improve risk management and the ability of investors to generate additional returns to meet their long-term liabilities. Yet, institutional investors may not undertake this effort alone without regulators strengthening reporting and other obligations on companies. As for asset managers, given their position as intermediaries, their role will always be limited to pursuing the interest of investors as expressed in their investment mandates, which act as the transmission mechanism of ESG considerations by institutional clients. Investors and managers should not be prescribed to act in certain ways on the basis of relevant ESG performance indicators, but rather should be required to consider those indicators and explain their actions with reference to them, in a way that is proportional to their size and their investment horizon.[178]

Figure 24. The intermediary role of asset managers in responsible investing

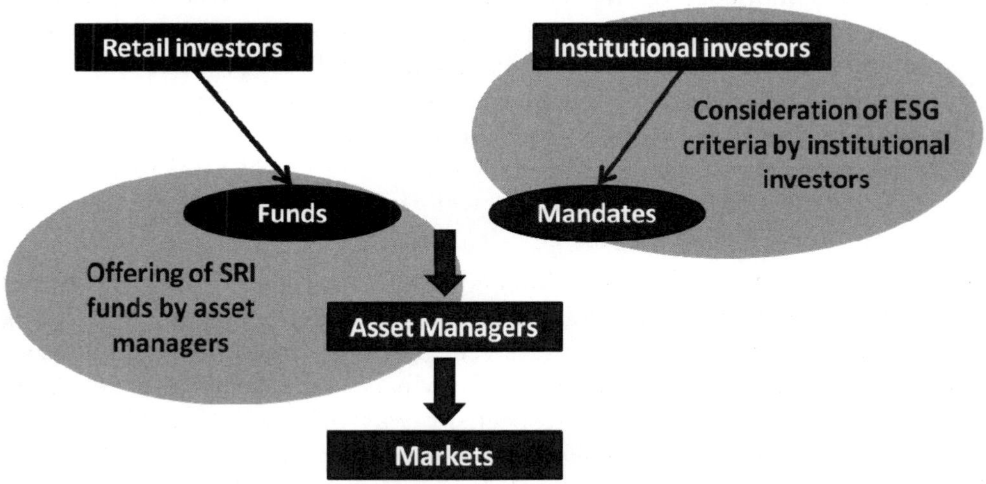

178 Such a requirement was adopted in France in 2010 by reforming Article 224 of the 'Code Monétaire et Financier' (under the so-called Grenelle II Act).

Box 12. Social entrepreneurship funds

The European Commission proposed in 2011 a Regulation on social entrepreneurship funds (SEFs) to facilitate cross-border marketing to professional investors that invest at least 70% of their assets in social projects.* SEFs will be positioned at the ethical end of the *responsible* investment spectrum and will be primarily aimed at achieving ESG goals rather than generating sizeable financial returns. The proposal, inserted in the framework of the Europe 2020 Strategy, takes stock of recent growth in this emerging subsector of the asset management industry and attempts to leverage the potential of the single market to the benefit of small and medium enterprises whose primary goal is to achieve positive and measureable social impacts.** In addition to fostering the participation of the asset management industry in social projects, the proposal also proves that asset management regulation may be employed to further public policy goals beyond the achievement of stable financial markets, investor protection or the promotion of capital markets. The proposal also shows that there is an untapped potential to foster *responsible* investing by devising appropriate regulatory frameworks, to which managers and investors may voluntarily ascribe.

* Article 3.1.1, COM (2001) 862 final (proposal social entrepreneurship funds).

** Article 3.d, COM (2001) 862 final (proposal social entrepreneurship funds).

5.4 Venture capital

Venture capital invests in equity or quasi-equity instruments from small and medium enterprises with a high growth potential. It intervenes early in the product or business cycle by providing seed funding and/or expansion capital. As it invests in innovative ideas that may not necessarily succeed, venture capital is high risk. The logic behind it is that under careful selection and experienced management the profits realised by successful projects are likely to exceed the costs of financing the projects that failed. Moreover, venture capital does not solely provide funding but also specialised advice and assistance to entrepreneurs in highly specialised areas such as biotechnology, health or sophisticated IT. When the product or business model reaches a critical stage of development, the fund will sell its equity investment and channel the principal towards new opportunities.

Venture capital can be very profitable where manager experience meets sufficient investor appetite and an attractive pool of investment opportunities. At the same time, venture capital benefits society and the wider economy by facilitating innovation, productivity and growth. Positive externalities are numerous and include increased expenditure in research and development, cluster formation and job creation (European Commission, 2007, p. 1). Venture capital invests in projects where traditional banking does not given a lack of sufficient expertise, risk-awareness or prudential requirements. It also finances ideas that threaten established products and services, and therefore would not be financed by established companies. Crucially, it is long-term investing that takes on average five to eight years to mature, that is, before the equity investment can be sold either privately of publicly.

Venture capital in Europe suffers from a problem in terms of size and performance. In effect, venture capital in Europe accounts for less than 3% of GDP in contrast to almost 15% in the US (see figure below). At the same time, the returns of European venture capital funds have been consistently weaker than in the US, both in periods of economic expansion and contraction (see Figures 25 and 26 below). A study by the European Investment Fund (EIF, 2006) explores the reasons that might explain the lower performance of venture capital in Europe. It suggests that industry size affects performance positively since it contributes to the build-up of specialised networks and expertise, is crucial to reach optimally sized investments, and allows more diversification. In effect the venture capital industry in Europe has not yet reached its critical size, given notably the fragmentation of national markets due to the absence of a pan-European vehicle and harmonised taxation, and prudential rules that very much limit the ability of institutional investors to invest in venture capital.

Figure 25. Venture capital as a % of GDP in Europe and the US, 2010

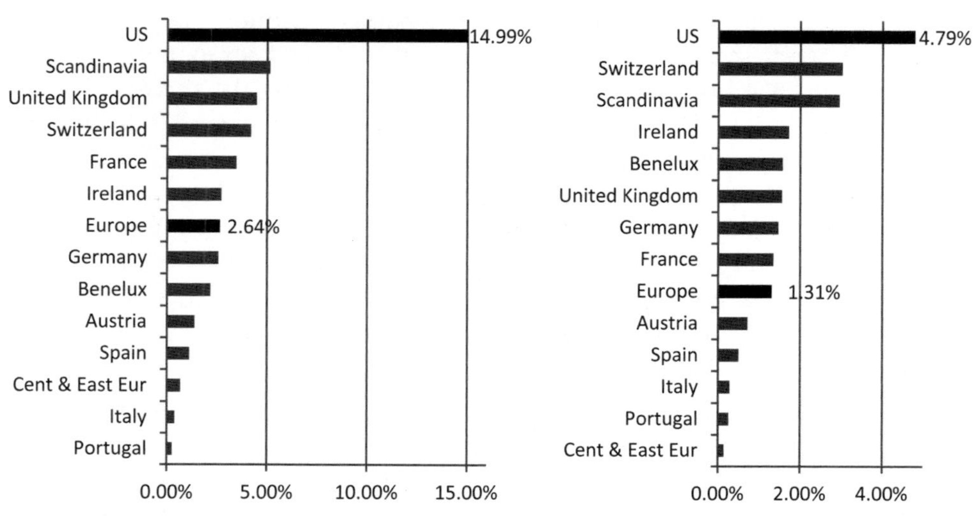

Source: EVCA.

Figure 26. Five-year rolling internal rate of returns (IRR) in venture capital

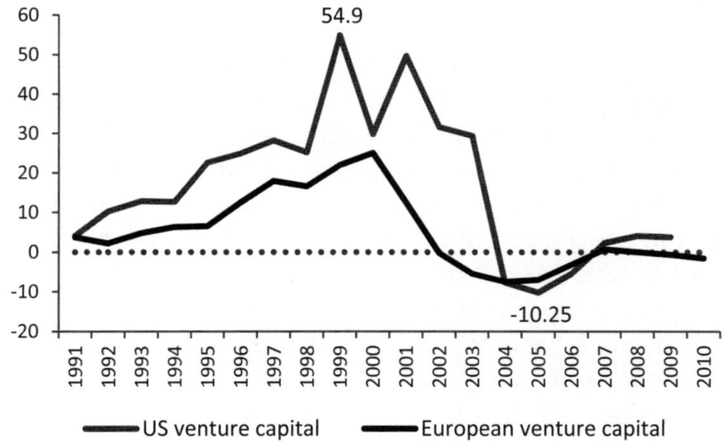

Source: EVCA.

Besides the size of the venture capital industry, lagging performance in Europe is also explained by factors such as (EIF, 2006):

- Dispersion of available funds into too many projects - European funds invest in nearly twice as many companies as US funds.
- The weight of government money in venture capital funds, which is much higher in Europe than in the US, may distort capital allocation in line with political considerations.
- The profile of venture capital managers - closer to finance in Europe, in contrast with engineering and science profiles in the US.
- The relative weight of seed investing. European funds prefer instead start-up and later-stage ventures with lower risks but possibly also lower returns.
- Fragmentation of European exit markets, given the absence of a small pan-European capitalisation market similar to NASDAQ.[179]
- The numerous legal and cultural barriers to entrepreneurship in Europe.

It follows that any policy response must be holistic and cut across all the elements above. Action at EU level to promote venture capital is not new and goes back as far as 1998 under the *Risk Capital Action Plan*. Despite its horizontal approach to risk capital and entrepreneurship, the progress

[179] The proposal of the European Commission to revise MiFID envisages the creation of an SME growth market (see Article 35, Legislative Proposal COM (2011) 656 final, MiFID II).

achieved by this plan during its implementation horizon, ending in 2003, was plainly insufficient. In 2007, the European Commission proposed to step up its work to facilitate the cross-border operation of venture capital funds based on the mutual recognition of the existing national frameworks (European Commission, 2007, p. 9). After the financial crisis and the adoption of the AIFMD, the policy changed in favour of fully harmonising the rules that apply to alternative fund managers, including also venture capital. Once the AIFMD was adopted in 2011, it became clear that its provisions would not kill venture capital but would not promote it either. In effect, 98% of venture managers will not be affected by the AIFMD but will fall under its *de minimis* €500 million threshold (see European Commission, 2011b, p. 2). Those who exceed this threshold will however bear the full compliance burden, even though it will probably be disproportionate to their size and/or untailored to the nature of their business model. Given this burden, the likelihood that small venture managers would opt into the AIFMD to benefit from its passport is virtually nil.

To overcome this impasse and create a single market for venture capital, the European Commission proposed in 2011 a Regulation on *European Venture Capital Funds* (EVCFs) that would allow these funds to be marketed cross-border in much the same way as in the AIFMD but under management and product rules tailored to the nature of their business models. If managers wish to benefit from the passport for their venture capital funds, these funds will have to invest at least 70% of their capital in qualifying investments in SMEs.[180] Cross-border marketing will be enabled only for eligible investors, that is, professional investors under MiFID but also those who satisfy certain conditions.[181] The proposal is aimed at reducing the administrative burden of managers in view of their relatively small size, their positive role in the economy and the need to facilitate entry and exit. It does not subject venture capital funds to depositary obligations, given the illiquidity of the equity instruments that they typically hold in their portfolios. In effect, most of these instruments cannot be freely traded given transfer restrictions. Moreover, these instruments are typically registered with the issuer directly or its agent, which would disqualify them from being held in custody, according to the implementation of the depositary rules in the AIFMD proposed by ESMA.[182]

---

180 Articles 3-4, Legislative Proposal COM (2011) 860 final (European Venture Capital Funds).

181 Article 6, Legislative Proposal COM (2011) 860 final (European Venture Capital Funds).

182 Box 79, ESMA Advice, ESMA 2011/379 (AIFMD implementation).

The introduction of EVCFs is no doubt an important step to overcome the fragmentation of national markets and allow the venture capital industry to gain critical size in Europe, but it will not suffice on its own. Notably, tax issues remain a major barrier to the operation of cross-border venture capital funds (European Commission, 2009d). The European Commission will work throughout 2012 with member states to find a solution to these issues (European Commission, 2011b, p. 3). It would be very unfortunate if a lack of agreement among member states on second-order tax issues would hinder the potential of venture capital to foster innovation and competitiveness in Europe. As tax rules stand today, the treatment applied to investments in venture capital is frequently less favourable than for investments in public equity, despite the well-known externalities of the former (European Commision, 2009, p. 1).

Europe will also need to reconsider prudential rules to better understand how to reconcile them with long-term investing, including investing in venture capital. Solvency charges for insurers and pension funds risk further undermining their ability to invest in venture capital and other long-term assets. Venture capital is a highly specialised asset class that requires building up sufficient in-house expertise to select and manage these investments. A reasonable objective for the average institutional investor would be to invest from 5 to 10% of his/her assets in venture capital. However, holdings of venture capital should not be artificially increased either. Professional investors should be given leeway to access venture capital as they see fit but under appropriate safeguards to mitigate related risks, including bubbles. The European 'venture capital ecosystem' will not be transformed overnight but will need much time to grow and consolidate, under appropriate incentives. Now is the time to create those incentives, including the revision of capital and solvency charges.

****

*

BIBLIOGRAPHY

AFG (2012), *Le marche français de la gestion financière en 2011*, Association Française de Gestion Financière, Paris.

AIEG (Alternative Investment Expert Group) (2006), *Report of the Alternative Investment Expert Group for the European Commission*, European Commission, Brussels.

Allen, W. and G. Wood (2006), "Defining and achieving financial stability", *Journal of Financial Stability*, 2(2), 152-172.

Amenc, Noël and S. Sender (2011), *Response to ESMA Consultation Paper to Implementing Measures for the AIFMD*, EDHEC-Risk Institute, Nice.

Amenc, Nöel, F. Ducoulombier, F. Goltz and L. Tang (2012), *What are the Risks of European ETFs?*, EDHEC-Risk Institute, Nice.

AMF (2011), *Risk and Trend Mapping for Financial Markets and Services*, Autorité des Marchés Financiers, Paris.

Bank of England (2011), *Financial Stability Report*, Issue No. 29, London.

Bannier, C.E., F. Fecht and M. Tyrell (2007), "Open-end real estate funds in Germany - genesis and crisis", Deutsche Bundesbank Discussion Paper Series 2: Banking and Financial Studies, No. 04.

BCG (2011), *Global Asset Management 2011: Building on Success*, Boston Consulting Group, Boston.

BIS (2003), *A glossary of terms used in payments and settlement systems*, Bank for International Settlements, Basel.

BIS (2006), *Growing exposure of institutional investors to alternative investments*, Bank for International Settlements, Basel.

——— (2010), *Review of the Differentiated Nature and Scope of Financial Regulation*, Bank for International Settlements, Basel Committee on Banking Supervision, Basel.

BlackRock (2011), *ETF Landscape - Industry Review*, end H1 2011.

Bodart, P. (2011), presentation to Task Force members.

CACEIS (2011), *Cross-border distribution of UCITS*, CACEIS Investor Services.

CACEIS and PwC (2011), *Rethinking Distribution: Creating competitive advantage in a new fund distribution paradigm*, CACEIS Investor Services & PriceWaterhouseCoopers.

Casey, J-P and K. Lannoo (2009), *Pouring old wine in new skins? UCITS and Asset Management after MiFID*, Centre for European Policy Studies, Brussels.

CEA (2012), *The European Life Insurance Market in 2010*, European Insurance and Reinsurance Federation, Brussels.

Cerulli Associates (2012), *European Distribution Dynamics 2012*, London.

Charter, N., H. Stefeen and I. Roman (2010), *Consumer Decision-Making in Retail Investment Services: A Behavioural Economics Perspective*, European Commission, Brussels.

Čihák, M. (2006), "Central Banks and Financial Stability: A Survey of Financial Stability Reports", IMF Working Paper, 1-31, International Monetary Fund, Washington, D.C.

City Fund Services (2010), "The Convergence of Traditional and Alternative Investment Products: Regulatory and Operational Considerations", *The Investment Lawyer*, 17(12).

DB (2011a), *Ninth Annual Alternative Investment Survey - Investor insights on the changing hedge fund landscape*, Deutsche Bank, Frankfurt.

——— (2011b), *ETF Research – Industry Perspective: In the ETF labyrinth, where does the thread begin?*, Deutsche Bank, Frankfurt.

de Larosière, J., L. Balcerowicz, O. Issing, R. Masera, C.M. Carthy, L. Nyberg, J. Pérez et al. (2009), *Report of the High-Level Group on Financial Supervision in the EU*, European Commission, Brussels.

Deli, D.N. and R. Varma (2002), "Contracting in the investment management industry: evidence from mutual funds", *Journal of Financial Economics*, 63(1), pp. 79–98.

de Meza, D., B. Irlenbusch and D. Reyniers (2008), *Financial Capability: A Behavioural Economics Perspective*, Financial Services Authority, London.

ECB (2011), Statistical Data Warehouse, European Central Bank, Frankfurt.

EDHEC-Risk (2010a), *The European fund management industry needs a better grasp of non-financial risks*, EDHEC-Risk Institute, Nice.

——— (2010b), *Are Hedge-Fund UCITS the Cure-All?*, EDHEC-Risk Institute, Nice.

EFAMA (2009), *Asset Management in Europe: Facts and Figures*, European Fund and Asset Management Association, Brussels.

——— (2011a), *Asset Management in Europe*, European Fund and Asset Management Association, Brussels.

——— (2011b), *Trends in the European Investment Fund Industry in the Third Quarter of 2011*, European Fund and Asset Management Association, Brussels.

——— (2011c), *The Evolving Investment Strategies of UCITS*, European Fund and Asset Management Association, Brussels.

——— (2012a), *International Statistical Release Q3 2011*, European Fund and Asset Management Association, Brussels.

——— (2012b), *Trends in the European Investment Fund Industry in the Fourth Quarter of 2011*, European Fund and Asset Management Association, Brussels.

EFAMA and IMMFA (2009), *Recommendation for a European Classification and definition of Money Market Funds*, European Fund and Asset Management Association & Institutional Money Market Funds Association, Brussels & London.

EFAMA and KPMG (2010), *Analysis of the Tax Implications of UCITS IV*, European Fund and Asset Management Association & Institutional Money Market Funds Association & KPMG.

EIF (2006), *Risk Capital Mandate (RCM) Investment Guidelines*, European Investment Fund, Luxembourg.

EIWG (European Investors Working Group) (2010), "Restoring Investor Confidence in European Capital Markets", European Capital Markets Institute (ECMI), Brussels.

ESMA (2010), *Inducements: Report on good and poor practices*, European Securities and Markets Authority, CESR/10-295, Paris.

——— (2011a), *Discussion Paper - Policy orientations on guidelines for UCITS Exchange-Traded Funds and Structured UCITS*, European Securities and Markets Authority, ESMA/2011/220, Paris.

——— (2011b), *Consultation paper - Guidelines on certain aspects of the MiFID suitability requirements*, European Securities and Markets Authority, ESMA 2011/445, Paris.

ESRB (2011), *Response to the ESMA discussion paper on policy orientations and guidelines for UCITS exchange-traded funds and structured UCITS*, European Systemic Risk Board, Frankfurt.

European Commission (2006), *White Paper on Enhancing the Single Market Framework for Investment Funds*, COM (2006) 686 final, European Commission, Brussels.

——— (2007), *Communication on Removing Obstacles to Cross-Border Investments by Venture Capital Funds*, COM(2007) 853 final, European Commission, Brussels.

——— (2009a), *Impact Assessment Accompanying the Proposal for a Directive on Alternative Investment Fund Managers*, COM (2009) 207, European Commission, Brussels.

——— (2009b), *Impact assessment accompanying the communication from the Commission on packaged retail investment products*, COM (2009) 204, European Commission, Brussels.

——— (2009c), *Communication on Packaged Retail Investment Products*, COM (2009) 204 final, European Commission, Brussels.

——— (2009d), *Report of Expert Group on Removing Tax Obstacles to Cross-border Venture Capital Investments*, European Commission, Brussels.

——— (2010), *Corporate governance in financial institutions and remuneration policies*, COM (2010) 284 final, European Commission, Brussels.

——— (2011a), *The Consumer Markets Scoreboard: Making Markets Work For Consumers* (6th ed.), European Commission, Brussels, October.

——— (2011b), *Impact assessment accompanying the document proposal for a directive on markets in financial instruments [recast] and the proposal for a regulation on markets in financial instruments*, COM (2011) 656 final, European Commission, Brussels.

——— (2011c), *The EU Corporate Governance Framework*, COM (2011) 164 final, European Commission, Brussels.

——— (2011d), *Proposal for a Regulation on European Venture Capital Funds*, COM (2011) 860 final, European Commission, Brussels.

——— (2012), *Consultation on the future of European Company Law*, European Commission, Brussels.

Eurosif (2010), *European Socially Responsible Investing Study*, European Sustainable Investing Forum.

Evans, D. (2007), *Unsafe Havens*, Bloomberg Markets October 2007.

EVCA (2011), *Private Equity and Venture Capital Statistics Database*, European Private Equity and Venture Capital Association.

FSA (2005), *Hedge funds: A discussion of risk and regulatory engagement*, Discussion Paper 05/4, Financial Services Authority, London.

——— (2007), *A Review of Retail Distribution*, Discussion Paper 07/1, Financial Services Authority, London.

——— (2009), *Distribution of retail investments: Delivering the RDR*, Consultation Paper 09/18, Financial Services Authority, London.

——— (2010a), *Financial Risk Outlook: Retail Intermediaries Sector Digest*, Financial Services Authority, London.

——— (2010b), *Distribution of retail investments: Delivering the RDR - feedback to CP09/18 and final rules*, Policy Statement 10/6, Financial Services Authority, London.

——— (2011a), *Assessing the Possible Sources of Systemic Risk from Hedge Funds*, Financial Services Authority, London.

——— (2011b), *Finalised guidance: assessing suitability*, Financial Services Authority, London.

——— (2011c), *Distribution of retail investments: Delivering the RDR – professionalism*, Policy Statement 11/1, Financial Services Authority, London.

FSB (2011a), *Shadow Banking: Scoping the Issues*, Financial Stability Board, Basel.

——— (2011b), *Shadow Banking: Strengthening Oversight and Regulation. October*, Financial Stability Board, Basel.

——— (2011c), *Potential financial stability issues arising from recent trends in Exchange-Traded Funds (ETFs)*, Financial Stability Board, Basel.

Fitch (2010), *European Asset Management: An Industry Under Pressure*, Fitch Ratings.

——— (2011a), *Hedge Fund and Absolute Return Strategies*, Fitch Ratings.

——— (2011b), *The European Debt Investor Landscape*, Fitch Ratings.

Grosman, S.J. and J.E. Stiglitz (1980), "On the impossibility of informationally efficient markets". *American Economic Review* 70, pp. 393-408.

ICI (2011), *Investment Company Fact Book*, Investment Company Institute, Washington, D.C.

IFF Research, YouGov and European Commission (2009), *UCITS Disclosure Testing Research Report*, European Commission, Brussels.

IMF (2008), *Global Financial Stability Report*, Washington, D.C., October.

IMF (2011), "Long-term investors and their asset allocation: Where are they now?", *Global Financial Stability Report*, International Monetary Fund, Washington, D.C., pp. 1-48.

IOSCO (2009), *Hedge Funds Oversight*, International Organisation of Securities Commission, Madrid.

———— (2011), *Principles on Suspensions of Redemptions in Collective Investment Schemes - Consultation Report*, International Organisation of Securities Commissions, Madrid.

Koski, J.L. and J. Pontiff (1996), "How Are Derivatives Used? Evidence from the Mutual Fund Industry", Wharton Financial Institutions Center Working Paper, The Wharton Financial Institutions Center, University of Pennsylvania, Philadelphia, PA.

Lipper (2010), *Symbiosis in the evolution of UCITS 1988-2018: Three Decades of Funds Industry Transformation*, Thomson Reuters.

———— (2012), *European Fund Market Review 2012 Edition*, Thomson Reuters.

McKinsey (2006), *The Asset Management Industry in 2010*, McKinsey & Company.

McCauley, R.N., N. Baba and S. Ramaswamy (2009), "US dollar money market funds and non-US banks", *BIS Quarterly Review*, March, pp. 65-81.

Mercer (2009), *Shedding light on responsible investment: Approaches, returns and impacts*, London.

Moisson, E. (2010), *Symbiosis in the evolution of UCITS 1988-2018: Three Decades of Funds Industry Transformation*, Lipper FMI and Thomson Reuters, London.

Moody's (2010), *Sponsor Support Key to Money Market Funds*, Moody's Investor Service.

OECD (2011), "Fostering Long-term Investment and Economic Growth: A Long-term Investor's View", *Financial Market Trends*, 2011(1), pp. 1-4, Organisation for Economic Co-operation and Development, Paris.

OEE (2011), *The Importance of Asset Management to the European Economy*, Observatoire de l'Eparge Européene, Paris.

Oxera (2009), *Retail Distribution Review proposals: impact on market structure and competition*, Financial Services Authority, London.

P&I (2011), Institutional investors pour into hedge funds, Published November 14 2011, Pensions & Investments, Chicago, IL.

PWGFM (2010), *Money Market Fund Reform Options*, US President's Working Group on Financial Markets.

PwC (2008a), *Investment funds in the European Union: Comparative analysis of use of investment powers, investment outcomes and related risk features in both UCITS and non-harmonised markets*, European Commission, Brussels.

——— (2008b), *The retailisation of non-harmonised investment funds in the European Union*, European Commission, Brussels.

——— (2011), *Benchmark your Global Fund Distribution*, PriceWaterhouseCooper.

Ramaswamy, S. (2011), "Market structures and systemic risks of exchange-traded funds", Bank for International Settlements Working Papers, BIS, Basel.

SEC (2011), *Use of Derivatives by Investment Companies Under the Investment Company Act of 1940*, Securities and Exchange Commission, Release No. IC-29776, File No. S7-33-11, Washington, D.C.

Schinasi, G.J. (2004), "Defining Financial Stability", International Monetary Fund Working Paper No. 04(187), IMF, Washington, D.C.

Strategic Insight (SI) (2010), *Alternative and Hedge Fund UCITS in the Next Decade*, SI Global Research Report, November.

Swan, E.J. (2000), *Building the Global Market: A 4000 Year History of Derivatives*, London: Kluwer Law.

Synovate (2011), *Consumer Market Study on Advice within the Area of Retail Investment Services*, European Commission, Brussels.

Tuchschmid, N.S., E. Wallerstein and L. Zanolin (2010), "Will alternative UCITS ever be loved enough to replace a hedge funds?", Haute Ecole de Gestion à Genève Working Paper, Geneva.

Turner, A. (2009), *The Turner Review*, Financial Services Authority, London.

Valiante, D. (2011), *MiFID 2.0 Casting New Light on Europe's Capital Markets*, Centre for European Policy Studies, Brussels.

WEF (2011a), *The Future of Long-term Investing*, World Economic Forum, location.

——— (2011b), *Accelerating the Transition towards Sustainable Investing - Strategic Options for Investors, Corporations and other Key Stakeholders*, World Economic Forum.

World Bank (2009), *Note Number 11: The leverage ratio*, Washington, D.C., December.

Zingales, L. (2008), "Testimony of Causes and Effects of the Lehman Brothers Bankruptcy", Testimony before the United States House of Representatives, Washington, D.C.

ANNEXES

Annex 1. Main provisions in the AIFMD

Scope (Art. 2.1)	- EU AIFM (Alternative Investment Fund Managers) - Non-EU AIFM if they manage an EU AIF or market a non-EU AIF in the EU
Full exemptions (Arts 2.3 and 3.1)	- Holding companies - Authorised managers of occupational retirement schemes (Directive 2003/41/EC) - Employee saving/participation schemes - Securitisation special purpose entities - AIF whose only investor are undertakings and subsidiaries of the AIFMD
Small funds (Art. 3.2)	- AuM < €100m or < €500m if 5 year lock-in - Compulsory registration (before national authority) - No passport but opt-in possible - Simplified reporting - Member states may adopt stricter requirements
Authorisation (Arts 5 -11)	- Distinction between externally appointed AIFM and internally managed AIF - Compatible with UCITS authorisation (but management of conflicts of interest) - Compatible with portfolio management for pension funds and occupational retirement schemes (under member state derogation) - Compatible with non-core services (under member state derogation) - No limitations in terms of investment strategies
Initial capital (Art. 9)	- €300m for internally managed AIFM / €125m for externally managed AIFM - 0.02% of AuM exceeding €250m (MS may allow 50% in the form of guarantees) - Additional own funds or insurance to cover professional liability risk
Risk management (Arts 15 and 16)	- Functionally and hierarchically separate (competent authority may provide exemption if not proportional) - Establish risk profile, liquidity profile (and redemption policy), maximum level of leverage and extent of the right to reuse collateral - Implement risk management and liquidity management systems - Carry-out due-diligence processes and stress testing - Rules on short-selling have moved out of the AIFMD and into horizontal legislation
Securitisation (Art. 17)	- Retention requirements of no less than 5% for originator, sponsor and original lender - Delegation to ESMA

Conduct of business (Arts 12 - 14)	- Rules similar to UCITS and MiFID on conduct of business and conflicts of interest - Binding annex on remuneration (under proportionality)

Delegation (Art. 20)	- Notification requirement (justification on objective reasons)
	- May not undermine effective supervision
	- Delegation of portfolio and risk management:
	  - Only to undertakings authorised or registered for asset management
	  - Subject to cooperation arrangements with third-country supervisor
	- No delegation to depositary
	- Sub-delegation subject to same requirements

Prime brokerage	- Defined (Art 4.af) and regulated indirectly with regard conflicts of interest (14.3), compatibility with depositary functions (21.4) and disclosure to investors (23) - No specific reporting requirements for the prime broker
Valuation (Art. 19)	- Either external or functionally separate (internal valuer) - National authorities may require verification by external valuer or auditor - AIFM retains full liability towards AIF and investors (no contractual discharge possible) - External valuer liable for negligent or intentional failure - External valuer may not be depositary except if functionally and hierarchically separate - External valuer may not sub-delegate
Depositary (Art. 21)	- Single external entity - UE credit institution, investment firm or other (according to national law) located in the home member state of the AIF - For non-EU AIF, it may be a non-EU entity if ESMA deems effective supervision exists in the relevant country - Responsible for checking valuation - Quasi-strict liability + reversal of the burden of proof - Delegation (and sub-delegation) possible under strict conditions - Contractual discharge of liability possible with regard to sub-custodians - Reporting upon request to supervisors
Passport (Arts 31 - 33)	- Passport granted to EU AIF with respect to marketing to professional investors - Passport granted to EU AIFM with respect to their management services - Member states may allow marketing of AIFs to retail investors (Art 43)
Third country rules (Arts 34 - 42)	- See Annex 2
Disclosure to investors (Arts 22 and 23)	- Before investing in the AIF: investment strategy, leverage, risk and liquidity management, valuation, conflicts of interest, fees and expenses, depositary liability... - Periodically: risk profile, liquidity and leverage - Annual report

Reporting to supervisors (Art. 24)	- Main markets, instruments, exposures and concentrations (per manager and fund) - Special arrangements for illiquid assets - Actual risk profile and management system - Results of stress tests - If leverage is used on a substantial basis: amount of leverage arising from borrowing of cash or securities and embedded in derivatives (and extent of re-use of AIF assets under leveraging agreements)
Supervisory authorities (Arts 45 - 55)	- Home member state of the AIFM responsible for prudential supervision - Host member state of the AIFM responsible for conduct of business and conflicts of interest - Wide powers of inspection and intervention - Power to impose limits on leverage or other restrictions to limit systemic risk or risks of disorderly markets - Powers of ESMA in line with Regulation 1095/2010 (banning of products, restrictions on management) - Enhanced co-operation procedures

Annex 2. Third country rules in the AIFMD

Timeline[1]	Article	Addresses	Purpose	Exemptions	Additional requirements	Procedure	Duration
From year 1 (22.07.2013)	34	- EU manager (authorised) - Non-EU fund - Marketing only outside the EU	Management	21 (depositary rules) 22 (annual report)	- Cooperation arrangement between competent authorities (home MS / third country)	None	-
Years 1 to 5 (Article 68)	36	- EU manager (authorised) - Non-EU fund - Marketing inside the EU	Marketing without passport	21 (depositary rules) subejct to caveats	- Main depositary tasks cannot be performed by the manager (duties in paragraps 7, 8 and 9 of Article 21) - Cooperation arrangements between competent authorities (home MS / third country) - Not listed as Non-Cooperative Country	Authorisation (National Law)	-
	42	- Non-EU manager - Both EU and non-EU funds - Marketing inside the EU		Full exemption apart from: 22 (annual report) 23 (disclosure to investors) 24 (reporting to authorities) 26-30 (private equity rules)	- Cooperation arrangements between competent authorities (MS / third country) - Not listed as Non-Cooperative Country	Authorisation (National Law)	-

From year 3 (Article 67)	35	- EU manager (authorised) - Non-EU fund - Marketing inside the EU	Marketing with passport	No exemptions	- Cooperation arrangements between competent authorities (home MS / third country) - Not listed as Non-Cooperative Country - OECD Model Tax Conventions (each MS where AIFM intends to be marketed / third country)	Notification (EU Law)	20 working days
	37	- Non-EU manager - Mangement of EU funds - Marketing of funds in the EU	Authorisation	Incompatible provisions[2]	- Legal reprentative established in MSR - Cooperation arrangements between competent authorities (MSR / third country) - Not listed as Non-Cooperative Country - OECD Model Tax Convention (MSR / third country) - Effective supervision is not impeded	Authorisation (EU Law)	At least 3 months (Article 8)
	41	- Non-EU manager (authorised) - EU fund (established in other member state than the MSR)	Management		- Communicate programme of operations - Communicate further details if establishing a branch	Notification (EU Law)	One month

39	- Non-EU manager (authorised) - EU fund - Marketing inside the EU	Marketing with passport		- No additional requirements	Notifcation (EU Law)	20 working days
40	- Non-EU manager (authorised) - Non-EU fund - Marketing inside the EU			- Cooperation arrangements between competent authorities (home MS / third country) - Not listed as Non-Cooperative Country - OECD Model Tax Conventions (each MS where AIFM intends to be marketed / third country)	Notification (EU Law)	20 working days

[1] Subject to Commissions decisions based on advice by ESMA with reference to the criteria set out in the Directive (Arts 67 and 68).

[2] Manager has to show: incompatibility of the AIFMD provision with a mandatory provision from its jurisdiction + existence of equivalent rule in that jurisdiction + compliance with that rule.

Abbreviations: MS refers to member state and MSR refers to member state of reference.

Annex 3. Task Force Participants

Task Force Members

Naïm Abou-Jaoude
Chief Executive Officer
Dexia Asset Management

Xavier Balthazar
Advisory Partner
Investment Management Regulatory
PriceWaterhouseCoopers

Massimiliano Castelli
Senior Strategist
UBS Global Asset Management

Simon Crown
Partner
Clifford Chance

Paul Cummins
Managing Director
Capital Markets Prime Services
Nomura International

James Cunningham
Global Network Management
BNY Mellon Asset Servicing

Robin Edme
Associé Gérant
Maqassar Socially Responsible Investment
On behalf of :
Eurosif (European Sustainable Investing Forum)

Malene Ehrenskjold
Global Head of Compliance & Operational Risk
Nordea

Daniel Enskat
Senior Director and Head of Global Consulting
Strategic Insight

Carey Evans
Account Executive
Fleishman-Hillard

Tony Freeman
Executive Director, Strategic Business Development and Industry Relations
OMGEO

Soren Gade
Executive Director
Danish Bankers Association (Finansraadet)

Rafael Gallegos
EU Affairs Manager
European Affairs Office
BBVA (Banco Bilbao Vizcaya Argentaria)

Vincent Gouverneur
Partner ERS-IMS
Deloitte

Didier Guennoc
Former Director
EVCA (European Private Equity and Venture Capital Association)

Samuel Hinton-Smith
Director Public Affairs
Prime Brokerage
Nomura International

Stéphane Janin
Head of International Affairs Division
AFG (Association Française de la Gestion Financière)

Mads Kaagaard
Head of Strategy Development & Support
Nordea Savings and Asset Management

Patrik Karlsson
Head of EU Public Affairs
Prudential

Agathe Legris
Associate
Kreab Gavin Anderson

Daniel Lehmann
Managing Director
Allianz Global Investors Product Solutions

Philippe Lenges
Partner - Assurance
Deloitte

Claudia Masbaum
General Manager European Strategic Relations
Winton Capital Management

Louise McDonald
Director of Product Development
Bank of New York Mellon

Andrew Mituzas
Professional Standards Manager
INREV (European Association for Investors in Non-listed Real Estate Vehicles)

Maxence Monot
Senior Manager
Deloitte Luxembourg

Celia Neves
Risk and Compliance Officer
Nordea

Martin Nijkamp
Member of the Management Committee
Strategic Business Development
ING Investment Management

Vesa Ollikainen
Risk and Compliance Officer
Savings and Asset Management
Nordea

Eric Pagniez
Deputy Chief Executive Officer
AFG (Association Française de la Gestion Financière)

John Parkhouse
Partner and Asset Management Leader
PriceWaterhouseCoopers

Francois Passant
Executive Director
Eurosif (European Sustainable Investing Forum)

Joao Pereira
Account Executive
Fleishman-Hillard

Romain Rard
Avocat
GLN Gide Loyrette Nouel
On behalf of:
EVCA (European Private Equity and Venture Capital Association)

David Reed
Partner
Kreab Gavin Anderson

Nickolas Reinhardt
Senior Policy Advisor
Fleishman-Hillard

Jeff Rupp
Director Public Affairs & Professional Standards
INREV (European Association for Investors in Non-listed Real Estate Vehicles)

Benoît Sauvage
Adviser, Financial Markets Regulation
ABBL (Luxembourg Bankers' Association)
On behalf of: EBF (European Banking Federation)

Hannes Sigurdsson
Deputy Director General
Confederation of Icelandic Employers

Dominique Sioen
Global Head of Public Legal Affairs
Dexia Asset Management

Roy Stockell
Partner - EMEIA Asset Management
Ernst & Young

Sandrell Sultana
Former Public and Regulatory Affairs
EVCA (European Private Equity and Venture Capital Association)

Giuseppe van der Helm
President
Eurosif (European Sustainable Investing Forum)

Maurice Vrolix
Partner - Audit
Deloitte Bedrijfsrevisoren

Steve Wallace
Director - Industry Relations - EMEA
CAIA (Chartered Alternative Investment Analyst Association)

Xavier Zaegel
Partner
Deloitte

Task Force Observers

Ugo Bassi
Director
Directorate Capital and Companies
European Commission - DG Internal Market
Former: Head of Unit - Asset Management
European Commission - DG Internal Market

Patrice Bergé-Vincent
Head of Regulation of Asset Management
AMF (Autorité des Marchés Financiers)
Also on behalf of: ESMA (European Securities and Markets Authority)

Jean-Pierre Casey
Director Investment Advisory - CISEE
Barclays Wealth

Sonia Catarinussi
Policy Officer
Asset Management Unit
European Commission - DG Internal Market

Charles Cronin
Former Head of Standards and Financial Market Integrity - EMEA
CFA Institute
And: Member of the Occupational Pensions Stakeholder Group
EIOPA (European Insurance and Occupational Pensions Authority)

Tom Fekete
Managing Director, Head of Investments Products - EMEA
Barclays Wealth

Christiane Grimm
Asset Management Unit
European Commission - DG Internal Market

Agnes Le Thiec
Director Capital Markets Policy
CFA Institute

Gaétan Parchliniak
Policy Officer
AMF (Autorité des Marchés Financiers)

Thomas Rostron
Global Head of Asset Management
Barclays Wealth

Rostislav Rozsypal
Policy Officer
Asset Management Unit
European Commission - DG Internal Market

Esther Wandel
Policy Officer
Asset Management Unit
European Commission - DG Internal Market

Invited Speakers

Paul Bodart
Executive Vice President
Bank of New York Mellon

Thomas Deinet
Executive Director
Hedge Funds Standards Board

Eric Derobert
Director of Public Affairs
Public Affairs
CACEIS Depositary Services

Alain Dubois
Chairman
Lyxor Asset Management
and:
Chair - ETFs and Structured Funds Committee
AFG (Association Française de la Gestion Financière)

Ulrich Hege
Professor of Finance
FBF Chair in Corporate Finance
Haute École de Commerce Paris

Wolfgang Mansfeld
Former Member of the Board
Union Asset Management Holding

Samuel Sender
Applied Research Manager
EDHEC-Risk Institute

Nils S. Tuchschmid
Professor of Banking and Finance
Haute École de Gestion Genève

CEPS and ECMI Researchers

Mirzha de Manuel Aramendía
Researcher
CEPS – ECMI

Angelo Fiorante
Research Assistant
CEPS – ECRI

Staffan Jerneck
Director of Corporate Relations
CEPS

Karel Lannoo
Senior Research Fellow and Chief Executive Officer
CEPS and ECMI

Elina Pyykko
Researcher
CEPS – ECRI

Diego Valiante
Research Fellow and Head of Research
CEPS – ECMI

Annex 4. Glossary of Abbreviations

AIF	Alternative Investment Fund
AIFMD	Alternative Investment Fund Managers Directive
AIMA	Alternative Investment Management Association
AMF	Autorité des Marchés Financiers
AuM	Assets under management
BIS	Bank for International Settlements
CDO	Collateralised debt obligation
CESR	Committee of European Securities Regulators
CPD	Continuing professional development
CSD	Central securities depositary
ECB	European Central Bank
EEA	European Economic Area
EFAMA	European Fund and Asset Management Association
EMIR	European Market Infrastructure Regulation
ESG	Environmental, social and governance
ESMA	European Securities and Markets Authority
ESRB	European Systemic Risk Board
ETF	Exchanged traded fund
ETP	Exchange traded product
EVCF	European Venture Capital Fund
FSB	Financial Stability Board
FSOC	Financial Stability Oversight Council
HFR	Hedge Fund Research
IFA	Independent financial adviser
IIRC	International Integrated Reporting Council
IMD	Insurance mediation Directive
IOSCO	International Organisation of Securities Commission
KIID	Key investor information document
KPI	Key Performance Indicator
LTRF	long-term retail fund
MCP	Management company passport
MiFID	Markets in Financial Instruments Directive
MMF	Money Market Fund
NAV	Net asset value
OEE	Observatoire de l'Epargne Européenne
OERE funds	Open-ended real estate funds
PRIPs	Packaged retail investment products
RDR	Retail distribution review
RM	Residual maturity
SEF	Social entrepreneurship fund
SIFI	Significantly important financial institution
SIPP	Self-invested personal pension
SLD	Securities law Directive
SRI	Socially responsible investment
TA	Transfer agent
UCITS	Undertakings for Collective Investment in Transferable Securities
WAL	Weighted average life
WAM	Weighted average maturity